Related Books of Interest

Enterprise Master Data Management
An SOA Approach to Managing Core Information

By Allen Dreibelbis, Eberhard Hechler, Ivan Milman, Martin Oberhofer, Paul Van Run, and Dan Wolfson

ISBN: 0-13-236625-8

The Only Complete Technical Primer for MDM Planners, Architects, and Implementers

Enterprise Master Data Management provides an authoritative, vendor-independent MDM technical reference for practitioners: architects, technical analysts, consultants, solution designers, and senior IT decision makers. Written by the IBM® data management innovators who are pioneering MDM, this book systematically introduces MDM's key concepts and technical themes, explains its business case, and illuminates how it interrelates with and enables SOA.

Drawing on their experience with cutting-edge projects, the authors introduce MDM patterns, blueprints, solutions, and best practices published nowhere else—everything you need to establish a consistent, manageable set of master data, and use it for competitive advantage.

The Art of Enterprise Information Architecture
A Systems-Based Approach for Unlocking Business Insight

By Mario Godinez, Eberhard Hechler, Klaus Koenig, Steve Lockwood, Martin Oberhofer, and Michael Schroeck

ISBN: 0-13-703571-3

Architecture for the Intelligent Enterprise: Powerful New Ways to Maximize the Real-time Value of Information

In this book, a team of IBM's leading information management experts guide you on a journey that will take you from where you are today toward becoming an "Intelligent Enterprise."

Drawing on their extensive experience working with enterprise clients, the authors present a new, information-centric approach to architecture and powerful new models that will benefit any organization. Using these strategies and models, companies can systematically unlock the business value of information by delivering actionable, real-time information in context to enable better decision-making throughout the enterprise—from the "shop floor" to the "top floor."

Related Books of Interest

The New Era of Business Intelligence
Using Analytics to Achieve a Global Competitive Advantage

By Mike Biere
ISBN: 0-13-707542-1

A Complete Blueprint for Maximizing the Value of Business Intelligence in the Enterprise

In *The New Era of Enterprise Business Intelligence*, top BI expert Mike Biere presents a complete blueprint for creating winning BI strategies and infrastructure and systematically maximizing the value of information throughout the enterprise.

This product-independent guide brings together start-to-finish guidance and practical checklists for every senior IT executive, planner, strategist, implementer, and the actual business users themselves.

Viral Data in SOA
An Enterprise Pandemic

By Neal A. Fishman
ISBN: 0-13-700180-0

"This book is a must read for any organization using data-integration or data-interchange technologies, or simply any organization that must trust data. Neal takes the reader through an entertaining and vital journey of SOA information management issues, risks, discovery, and solutions. He provides a fresh perspective that no corporation should overlook; in fact, corporations might head blindly into SOA implementations without this awareness."

—Kevin Downey, Senior Partner, Xteoma Inc., Canada

Leading IBM information forensics expert Neal Fishman helps you identify the unique challenges of data quality in your SOA environment—and implement solutions that deliver the best results for the long term at the lowest cost.

Listen to the author's podcast at:
ibmpressbooks.com/podcasts

Related Books of Interest

DB2 pureXML Cookbook
Master the Power of the IBM Hybrid Data Server

By Matthias Nicola and Pav Kumar-Chatterjee
ISBN: 0-13-815047-8

Hands-On Solutions and Best Practices for Developing and Managing XML Database Applications with DB2

Two leading experts from IBM offer the practical solutions and proven code samples that database professionals need to build better XML solutions faster. Organized by task, this book is packed with more than 700 easy-to-adapt "recipe-style" examples covering the entire application lifecycle—from planning and design through coding, optimization, and troubleshooting. This extraordinary library of recipes includes more than 250 XQuery and SQL/XML queries. With the authors' hands-on guidance, you'll learn how to combine pureXML "ingredients" to efficiently perform virtually any XML data management task, from the simplest to the most advanced.

Understanding DB2 9 Security

Bond, See, Wong, Chan
ISBN: 0-13-134590-7

DB2 9 for Linux, UNIX, and Windows

DBA Guide, Reference, and Exam Prep, 6th Edition
Baklarz, Zikopoulos
ISBN: 0-13-185514-X

Lotus Notes Developer's Toolbox

Elliott
ISBN: 0-13-221448-2

IBM Lotus Connections 2.5

Planning and Implementing Social Software for Your Enterprise
Hardison, Byrd, Wood, Speed, Martin, Livingston, Moore, Kristiansen
ISBN: 0-13-700053-7

Mining the Talk

Unlocking the Business Value in Unstructured Information
Spangler, Kreulen
ISBN: 0-13-233953-6

Data Integration Blueprint and Modeling

Data Integration Blueprint and Modeling:

Techniques for a Scalable and Sustainable Architecture

Anthony David Giordano

IBM Press Pearson plc

Upper Saddle River, NJ • Boston • Indianapolis • San Francisco
New York • Toronto • Montreal • London • Munich • Paris • Madrid
Cape Town • Sydney • Tokyo • Singapore • Mexico City

ibmpressbooks.com

IBM Press Program Managers: Steven M. Stansel, Ellice Uffer

Cover design: IBM Corporation

Editor in Chief: Mark Taub

Marketing Manager: Stephane Nakib

Publicist: Heather Fox

Acquisitions Editors: Bernard Goodwin, Michael Thurston

Development Editor: Michael Thurston

Managing Editor: Kristy Hart

Designer: Alan Clements

Project Editor: Betsy Harris

Copy Editor: Karen Annett

Senior Indexer: Cheryl Lenser

Senior Compositor: Gloria Schurick

Proofreader: Language Logistics, LLC

Manufacturing Buyer: Dan Uhrig

Published by Pearson plc

Publishing as IBM Press

IBM Press offers excellent discounts on this book when ordered in quantity for bulk purchases or special sales, which may include electronic versions and/or custom covers and content particular to your business, training goals, marketing focus, and branding interests. For more information, please contact:

U.S. Corporate and Government Sales
1-800-382-3419
corpsales@pearsontechgroup.com

For sales outside the U.S., please contact:

International Sales
international@pearson.com

Library of Congress Cataloging-in-Publication Data

Giordano, Anthony, 1959-

 Data integration : blueprint and modeling techniques for a scalable and sustainable architecture / Anthony Giordano.

    p. cm.

 ISBN-13: 978-0-13-708493-7 (hardback : alk. paper)

 ISBN-10: 0-13-708493-5 (hardback : alk. paper)

 1. Data integration (Computer Science) 2. Data structures (Computer science) I. Title.

 QA76.9.D338G56 2010

 005.7'3—dc22

                    2010041861

   Pearson Education, Inc
   Rights and Contracts Department
   501 Boylston Street, Suite 900
   Boston, MA 02116
   Fax (617) 671-3447

First printing December 2010

ISBN-13: 978-0-13-708493-7

ISBN-10: 0-13-708493-5

I would like to dedicate this book to my family, Jenny, Happy, Raleigh, Katie, and Kelsie. It is their patience with my 80–90 hour work weeks that have provided me with the experiences necessary to write this book.
Lest I forget, I must also thank my two wolf hounds, Rupert and Switters, who kept me company during the long hours writing this book.

Contents

Appendix D is an online-only appendix. Print-book readers can download the appendix at www.ibmpressbooks.com/title/9780137084937. For eBook editions, the appendix is included in the book.

Preface

This text provides an overview on data integration and its application in business analytics and data warehousing. As the analysis of data becomes increasingly important and ever more tightly integrated into all aspects of Information Technology and business strategy, the process to combine data from different sources into meaningful information has become its own discipline. The scope of this text is to provide a look at this emerging discipline, its common "blueprint," its techniques, and its consistent methods of defining, designing, and developing a mature data integration environment that will provide organizations the ability to move high-volume data in ever-decreasing time frames.

Intended Audience

This text serves many different audiences. It can be used by an experienced data management professional for confirming data integration fundamentals or for college students as a textbook in an upper-level data warehousing college curriculum. The intended audience includes the following:

- Data warehouse program and project managers
- Data warehouse architects
- Data integration architects
- Data integration designers and developers
- Data modeling and database practitioners
- Data management-focused college students

Scope of the Text

This book stresses the core concepts of how to define, design, and build data integration processes using a common data integration architecture and process modeling technique.

With that goal in mind, *Data Integration Blueprint and Modeling*

- Reviews the types of data integration architectural patterns and their applications
- Provides a data integration architecture blueprint that has been proven in the industry
- Presents a graphical design technique for data integration based on process modeling, data integration modeling
- Covers the Systems Development Life Cycle of data integration
- Emphasizes the importance of data governance in data integration

Organization of the Text

The text is organized into three parts, including the following:

- **Part 1: Overview of Data Integration**

  The first part of this text provides an overview of data integration. Because of the operational and analytic nature of integrating data, the frequency and throughput of the data integration processes have developed into different types of data integration architectural patterns and technologies. Therefore, this part of the text begins with an investigation of the architectural types or patterns of data integration.

  Regardless of the type of architecture or supporting technology, there is a common blueprint or reference architecture for the integrating data. One of the core architectural principles in this text is that the blueprint must be able to deal with both operational and analytic data integration types. We will review the processes and approach to the data integration architecture.

  The final concept focuses on a graphical process modeling technique for data integration design, based on that reference architecture.

  To complete this section, we provide a case study of designing a set of data integration jobs for a banking data warehouse using the Data Integration Modeling Technique.

- **Part 2: The Data Integration Systems Development Life Cycle**

  The second part of the text covers the Systems Development Life Cycle (SDLC) of a data integration project in terms of the phases, activities, tasks, and deliverables. It explains how the data integration reference architecture is leveraged as its blueprint, and data integration modeling as the technique to develop the analysis, design, and development deliverables. This section begins the next of a multichapter case study on building an end-to-end data integration application with multiple data integration jobs for the Wheeler Automotive Company, which will require the reader to work through the entire data integration life cycle.

- **Part 3: Data Integration and Other Information Management Disciplines**

  The third part of this text discusses data integration in the context of other Information Management disciplines, such as data governance, metadata, and data quality. This part investigates the definition of data governance and its related disciplines of metadata and data quality. It reviews how both the business and IT are responsible for managing data governance and its impact on the discipline of data integration.

  For metadata, this part provides an overview of what metadata is, the types of metadata, and which types of metadata are relevant in data integration.

  Finally, this part reviews concepts of data quality in terms of the types, approaches to prevent bad data quality, and how to "clean up" existing bad data quality.

- **End-of-Chapter Questions**

  Each chapter provides a set of questions on the core concepts in the book to test the reader's comprehension of the materials. Answers to the questions for each chapter can be found in Appendix A, "Chapter Exercise Answers."

- **Appendices**

  Much of the supporting materials to the text can be found in the appendices, which include the following:

  - Appendix A, "Chapter Exercise Answers"—This appendix contains answers to the questions found at the end of each chapter.

  - Appendix B, "Data Integration Guiding Principles"—This appendix contains the guiding principles of data integration that were referenced throughout the book.

  - Appendix C, "Glossary"—This appendix contains the glossary of terms used in the book.

  - Appendix D, "Case Study Models"—This appendix can be found in the eBook versions of this book, or it can be downloaded from the book's companion Web site (www.ibmpressbooks.com/title/9780137084937). It contains the detailed data models, entity-attribute reports, subject area file layouts, data mappings, and other artifacts that were created and used throughout the book in the Wheeler case studies.

Acknowledgments

As with most Information Technology concepts, no one person invents a new architectural concept; they observe and document that concept in the workplace. The data integration architectural concepts discussed in this book are no different. This book is a result of the collaboration of many skilled and committed data integration practitioners. In particular, I would like to acknowledge Mike Schroeck, Mark Sterman, Ed Sheehy, and Bruce Tyler who started me on this journey; Joe Culhane, Jay Whitley, and Jay Houghton for believing and committing to my vision of data integration modeling; and Glenn Finch for sponsoring and mentoring this vision. I also need to thank Greg Transchida, Mike Spencer, and Ron Nitschke for believing.

I would also like to acknowledge Si Prather and Dr. Don Gottwald in their help reviewing, editing, and forming the content of this effort.

About the Author

Anthony Giordano is a partner in IBM's Business Analytics and Optimization Consulting Practice and currently leads the Enterprise Information Management Service Line that focuses on data modeling, data integration, master data management, and data governance. He has more than 20 years of experience in the Information Technology field with a focus in the areas of business intelligence, data warehousing, and Information Management. In his spare time, he has taught classes in data warehousing and project management at the undergraduate and graduate levels at several local colleges and universities.

Introduction: Why Is Data Integration Important?

Today's business organizations are spending tens to *hundreds* of millions of dollars to integrate data for transactional and business intelligence systems at a time when budgets are severely constrained and every dollar of cost counts like never before. There are organizations that have thousands of undocumented point-to-point data integration applications that require significant runtime, CPU, and disk space to maintain and sustain. Consider the cost of an average Information Technology worker at $100,000; the larger the environment, the more workers are needed to support all these processes. Worse, a majority of these processes are either redundant or no longer needed.

This unprecedented rate of increased cost in data integration is felt especially in those organizations that have grown rapidly through acquisition. It is also observed where there is an absence of corporate-level strategy and operational processes regarding the management and maintenance of corporate data assets. Businesses are relying more heavily on analytic environments to improve their efficiency, maintain market share, and mine data for opportunities to improve revenue and reduce cost.

One of the main reasons for excessive cost within the data integration domain is the absence of a clear, consistent, and effective approach to defining, designing, and building data integration components that lead to a more effective and cost-efficient data integration environment. Having a well-documented environment with fewer data integration processes will ensure that both cost and complexity will be reduced.

The intent of this book is to describe a common data integration approach that can substantially reduce the overall cost of the development and maintenance of an organization's data integration environment and significantly improve data quality over time.

Data Integration...An Overlooked Discipline

You can go into any bookstore or surf www.Amazon.com on the Web and you will find volumes of books on Information Management disciplines. Some of these will be data modeling texts that cover all the different types of data modeling techniques from transactional, dimensional, logical, and physical types of models and their purposes in the process of data integration.

There are very few books that cover the architecture, design techniques, and methodology of the Information Management discipline of data integration. Why? Because data integration isn't sexy. The front-end business intelligence applications provide the "cool," colorful, executive dashboards with the multicolored pie and bar charts. Data modeling is a technology focal point for all data-related projects. But the processes or "pipes" that integrate, move, and populate the data have been largely ignored or misunderstood because it is simply hard, tedious, and highly disciplined work.

This emerging discipline has developed from the old programming technologies such as COBOL that moved data with traditional programming design patterns or from database technologies that move data with stored SQL procedures. It is a discipline that is in dire need of the same focus as data modeling, especially because data integration has consistently made up 70% of the costs and risks of all data warehousing and business intelligence projects over the past 15 years.

The cost of maintenance for these data integration environments can be staggering with documented cases of ongoing maintenance cost into the hundreds of millions of dollars. Most data integration environments are poorly documented, with no repeatable method of understanding or clear ability to view the data integration processes or jobs. This leads to unnecessary rework that results in massive redundancy in the number of data integration processes or jobs we see in many organizations. Every unnecessary or duplicative data integration process results in excessive data, increased maintenance, and staff cost, plus the dreaded word, *bad* when it comes to trust in and the measurement of data quality. Anytime an organization has competing data integration processes that perform the same task, it is inevitable that there will be different results, causing the user community to doubt the validity of the data.

As with any engineering discipline, when an organization uses an architecture-specific blueprint, with common processes and techniques to build out and sustain an environment, it reaps the benefits of adhering to that discipline. The benefits are improved quality, lower costs, and sustainability over the long term. Organizations that use a common data integration architecture or blueprint and build and maintain their data integration processes have reaped those benefits.

Data Integration Fundamentals

Data integration leverages both technical and business processes to combine data into useful information for transactional analytics and/or business intelligence purposes. In the current environment, the volume, velocity, and variety of data are growing at unprecedented levels. Yet most organizations have not changed the approach to how they develop and maintain these data integration processes, which has resulted in expensive maintenance, poor data quality, and a limited ability to support the scope and ever-increasing complexity of transactional data in business intelligence environments.

Data integration is formally defined as the following:

> **Data integration** is a set of procedures, techniques, and technologies used to design and build processes that extract, restructure, move, and load data in either operational or analytic data stores either in real time or in batch mode.

Challenges of Data Integration

Of all the Information Management disciplines, data integration is the most complex. This complexity is a result of having to combine similar data from multiple and distinct source systems into one consistent and common data store for use by the business and technology users. It is this integration of business and technical data that presents the challenge. Although the technical issues of data integration are complex, it is conforming (making the many into one) the business definitions or *metadata* that prove to be the most difficult. One of the key issues that leads to poor data quality is the inability to conform multiple business definitions into one enterprise or canonical definition, as shown in Figure I.1.

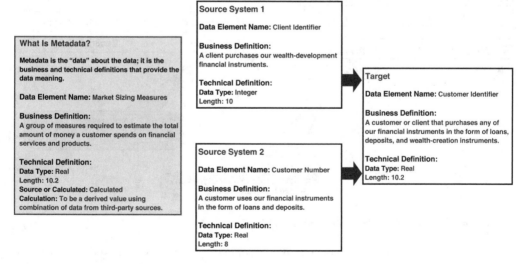

Figure I.1   Example of integrating data into information

A major function of data integration is to integrate disparate data into a single view of information. An example of a single view of information is the concept of a bank loan.

For a bank (or other financial institution) to have a single view of information, they need to integrate their different types of loans. Most U.S. banks leverage packaged applications from vendors such as AFS for commercial loans and ACLS for retail loans for their loan origination and processing. To provide these banks a holistic view of their loan portfolios, the AFS-formatted loan data and ACLS-formatted loan data need to be conformed into a common and standard format with a universal business definition.

Because the major focus of this text is integrating data for business intelligence environments, the target for this loan type example will be a data warehouse.

For this data warehouse, there is a logical data model complete with a set of entities and attributes, one of which is for the loan entity. One of the attributes, "Loan Type Code" is the unique identifier of the loan type entity. A loan type classifies the valid set of loans, such as commercial loan and retail loan.

Figure I.2 demonstrates the issues caused by the complexity of simply integrating the Loan Type attribute for commercial loans (AFS) and retail loans (ACLS), into a common Loan Type field in the data warehouse.

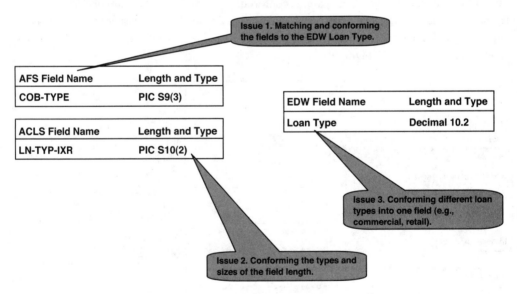

Figure I.2 Complexity issues with integrating data

In addition to discussing topics such as conforming technical and business definitions, this book covers core data integration concepts and introduces the reader to new approaches such as data integration modeling. This set of activities will help an institution organize its data integration environments into a set of common processes that will ultimately drive unnecessary cost out of their analytic environments and provide greater information capabilities.

PART 1

Overview of Data Integration

CHAPTER 1

Types of Data Integration

The first part of this text provides an overview of data integration. We know from our definition that data integration is a set of processes used to extract or capture, restructure, move, and load or publish data, in either operational or analytic data stores, in either real time or in batch mode. Because of the operational and analytic nature of integrating data, the frequency and throughput of the data have developed into different types of data integration architectural patterns and technologies. Therefore, this section begins with an investigation of the architectural types or "patterns" of data integration.

We also know that regardless of the type of architecture or supporting technology, there is a common "blueprint" for integrating data. One of the core architectural principles in this text is that the blueprint must be able to deal with both operational and analytic data integration types. We will review the processes and approach to our data integration architecture.

The final concept in Part I, "Overview of Data Integration," focuses on the need for a common technique for designing databases. We believe that there needs to be the same sort of rigor and discipline for the definition and design of data integration processes. We will review a graphical approach for designing data integration processes using existing process modeling techniques called data integration modeling.

Data Integration Architectural Patterns

The major focus of this book is data integration for data warehousing and analytics environments. At the same time, it is important to define all the types of data integration, both transactional and business intelligence, along with the types of data integration architectural models.

First, there are different methods or patterns of integrating data based on the types of processing being performed, which includes the following:

- **Transactional data integration**—Focuses on how transactions are created, updated, modified, and deleted

- **Business intelligence data integration**—Focuses on the collection of those transactions and forming them into a database structure that facilitates analysis

Transactional and business intelligence types of data integration are reflected in the following architecture models.

Enterprise Application Integration (EAI)

The first architectural pattern we review is known as *Enterprise Application Integration* or *EAI*. EAI provides transactional data integration for disparate source systems, both custom and package. EAI would be a relatively simple architectural pattern in a perfect world. One application would create a transaction, review and update the "lookup data" (e.g., List of Values) for the transaction, and, finally, commit the transaction. The existing application environment consists of enterprise resource planning (ERP) package applications, from vendors such as SAP® and Oracle® as well as others, in addition to internally developed custom applications. Because in many organizations there are multiples of these internally developed and packaged ERP applications, the simple act of creating, populating, and committing a transaction is a much more complex event. For example, many organizations may have multiple copies of SAP's Order Management system by Geography. An update to one system may require an update to all Order Management systems.

What Are the Complexities of EAI?

The complexities of EAI involve the requirement to bring together, in a high-performing manner, disparate technologies. The classic EAI implementation example is a large, complex multinational corporation that uses SAP for its General Ledger, Oracle Applications for its Order Entry, and the IBM® MDM package for its customer hub, as portrayed in Figure 1.1.

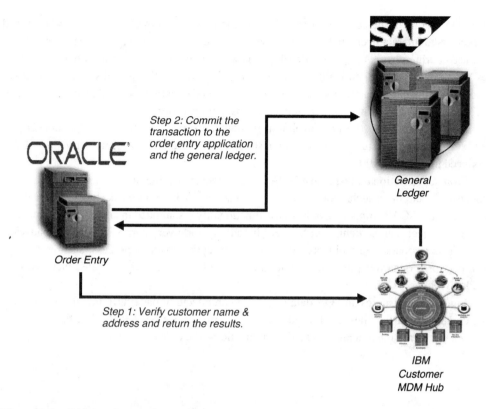

Figure 1.1 EAI data integration architectural pattern example

In this scenario, when a customer places an order through the Oracle Order Entry Application, the customer name and address must be verified through the customer hub. Once verified, the transaction must be submitted to the system of origin, the Oracle Order Entry system, and also the SAP General Ledger. Multiply this complexity by two or more Order Entry Systems and General Ledgers all in one organization. It is the challenge of the multiple versions of technology integration that EAI attempts to address.

When Should EAI Be Considered?

EAI as a data integration architectural pattern is best leveraged in environments where there are multiple, disparate transactional systems that need to share the same transactional information.

Service-Oriented Architecture (SOA)

Service-oriented architecture (SOA) is a transactional data integration pattern that routes or "orchestrates" messages to instantiate objects that will perform at different levels on a common network interface called a service bus. These objects represent functional business components, which are created or instantiated at different layers of granularity.

SOA can really be considered more of a framework that allows the previously discussed components to interact over a network. It provides a set of guiding principles for governing concepts used during phases of systems development and integration. It is a framework that "packages" the component functionality as interoperable services: Components either within or without the firewall can be provided as a service that can be integrated or used by other organizations, even if their respective client systems are substantially different.

SOA is considered the next evolution of both EAI and CORBA (the Common Object Request Broker Architecture) that has shown some level of adoption in the industry since it was introduced in the mid-1990s.

From an operational perspective, SOA requires loose coupling of services within the operating systems and other technologies within a framework. This framework directs, controls, or orchestrates the SOA components or business functionality instantiated in an on-demand manner.

SOA objects can be defined either very broadly or for a very narrow process. Broad-view SOA objects or coarse-grain objects can represent an entire business process, such as "Create Customer," or very narrow processes or fine-grain SOA objects with very discrete functions, such as address lookup or account total.

Figure 1.2 illustrates an SOA data integration architectural pattern. In this illustration, the SOA components are orchestrated through an enterprise service bus (ESB). The ESB provides that layer of abstraction that allows existing applications to interact as components.

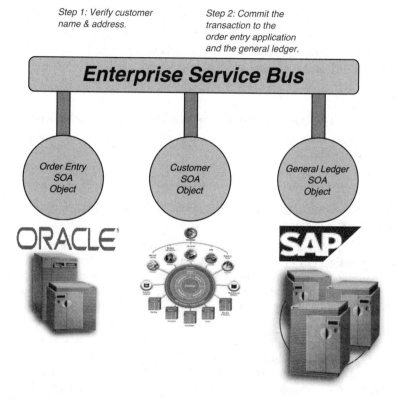

Step 1: Verify customer name & address.

Step 2: Commit the transaction to the order entry application and the general ledger.

Figure 1.2   SOA data integration architectural pattern example

What Are the Complexities of SOA?

There are multiple challenges to the design and implementation of an SOA environment. First is *Rigidity and Rigor*—the same disciplines that have caused issues with the success of earlier object-based architectures such as CORBA. Rigidity indicates that set patterns must be followed with little variance. Rigor indicates that adherence to standards must be absolute for a component to work. Although both of these principles are those that are the goals for all software development shops, it has only taken hold in the most mature Information Technology environments. The requirement for the strict adherence to the architecture and the standards of SOA are well beyond most Information Technology Departments' current levels of technical maturity. SOA requires an extremely disciplined approach to the design process to ensure that the components developed can be leveraged in this architectural pattern.

When Should SOA Be Considered?

SOA should be considered by organizations that are mature enough to manage a portfolio of both in-house custom SOA objects and external SOA objects. SOA is not for beginners; organizations need to have some level of maturity in their development, architecture, and portfolio management processes. Cutting-edge companies that are investigating and implementing a Software As A Service (**SAAS**) application such as Salesforce.com, will be able to integrate SAAS applications into their organizations by leveraging their SOA service bus. Although it is yet to be determined whether SOA will ultimately succeed as a ubiquitous architecture in everyday environments, many organizations have had different levels of success in implementing SOA, and some are currently reaping its benefits.

Although SOA is not the major focus for this book, we do investigate and discuss how you can instantiate data integration components as fine-grain SOA objects in Chapter 8, "Data Integration Logical Design Case Study."

TRANSACTION-FOCUSED DATA INTEGRATION PROCESSING AND BUSINESS INTELLIGENCE

EAI and SOA truly are transaction-focused architectures. There is much discussion about how these transaction-focused architectural patterns will more tightly integrate into the business intelligence space. We believe this is partly true. Business intelligence is based entirely on analyzing aggregated transactions. If a system is *truly* real-time, those transactions can be captured and consolidated in real time for analysis.

When considering real-time data integration for business intelligence, let prudence and pragmatism rule the day. Let the business requirements dictate whether a downstream database or application requires real-time data integration. One example of overenthusiasm in applying real time is an example of a department head, who upon hearing about the opportunities in real-time data integration stated, "Stop the project, we need to build real-time data integration processes for our data warehouse so that we can analyze information in real time." Unfortunately, they were building an employee data warehouse, where the major transactions were the biweekly payroll updates with fairly infrequent employee information (e.g., address) updates. His staff informed him of the extra time and cost of building real-time data integration interfaces and questioned the business benefit of spending the additional money on building real-time data integration interfaces for biweekly updates. Upon reflection of the cost/benefit, he abandoned the idea. The lesson is that each of these architectural patterns has its place, based on what is the right pattern for a real business need, not marketing hype.

Federation

Federation is a data integration pattern that has been in the industry since the mid-1980s. Federation combines disparate data into a common logical data structure, typically a relational database, not by moving data, but by providing a uniform view of the data, as shown in Figure 1.3.

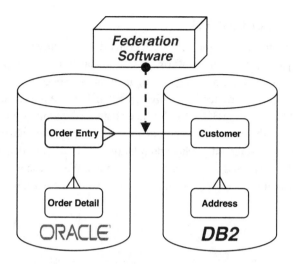

Figure 1.3   Federated data integration architectural pattern example

It is the idea of connecting disparate database technologies through a "bridge" concept that provides a "virtual" database. Connected at the database table level, it provides the ability to develop logical data models across the enterprise regardless of location and technology across the network.

What Are the Complexities of Federation?

The commercial software packages for federation can be notoriously difficult to implement and configure and are bandwidth-intensive. One of the primary problems of a federated solution is getting all the disparate hardware, software, and network configured properly to provide acceptable performance. Another problem is managing expectations. There are both business and technical users that will expect a federated solution to perform at the same level as a homogenous database solution. A query, however, that is performed intradatabase in the same database engine and platform will always perform faster than a query that is assembled over a network. Also if a high level of transformation is required, then federation will have the bandwidth challenges of attempting to perform transformation on the network.

When Should Federation Be Considered?

The key word here is expediency. When developing a solution that requires data from disparate environments, the time and cost of redevelopment are not justified, and the usage of the data is not transactional, then federation is a viable option. A classic example as described here is in environments in which the organization wants to leverage a common customer table over multiple geographic locations, such as London, New York, and Washington. Using a data federation product, location-specific order management packages can use the same customer database in a remote location.

Extract, Transform, Load (ETL)

ETL is the collection and aggregation of transactional data, as shown in Figure 1.4, with data extracted from multiple sources to be conformed into databases used for reporting and analytics. Most of the cost and maintenance of complex data integration processing occurs in the bulk data movement space. ETL has experienced explosive growth in both frequency and size in the past 15 years. In the mid-1990s, pushing 30GB to 40GB of data on a monthly basis was considered a large effort. However, by the twenty-first century, moving a terabyte of data on a daily basis was a requirement. In addition to standard flat file and relational data formats, data integration environments need to consider XML and unstructured data formats. With these new formats, along with the exponential growth of transactional data, multi-terabyte data integration processing environments are not unusual.

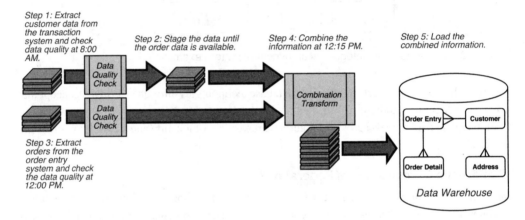

Figure 1.4   ETL data integration architectural pattern

What Are the Complexities of ETL?

There are several complexities in ETL data integration, including the following:

- **Batch window processing**—In addition to the common data integration issues of integrating business and technical metadata, integrating data from different source systems that have different batch windows of available data for extraction or capture create latency issues on when the combined data can be made available for end-user access.

- **Duplicative processes**—The old traditional programming design patterns used in this architecture (also found in the others as well) lead to massive redundancies in all aspects of the ETL job design. The current traditional programming design approach for developing ETL data integration processes is that a single data integration process will be developed to extract the customer data, check (or more often than not, not check) some sort of data quality criteria, and then load that data. A separate data integration process performs another extract, a quality check, and data load. This duplication may result in data quality issues as well as make it highly unlikely that the two processes remain in sync over time.

- **Change data capture processing**—The process of capturing transactional changes to source systems (adds, changes, deletes) is both complicated and process-intensive in terms of how to capture the changes and process them into the target data warehouse environment.

When there are two different data quality processes with different criteria/business rules, you not only have inconsistent data quality, but you also have expensive duplication of processes, data, maintenance, and, ultimately, costs. Chapter 3, "A Design Technique: Data Integration Modeling," provides in-depth coverage of a different design paradigm, called Physical Data Integration Modeling, that addresses the data quality duplication issue where much of the hidden cost of data integration can be found and addressed.

When Should ETL Be Considered?

For non-real-time, transactional data that accumulates, ETL is the preferred data integration architectural pattern, especially where there is a lag between the times when the transactions are created and the time when the data is needed.

It is also the preferred approach when there are multiple extracts of accumulated data with different frequencies of data that require aggregation to a common file format.

For example, customer data is updated once a week, but order management data is updated daily; the differences in frequencies require an architectural pattern such as bulk ETL that can store and then simultaneously process the different sources of data.

It should be noted that with the maturation of Change Data Capture (CDC) capabilities being added to commercial data integration technologies, the line between EAI and ETL is becoming increasingly blurred. Change Data Capture is covered in more detail in Chapter 8.

Common Data Integration Functionality

In this chapter, we have reviewed the various architectural patterns for data integration based on transactional and business intelligence requirements.

Regardless of the pattern being used for transactional or business intelligence purposes, the following clear and common functions exist in each of the patterns:

- **Capture/extract**—All patterns need to acquire data, either as a transaction or as groups of transactions.
- **Quality checking**—All patterns encourage the qualification of the data being captured.
- **Change**—All patterns provide the facility to change the data being captured.
- **Move**—All patterns provide the capabilities to move and load the data to an end target.

We use this concept of these common functions as a foundation in the forthcoming chapters on what is needed for a common architecture for data integration.

Summary

So the question is, "What architectural patterns do you focus on?" The question is as clear as mud. Today's data integration environments must be able to deal with all these architectural patterns, based on the type of data integration required. There are clear challenges to implementation of any of these architectural patterns, from organizational maturity to technical constraints. These are common challenges not just in data integration environments, but also in most Information Technology organizations; it is just more pronounced in a data integration environment (remember the 70% cost and risk factor), especially for business intelligence projects.

At the same time, there is a true convergence of business needs that is causing these patterns to converge. The business need for real-time analytics that are being embedded into operational processes is driving the need to be able to leverage both the real-time and batch data integration capabilities.

Because of this convergence, many of the data integration environments that extract, transform, and load multiterabytes of data now need to process near-real-time transactional feeds often at the same time. Fortunately, the required ability to provide both EAI and ETL functionality in current data integration software is improving. The data integration software vendors are adding the capability to perform both EAI and ETL processing in their software packages.

What is needed is an architectural blueprint that will accommodate both EAI and ETL processing in a more cost-effective manner, while providing the ability to also instantiate fine-grain SOA components on an enterprise service bus.

Chapter 2, "An Architecture for Data Integration," focuses on just such a blueprint for data integration.

End-of-Chapter Questions

Question 1.
What is the formal definition of data integration?

Question 2.
What are the three problems noted in the complexity issue in integrating data displayed in the Introduction that are caused by the complexity of simply integrating the Loan Type attribute for commercial loans and retail loans into a common Loan Type field in the data warehouse?

Question 3.
What are the four data integration architectural patterns?

Question 4.
Regardless of data integration purpose (transactional or business intelligence), what are the clear and common functions in each of the patterns?
Question 5.
For two of the four data integration architectural patterns, provide a rationale of when it is appropriate to use that particular pattern.

Please note that the answers to all end-of-chapter questions can be found in Appendix A, "Chapter Exercise Answers."

An Architecture for Data Integration

If there is one key chapter in this book to read and internalize, it is this one. Understanding how to build to a component-based data integration architecture is the differentiator between a flexible, low-maintenance\cost environment and ever-spiraling maintenance costs.

In this chapter, we will review a reference architecture for data integration that can be leveraged for most of the data integration architectural patterns we reviewed in Chapter 1, "Types of Data Integration." We will discuss what reference architecture is, and how it is simply a blueprint, not a dogmatic discipline, but a suggested best-practice method of building out data integration applications based on business requirements. As we review this chapter, we will define and review the specific processes and landing zones (a defined directory or area where data is staged) that makes up the data integration reference architecture.

What Is Reference Architecture?

We cannot fathom building a house or high-rise without a picture or blueprint that communicates the requirements within the boundaries of commonly accepted engineering principles.

In fact whether you are building a three-bedroom house or a one-hundred-story skyscraper, there are certain common subsystems or layers, such as the following:

- Water infrastructure
- Electrical infrastructure

- Telecommunications

- Heating and cooling

Because of these common layers, most builders have been able to understand how to build a structure. However, the design is still dependent on the user's requirements, for example, a family may choose between a ranch-style, a tri-level, or a colonial-style house, based on financing and family size. Regardless of what design is chosen, all buildings will still have those common layers. The same is true of a data integration environment; there are common layers that all data integration environments share. The requirements will dictate the design of the data integration components that will leverage the architectural patterns within these layers, whether it is transactional or business intelligence-oriented.

The following data integration reference architectures follow these principles of common layers.

Reference Architecture for Data Integration

The data integration reference architecture, shown in Figure 2.1, defines the processes and environments that support the capture, quality checking, processing, and movement of data whether it is transactional or bulk to one or many targets.

This architecture or blueprint has been implemented and proven in the field as operational data integration environments that process terabytes of information for analytic data stores such as data warehouses, operational data stores, and data marts using all the commercial data integration technologies, such as Ab Initio, IBM Data Stage, and Informatica.

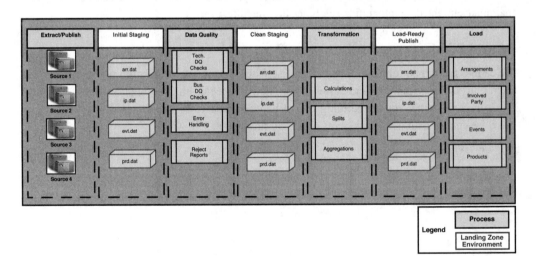

Figure 2.1   Data integration reference architecture

Objectives of the Data Integration Reference Architecture

Whether a data integration environment has applications that have been designed and built to a planned blueprint or has evolved organically, it has a design pattern. Many early data integration environments suffer from significant complexity and poor performance by not having been built to any plan or blueprint.

This blueprint or reference architecture for data integration in Figure 2.1 has been developed over time through both observing high-performance data integration application environments and experience in the field in designing, building, and maintaining large, complex data integration application environments. This data integration reference architecture has been developed to ensure two main objectives: simplicity and scalability.

Simplicity in Common Architectural Layers

Communicating commonly understood concepts is a key factor in the success of any project, whether creating a data integration project or designing a relational database. A part of the success of modeling data with entity-relationship diagrams is the simplicity of the notation and its understandability. An entity relationship contains simply entities, attributes, and relationships. The common layers of the data integration reference architecture are meant to provide that same communication medium of common understanding of the stages and processes found in data integration.

Using the data integration reference architecture, there is always an extract layer to an initial stage, then data quality layer to a clean stage, then a transformation layer to a load-ready stage, and then a load-ready publish layer. Each layer and stage have a specifically defined purpose and usage; all drive the concepts of reusability. By tightly defining the functionality of each layer and stage, best practices, techniques, and assets can be developed and refined at that layer or stage.

It is important to note that these layers are not necessarily sequential or even necessary. Not every data integration process will need to have transformations or even data quality checks, based on the particular business requirements of that data integration process.

The data integration reference architecture has proven extremely useful for development planning. The extract and loading layers usually require simpler design and development skills, where a project manager can leverage junior developers, allowing the project manager to focus more senior resources on the more complex data quality and transformation layers.

Simplicity in Providing a Layer of Encapsulation from the Source to Target

Brian Kernighan and Dennis Ritchie in their seminal book *An Introduction to C Programming* stated it best in that "a function should do one and only one thing." The data integration architecture promotes that concept to ensure the encapsulation of changes in data structure between the sources and targets, creating a flexible environment that can be more easily managed, maintained, and expanded.

Much of the cost and expense of building and maintaining data integration jobs is due to traditional application programming design techniques that they were developed in. Much of the existing data integration jobs that have been developed are the result of traditional third-generation language (3GL) programmers or database administrators with a procedural SQL background. They use their single-purpose, traditional design approaches for COBOL programs or PL/SQL scripts when designing and building stand-alone data integration jobs.

This design approach creates highly inflexible code that is difficult to extend due to its lack of modularity, which makes it easier to just build a duplicative process, hence the cost and redundancy found in most data integration environments today, as portrayed in Figure 2.2.

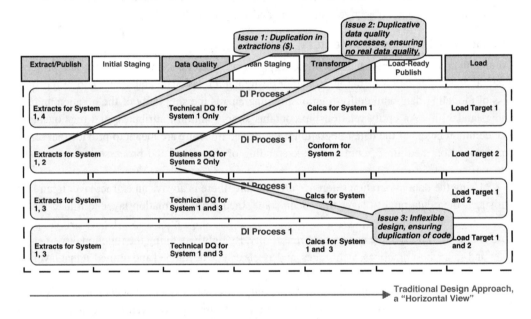

Figure 2.2   Traditional application-focused design approach

The Data Subject Area-Based Component Design Approach

To avoid the preceding sample scenario with redundant code, the goal of a mature data integration environment is to have as little code as possible that provides as much capability as possible. The key to not having inflexible application-based data integration processes is to break up the functionality into discrete, reusable components.

The data integration reference architecture provides the basis or blueprint for breaking up processes into discrete, highly modular, highly flexible components.

One of the key architectural principles used for increasing the modularity and flexibility in the design of a data integration architecture is to encapsulate both data and function in the staging layers using common file formats using the target data model's data subject areas.

The concept of subject area files is one where a common file format is used based on a business concept (such as customer) within each of the staging areas. This approach provides both the design modularity desired as well as the encapsulation of source data formats from the targets.

Subject area files (displayed in Figure 2.3) provide a simple generic layout, which allows information to be easily mapped by business concepts rather than source systems. This greatly reduces the complexities of traditional mapping exercises as all dependencies are determined well ahead of this design.

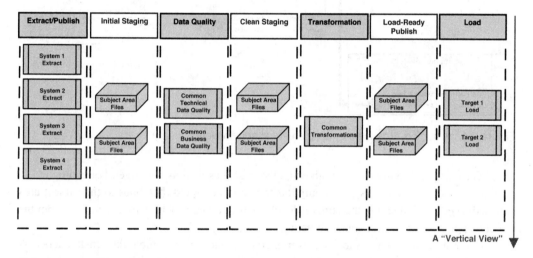

Figure 2.3   Using subject area files to provide a layer of encapsulation from the source to target

Target data stores provide a common file format for disparate sources and provide a layer of encapsulation between the sources and the ultimate target, as demonstrated in Figure 2.4.

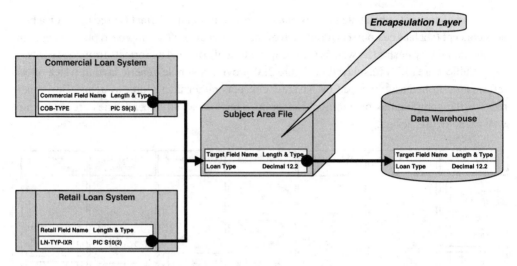

Figure 2.4   A subject area file providing an encapsulation layer

The encapsulation occurs at both ends: the source as well as the target. For example, if a change occurs in the source system, only the source system field that maps to the subject area load will need to change. On the target side, changes to a target field will only impact from the target mapping to the subject area load field.

Leveraging subject area files as a layer of conformance to a common file format that occurs on extract, plus changes that may occur in the target, such as collapsing tables, are shielded from the extract and transformation logic. An example of a subject area file is a customer subject area file or loan subject area file.

A Scalable Architecture

The requirements for scalability and stability have increased considerably in the past ten years. Business intelligence environments such as enterprise data warehouses are no longer 9 to 5 departmental reporting environments. They are now 24/7 global analytic environments that certainly cannot be down for two or three weeks or even two or three days. They need to be available for a much wider group of users who need daily access to do their jobs.

Modern data warehouse environments are also facing exponential increases in data volumes due to many reasons, including unstructured file formats such as XML.

To handle the growth of data and the ever-shorter downtime, the data integration reference architecture has been designed as a logical blueprint that can be instantiated across one or many physical machines, providing the ability to limit scalability to only the number of CPUs that are clustered.

The data integration reference architecture has a proven track record of scaling in the multiterabyte range across multiple machines.

Please note that CPU usage, memory usage, network, and backplane connectivity sizing must be thoroughly estimated based on current and expected volumes for the planned environment.

Figure 2.5 illustrates how the data integration reference architecture can be scaled over multiple CPUs.

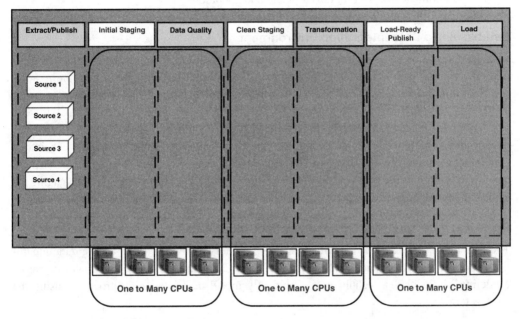

Figure 2.5   Scaling a data integration environment over multiple hardware platforms

The ability to scale the data integration over physical environments provides a data integration architect multiple options on how to configure an environment, including the following:

- **Environment 1: sharing an environment**—In this scenario, the data integration environment is hosted on a 24-way UNIX midrange, with 12 CPUs logically partitioned for the data integration environment and the other 12 CPUs dedicated to the database server.

- **Environment 2: dedicated environment**—In this scenario, the data integration environment is hosted and fully dedicated on the same 24-way CPU hardware platform.

- **Environment 3: managed environment**—In this scenario, the data integration environment is distributed between multiple Linux environments.

Purposes of the Data Integration Reference Architecture

The data integration architecture has two purposes:

- Establishing a data integration environment
- Providing a blueprint for development and operations

Establishing a Data Integration Environment

The data integration architecture provides a blueprint or framework for setting up a data integration environment with a data integration software package. It provides a basis for the requirements of a proposed data integration environment in terms of how the requirements are to be satisfied in a physical hardware infrastructure. These representations include conceptual, logical, and physical architecture diagrams; high-level platform definitions; key subject areas; the estimated number of files; and high-level volumes estimations. The primary audience consists of data integration architects, DBAs, systems administrators, project managers, data quality managers, and operations managers who have the responsibility for creating, using, and managing the environment.

Providing a Blueprint for Development and Operations

The data integration reference architecture also provides a blueprint for designing data integration processes in a consistent manner. In fact, Chapter 3, "A Design Technique: Data Integration Modeling," introduces a technique to graphically model data integration processes using the architecture.

The Layers of the Data Integration Architecture

The data integration architecture consists of conceptual layers of processes and landing zones, as portrayed in Figure 2.6.

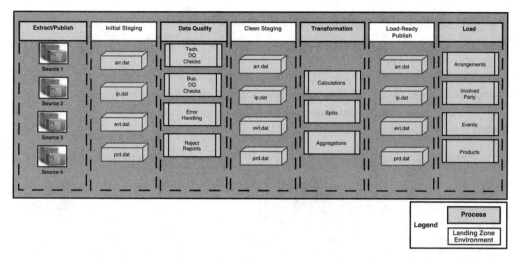

Figure 2.6 The processes and staging areas of the data integration reference architecture

The number-one question asked when first reviewing the data integration architecture is, "Do we need all the processes and landing zones?" The classic answer is, "It depends." It depends on the data integration process you are designing, it depends on the types of processing, and it depends on the frequency and volumes of data that will be moved through the process.

The best practice is that the larger the throughput data volume, the more likely landing data between processes is a good idea. For environmental sizing purposes, it is suggested that the environment be sized for the space and directories needed to accommodate all the recommended landing zones in the architecture. For individual data integration process designs, using the landing zones is on a process-by-process basis. The next sections of this chapter focus on the defined process layers and landing zones of this architecture.

Extract/Subscribe Processes

"Extract/subscribe" represents a set of processes that captures data, transactional or bulk, structured or unstructured, from various sources and lands it in an initial staging area. It follows the architectural principles of "read once, write many" to ensure that the impact on source systems is minimized, and data lineage is maintained.

Much of the excessive cost found in a data integration environment is the redundancy found in the extract/subscribe data integration processes. There are some **data integration guiding principles** that we follow in the development of this environment to prevent these costs.

Data Integration Guiding Principle: "Read Once, Write Many"

There is a reason why extract (either internal or external) costs are often so high. It is often the result of requests for multiple extracts from their source systems for the same data. One of the major issues in terms of cost and maintenance data integration is the number of uncontrolled, undocumented, and duplicative data integration extraction routines for the same data.

The goal is to have one data integration component per source type (flat file, relational), as portrayed in Figure 2.7.

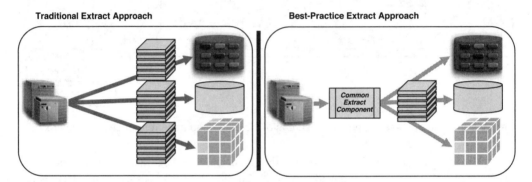

Figure 2.7   Traditional versus best-practice extract approaches

Data Integration Guiding Principle: "Grab Everything"

When developing extract requirements, it is easy to focus on only extracting the fields needed for the intended application or database. A best practice is to evaluate the data source in its entirety and consider extracting all potentially relevant data for the current and potential future sourcing needs, as shown in Figure 2.8. When extracting only data needed for a single application or database, it is highly probable that there will be the need to extend the application, rewrite the application, or in the worst case, write another extract from the same source system.

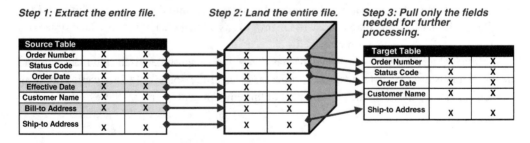

Figure 2.8   Staging the entire file, moving what is needed technique

As stated, the best practice is to extract all columns/data fields from the entire file and only use what is needed. It also helps in resource planning to have sufficient space planned for in the initial staging landing zone.

Initial Staging Landing Zone

Initial staging is the first optional landing zone, where the copy of the source data is landed as a result of the extract/subscribe processing.

The main objective of the initial staging area is to persist source data in nonvolatile storage to achieve the "pull it once from source" goal as well as the read once, write many principle.

Note that transactional data from real-time sources intended for real-time targets is captured through the extract/subscribe processes and might or might not land in the initial staging area, again based on the integration requirements.

Why land it? In situations where transactional data is passed to a transactional target and a business intelligence target, the requirements of aggregation will necessitate that the transactional data be combined with data that is not yet present and will require that the transactional data be staged and accumulated, as demonstrated in Figure 2.9.

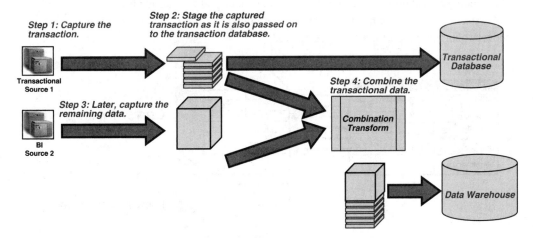

Figure 2.9 Store and forward: a rationale for landing data

Although many organizations have implemented landing zones, not many have truly thought through how to best exploit this layer of their data integration environment. For example, it is a great place to profile data for technical metadata and data quality criteria. The initial landing zone can become a data "junkyard" if not planned properly. It is not a place to store data indefinitely.

The disk space requirements for initial staging should be planned in advance by determining the volumetrics on every file.

The simple volumetrics formula is shown in Figure 2.10.

Source Table							
Order Number	Status Code	Order Date	Effective Date	Customer Name	Bill-to Address	Ship-to Address	
20	5	10	10	30	30	30	

Total Bytes

135

Number of Rows

30,000,000

4.05 GB

30% Yearly Growth

5.265 GB

Figure 2.10   Volumetrics formula

This should be done for all expected extract files and multiplied by the potential number of other landing zones this data may be staged in (e.g., data quality, load-ready).

Also the sizing plan needs to consider the number of file generations needed for disaster recovery planning, as portrayed in Figure 2.11.

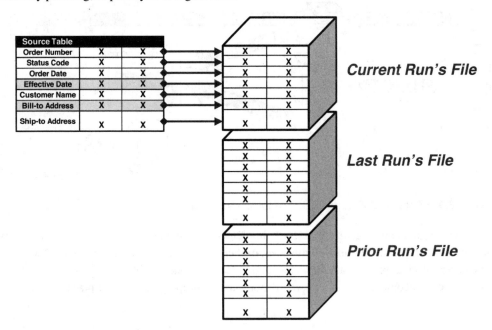

Figure 2.11   Storing generations of subject area files

When developing an operations plan, a subject area file cleanup schedule and process will be required to manage unwanted file proliferation and disk space size.

Data Quality Processes

Data quality processes are those data integration processes that qualify and cleanse the data, based upon technical and business process rules. These rules or **data quality criteria** are built in to the data integration jobs as data quality criteria or "checks."

You will find that data quality is a common architectural "thread" that is discussed in several different chapters of this book in terms of its impact on data integration processes and the data governance processes that are needed for a robust data integration environment.

What Is Data Quality?

Data quality is the commonly understood business and technical definition of data within defined ranges. It is measured by how effectively the data supports the transactions and decisions needed to meet an organization's strategic goals and objectives, as embodied in its ability to manage its assets and conduct its core operations.

The level of data quality required to effectively support operations will vary by information system or business unit, depending upon the information needs to conduct that business unit's operations. For example, financial systems require a high degree of quality data due to the importance and usage of the data, but a marketing system may have the latitude to operate with a lower level of data quality without significantly impacting the use of the information in measuring marketing success. Because the purpose varies, so does the bar that is used to measure fitness to purpose.

Causes of Poor Data Quality

Causes for bad data quality can be categorized as business-process and technology-defined data quality issues, as demonstrated in Figure 2.12.

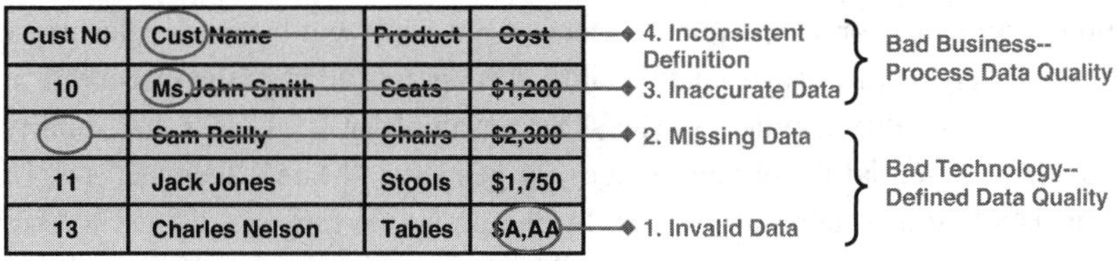

Figure 2.12   Examples of bad data quality types

Technology-driven poor data qualities are those types that are caused by not applying technology constraints either database or data integration. These types include the following:

- **Invalid data**—Data that in incorrect in that field. For example, by not applying constraints, alphanumeric data is allowed in a numeric data field (or column).

- **Missing data**—Data that is missing in that field. For example, by not applying key constraints in the database, a not-null field has been left null.

Business-driven bad data qualities are those types that are caused by end users inaccurately creating or defining data. Examples include the following:

- **Inaccurate data**—Invalid data due to incorrect input by business users. For example, by inaccurately creating a record for "Ms. Anthony Jones," rather than "Mr. Anthony Jones," poor data quality is created. Inaccurate data is also demonstrated by the "duplicate data" phenomenon. For example, an organization has a customer record for both "Anthony Jones" and Tony Jones," both the same person.
- **Inconsistent definitions**—Where stakeholders have different definitions of the data. By having disparate views on what the definition of poor data quality is, perceived bad quality is created, for example when the Sales Department has a different definition of customer profitability than the Accounting Department.

Data Quality Check Points

Poor data quality can be prevented by determining key data quality criteria and building those rules into data quality "checks." There are two types of data quality checks:

- **Technical data quality checkpoints**—Technical data quality checkpoints define the data quality criteria often found in both the entity integrity and referential integrity relational rules found in logical data modeling. They address the invalid and missing data quality anomalies. Technical data quality criteria are usually defined by IT and Information Management subject matter experts. An example includes the primary key null data quality checkpoint.
- **Business data quality checkpoints**—The business data quality checkpoints confirm the understanding of the key data quality elements in terms of what the business definition and ranges for a data quality element are and what business rules are associated with that element. Business data quality checkpoints address the inaccurate and inconsistent data quality anomalies. The classic example of a business data quality check is gender. A potential list of valid ranges for gender is "Male," "Female," or "Unknown." This is a business definition, not an IT definition; the range is defined by the business. Although many organizations find the three values for gender sufficient, the U.S. Postal Service has seven types of gender, so their business definition is broader than others.

Where to Perform a Data Quality Check

One of the best practices for data quality is that it should be checked before any transformation processing because there is usually no reason to process bad data. However, there are data integration environments that check data quality after transformations are complete due to business rules and legitimate technical reasons. An example is check total ranges, where a check occurs after a total sales calculation, ensuring that the amount is within a business-defined range.

Pragmatism dictates that the location of data quality checks in the architecture should be based on the data integration requirements, especially when there is a high degree of cycling logic, as portrayed in Figure 2.13.

*Iteratively Processing
Records in a Subject Area
File*

Figure 2.13 Iterative transform and data quality checkpoint processing scenario

Regardless of where the data quality rules and the data quality layer are executed, the following data quality checkpoint processing functionality should be provided, as shown in Figure 2.14:

- **Cleansed data files**—Using the data quality criteria, the good records are filtered into the "clean" file.

- **Reject data files**—Data records that fail are logged in the "reject" file.

- **Reject reports**—Data records that fail are listed in a tabular report with reason codes for review and renovation.

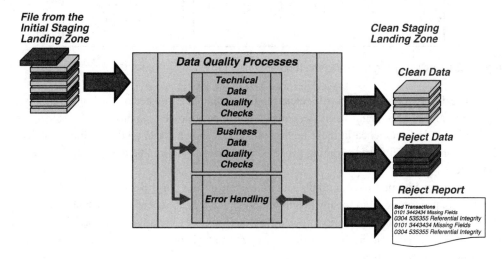

Figure 2.14 Data quality checkpoint processing architecture best practice

A discussion on whether records that fail the data quality process should stop the data integration process or whether the records should be flagged and passed or fail (absolute versus optional data quality) is located in Chapter 11, "Data Integration Development Cycle."

Clean Staging Landing Zone

The clean staging area is the next optional landing zone and it contains files that have clean data, flagged data, or rejected data. This data is either used for transformation processing or loaded directly to the final destination.

Figure 2.15 demonstrates both a simple pass-through or straight move and staging for transformation processing. Option 1 portrays how data may be passed directly to processes that build load-ready files. Option 2 demonstrates how the data becomes input to transformation processes, which, in turn, may produce new data sets.

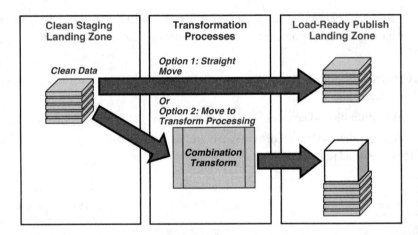

Figure 2.15   Clean staging land zone usages

The disk space requirements for clean staging should be estimated on the initial staging sizing requirements. This sizing should be considered for peak processing only, not for storing generations of files. Experience in these environments has shown when (and if) a file is landed in clean staging, it is only needed during processing of that file and can be deleted after processing completes.

Environments that have initially saved their clean files for a period of time have subsequently stopped saving them for any length of time due to a lack of need and use because it is easier to simply rerun the data quality processes. Therefore, file deletion upon process completion should be the default for clean stage files for operations planning. Any changes to that default should be based on business requirements.

Transform Processes

Transformations can mean many different things. For this text, transformations are defined as follows:

> **Transformation** is a data integration function that modifies existing data or creates new data through functions such as calculations and aggregations.

On the surface, the term **transform** appears to be a very simple definition in data integration. It is, in fact, the most complex aspect of data integration due in part to the very many different types of transformations. A transformation can be anything from reformatting information from **Char** to **Varchar**, to totaling a loan balancing column into an aggregation table.

There are a several types of transform patterns or types, which are discussed in the following sections.

Conforming Transform Types

Figure 2.16 portrays a common transformation type that maps or translates data from multiple data types into a common data type.

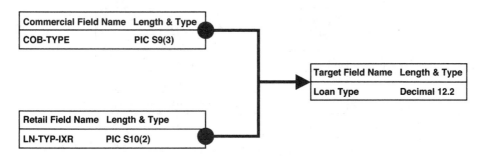

Figure 2.16   Conforming transformation example

Care needs to be used in determining data types. Conforming different data types requires trade-offs on efficiency in queries based on the category of data type used. For example, numeric data that will not be used for calculations, such as a Social Security number, can be stored in either VarChar or Integer; however, for queries, integer-defined columns are more efficient than VarChar.

Calculations and Splits Transform Types

Calculations and splits allow for the creation of new data elements (that extend the data set), or new data sets, that are derived from the source data. The enrichment capability includes the following functions:

- **Calculations**—Calculations process data in a data set to produce derived data based on data transforms and computations, as demonstrated in Figure 2.17.

Record Number	Date	Transaction Amount	Status	Customer Name
001	06/02/2005	$15,000	New	JP Morgan
002	06/02/2005	$35,000	Open	Citicorp
003	06/02/2005	$27,000	Open	Wachovia

Calculate Total	= Sum (Transaction Amount) $77,000

Figure 2.17   Calculation transformation example

- **Splits**—The architecture supports splitting data sets. Splitting is a technique used to divide a data set into subsets of fields that are then stored individually, as demonstrated in Figure 2.18.

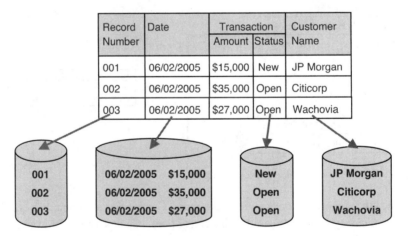

Figure 2.18   Splits calculation transformation example

Processing and Enrichment Transform Types

A transformation operational type is one that creates new data at the end of the process; these operational types include the following:

- **Joins**—Combines data fields from multiple sources and stores the combined data set, as portrayed in the example in Figure 2.19

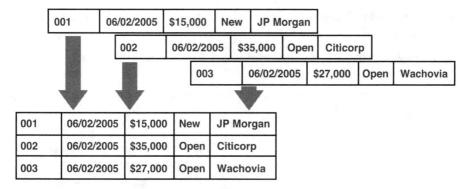

Figure 2.19 Join transformation example

- **Lookups**—Combines data fields from records with values from reference tables and stores the combined data set, as portrayed in the example in Figure 2.20

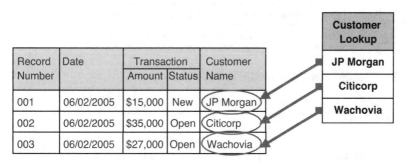

Figure 2.20 Lookup transformation example

- **Aggregations**—Creates new data sets that are derived from the combination of multiple sources and/or records, as portrayed in the example in Figure 2.21

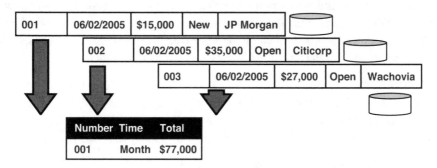

Figure 2.21 Aggregation transformation example

- **Change Data Capture**—Change Data Capture or CDC is the complex transform process that:

  - Identifies changed records from a source data set by comparing the values with the prior set from the source

  - Applies those changed records to the target database, as portrayed in the example in Figure 2.22

Data Warehouse Append

Record Number	Date	Transaction Amount	Status	Customer Name
001	06/02/2005	$15,000	New	JP Morgan
002	06/02/2005	$35,000	Open	Citicorp
003	06/02/2005	$27,000	Open	Wachovia
004	06/07/2005	$29,000	Edit	Wachovia
005	06/07/2005	$40,000	New	Wells Fargo

Figure 2.22   Change Data Capture transformation example

NOTE

We devote significant time to the types and approaches to Change Data Capture (**CDC**) in Chapter 8, "Data Integration Logical Design Case Study."

Target Filters Transform Types

Target filters format and filter data based on vertical (columns-level) and horizontal (row-level) business rules. Filtering is a powerful formatting tool and there can be instances where both vertical and horizontal filtering is performed on the same data file based on business rules. The following list presents some of the most-used filter types used in transformations:

- **Vertical filtering**—Passes only the data columns the target needs. In the example in Figure 2.23, only the three columns are passed.

- **Horizontal filtering**—Passes only the records that conform to the target rules. In the example in Figure 2.23, only the records with an "Open" status are passed.

Figure 2.23 depicts both vertical and horizontal filtering examples.

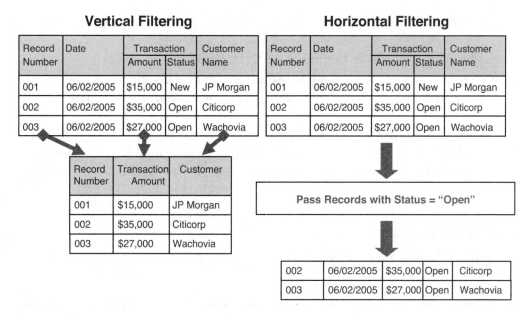

Vertical Filtering

Record Number	Date	Transaction Amount	Status	Customer Name
001	06/02/2005	$15,000	New	JP Morgan
002	06/02/2005	$35,000	Open	Citicorp
003	06/02/2005	$27,000	Open	Wachovia

Record Number	Transaction Amount	Customer
001	$15,000	JP Morgan
002	$35,000	Citicorp
003	$27,000	Wachovia

Horizontal Filtering

Record Number	Date	Transaction Amount	Status	Customer Name
001	06/02/2005	$15,000	New	JP Morgan
002	06/02/2005	$35,000	Open	Citicorp
003	06/02/2005	$27,000	Open	Wachovia

Pass Records with Status = "Open"

| 002 | 06/02/2005 | $35,000 | Open | Citicorp |
| 003 | 06/02/2005 | $27,000 | Open | Wachovia |

Figure 2.23   Horizontal and vertical filtering transformation examples

Please note that all the transform types presented represent the major types of transforms used in data integration. There are many other transformation types as well as permutations of the ones previously discussed.

Load-Ready Publish Landing Zone

Load-ready publish is an optional staging area (also called landing zone) that is utilized to store target-specific, load-ready files, which is depicted in Figure 2.24.

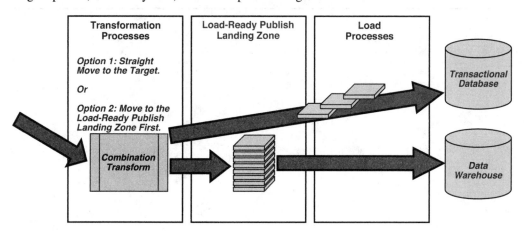

Figure 2.24   Example of a load-ready publish landing zone

If a target can take a direct output from the data integration tool first without storing the data, then storing it in a load-ready staging area might not be required.

There are two key areas to consider for load-ready publish:

- **Sizing**—Just as with the clean staging land zone, it is important to determine sizing. In this stage, there might be justification for keeping more than one generation of the load-ready files.

- **Disaster recovery**—At this point in the process, the load-ready files are essentially flat-file images of the tables that are going to be loaded. Saving these files on a data integration server that is separated from the database provides another layer of database recovery.

Load/Publish Processes

"Load/publish" is a set of standardized processes that loads either transactional or bulk updates.

DI GUIDING PRINCIPLE: "TARGET-BASE LOAD DESIGN"

The design principle for load processes is based on first, defining a target data store and second, defining by subject area within that data store.

To better explain this architectural concept, Figure 2.25 displays two files to load. One is for a stand-alone customer profitability data mart, and the second is for the enterprise data warehouse.

Designing the load processes by target data store and then subject area provides for the ability to design and extend tightly focused **target-based** load jobs.

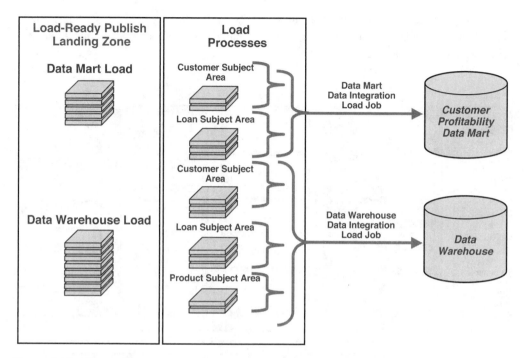

Figure 2.25   Target-based load design example

Physical Load Architectures

There are five types of physical load architectures:

- **FTP to target**—In this type of load, the process is only responsible for depositing the output to the target environment.
- **Piped data**—This process executes a load routine on the target that takes the data directly piped in from the target-specific filter.
- **RDBMS utilities**—The RDMS middleware utilities are used to load directly into the tables.
- **SQL**—SQL writes directly to the target database.
- **Message publishing**—This is used for loading real-time data feeds to message queues.

An Overall Data Architecture

They say that "no man is an island," and the same is true for the data integration architecture; it is simply an aspect of a larger architecture.

Within the data warehousing space in the IBM Global Business Services® Business Intelligence Practice, the data integration architecture is simply a layer of a broader architectural blueprint, as shown in Figure 2.26.

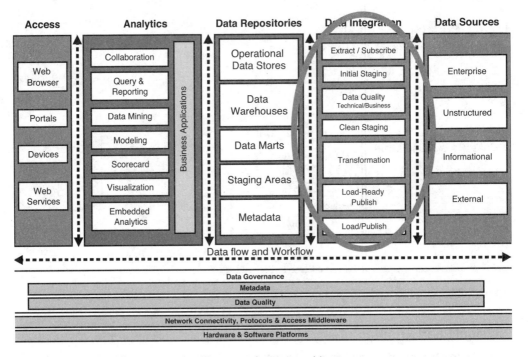

Figure 2.26 The IBM business intelligence reference architecture

Summary

This chapter presented the core foundation for an engineered approach for high-volume data integration environments with the data integration reference architecture.

It discussed how this blueprint is organized into a series of optional layers of process and landing areas, each with its own set of purpose and unique processing logic.

This chapter also discussed the rationale and advantages of using the data integration reference architecture.

Finally, it discussed how the data integration reference architecture itself is simply a layer in a broader reference architecture for business intelligence.

Chapter 3 reviews a design technique to graphical pattern data integration jobs as models using the data integration reference architecture as a blueprint.

End-of-Chapter Questions

Question 1.
Identify and name the staging processes of the data integration reference architecture.
Question 2.
Identify and name the staging layers of the data integration reference architecture.
Question 3.
What are the two primary uses of the data integration architecture?
Question 4.
What are the four types of bad data quality?
Question 5.
Define and explain the transformation types discussed.
Question 6.
What are the two key areas to consider for the load-ready publish layer?

A Design Technique: Data Integration Modeling

This chapter focuses on a new design technique for the analysis and design of data integration processes. This technique uses a graphical process modeling view of data integration similar to the graphical view an entity-relationship diagram provides for data models.

The Business Case for a New Design Process

There is a hypothesis to the issue of massive duplication of data integration processes, which is as follows:

> If you do not see a process, you will replicate that process.

One of the main reasons why there is massive replication of data integration processes in many organizations is the fact that there is no visual method of "seeing" what data integration processes currently exist and what is needed. This is similar to the problem that once plagued the data modeling discipline.

In the early 1980s, many organizations had massive duplication of customer and transactional data. These organizations could not see the "full picture" of their data environment and the massive duplication. Once organizations began to document and leverage entity-relationship diagrams (visual representations of a data model), they were able to see the massive duplication and the degree of reuse of existing tables increased as unnecessary duplication decreased.

The development of data integration processes is similar to those in database development. In developing a database, a blueprint, or model of the business requirements, is necessary to ensure that there is a clear understanding between parties of *what* is needed. In the case of data integration, the data integration designer and the data integration developer need that blueprint or project artifact to ensure that the business requirements in terms of sources, transformations, and targets that are needed to move data have been clearly communicated via a common, consistent approach. The use of a process model specifically designed for data integration will accomplish that requirement.

Figure 3.1 depicts the types of data models needed in a project and how they are similar to those that could be developed for data integration.

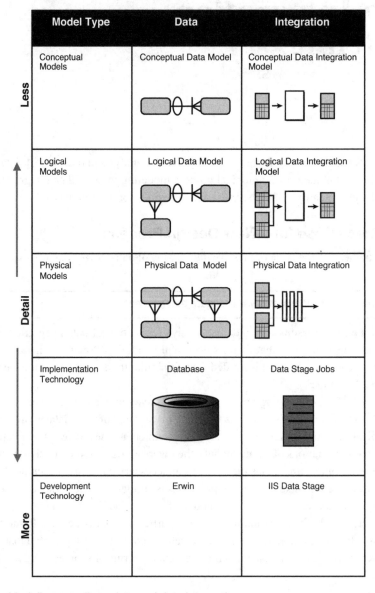

Figure 3.1   Modeling paradigm: data and data integration

The usual approach for analyzing, designing, and building ETL or data integration processes on most projects involves a data analyst documenting the requirements for source-to-target mapping in Microsoft® Excel® spreadsheets. These spreadsheets are given to an ETL developer for the design and development of maps, graphs, and/or source code.

Documenting integration requirements from source systems and targets manually into a tool like Excel and then mapping them again into an ETL or data integration package has been proven to be time-consuming and prone to error. For example:

- **Lost time**—It takes a considerable amount of time to copy source metadata from source systems into an Excel spreadsheet. The same source information must then be rekeyed into an ETL tool. This source and target metadata captured in Excel is largely non-reusable unless a highly manual review and maintenance process is instituted.

- **Nonvalue add analysis**—Capturing source-to-target mappings with transformation requirements contains valuable navigational metadata that can be used for data lineage analysis. Capturing this information in an Excel spreadsheet does not provide a clean automated method of capturing this valuable information.

- **Mapping errors**—Despite our best efforts, manual data entry often results in incorrect entries, for example, incorrectly documenting an INT data type as a VARCHAR in an Excel spreadsheet will require a data integration designer time to analyze and correct.

- **Lack of standardization: inconsistent levels of detail**—The data analysts who perform the source-to-target mappings have a tendency to capture source/transform/target requirements at different levels of completeness depending on the skill and experience of the analyst. When there are inconsistencies in the level of detail in the requirements and design of the data integration processes, there can be misinterpretations by the development staff in the source-to-target mapping documents (usually Excel), which often results in coding errors and lost time.

- **Lack of standardization: inconsistent file formats**—Most environments have multiple extracts in different file formats. The focus and direction must be toward the concept of *read once, write many,* with consistency in extract, data quality, transformation, and load formats. The lack of a standardized set of extracts is both a lack of technique and often a result of a lack of visualization of what is in the environment.

To improve the design and development efficiencies of data integration processes, in terms of time, consistency, quality, and reusability, a graphical process modeling design technique for data integration with the same rigor that is used in developing data models is needed.

Improving the Development Process

Process modeling is a tried and proven approach that works well with Information Technology applications such as data integration. By applying a process modeling technique to data integration, both the visualization and standardization issues will be addressed. First, let's review the types of process modeling.

Leveraging Process Modeling for Data Integration

Process modeling is a means of representing the interrelated processes of a system at any level of detail, using specific types of diagrams that show the flow of data through a series of processes. Process modeling techniques are used to represent specific processes graphically for clearer understanding, communication, and refinement between the stakeholders that design and develop system processes.

Process modeling unlike data modeling has several different types of process models based on the different types of process interactions. These different model types include process dependency diagrams, structure hierarchy charts, and data flow diagrams. Data flow diagramming, which is one of the best known of these process model types, is further refined into several different types of data flow diagrams, such as context diagrams, Level 0 and Level 1 diagrams and "leaf-level" diagrams that represent different levels and types of process and data flow.

By leveraging the concepts of different levels and types of process modeling, we have developed a processing modeling approach for data integration processes, which is as follows:

> *Data integration modeling* is a process modeling technique that is focused on engineering data integration processes into a common data integration architecture.

Overview of Data Integration Modeling

Data integration modeling is a technique that takes into account the types of models needed based on the types of architectural requirements for data integration and the types of models needed based on the Systems Development Life Cycle (SDLC).

Modeling to the Data Integration Architecture

The types of process models or data integration models are dependent on the types of processing needed in the data integration reference architecture. By using the reference architecture as a framework, we are able to create specific process model types for the discrete data integration processes and landing zones, as demonstrated in Figure 3.2.

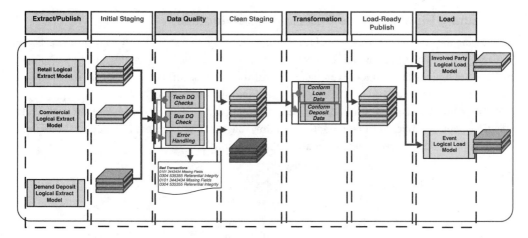

Figure 3.2 Designing models to the architecture

Together, these discrete data integration layers become process model types that form a complete data integration process. The objective is to develop a technique that will lead the designer to model data integration processes based on a common set of process types.

Data Integration Models within the SDLC

Data integration models follow the same level of requirement and design abstraction refinement that occurs within data models during the SDLC. Just as there are conceptual, logical, and physical data models, there are conceptual, logical, and physical data integration requirements that need to be captured at different points in the SDLC, which could be represented in a process model.

The following are brief descriptions of each of the model types. A more thorough definition along with roles, steps, and model examples is reviewed later in the chapter.

- **Conceptual data integration model definition**—Produces an implementation-free representation of the data integration requirements for the proposed system that will serve as a basis for determining how they are to be satisfied.

- **Logical data integration model definition**—Produces a detailed representation of the data integration requirements at the data set (entity/table)level, which details the transformation rules and target logical data sets (entity/tables). These models are still considered to be technology-independent.

  The focus at the logical level is on the capture of actual source tables and proposed target stores.

- **Physical data integration model definition**—Produces a detailed representation of the data integration specifications at the component level. They should be represented in terms of the component-based approach and be able to represent how the data will optimally flow through the data integration environment in the selected development technology.

Structuring Models on the Reference Architecture

Structuring data models to a Systems Development Life Cycle is a relatively easy process. There is usually only one logical model for a conceptual data model and there is only one physical data model for a logical data model. Even though entities may be decomposed or normalized within a model, there is rarely a need to break a data model into separate models.

Process models have traditionally been decomposed further down into separate discrete functions. For example, in Figure 3.3, the data flow diagram's top process is the context diagram, which is further decomposed into separate functional models.

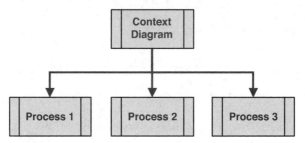

Figure 3.3   A traditional process model: data flow diagram

Data integration models are decomposed into functional models as well, based on the data integration reference architecture and the phase of the Systems Development Life Cycle.

Figure 3.4 portrays how conceptual, logical, and physical data integration models are broken down.

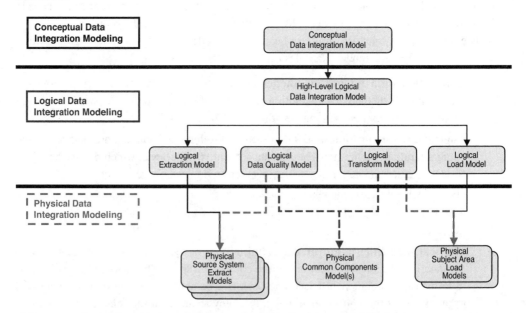

Figure 3.4   Data integration models by the Systems Development Life Cycle

Conceptual Data Integration Models

A conceptual data integration model is an implementation-free representation of the data integration requirements for the proposed system that will serve as a basis for "scoping" how they are to be satisfied and for project planning purposes in terms of source systems analysis, tasks and duration, and resources.

At this stage, it is only necessary to identify the major conceptual processes to fully understand the users' requirements for data integration and plan the next phase.

Figure 3.5 provides an example of a conceptual data integration model.

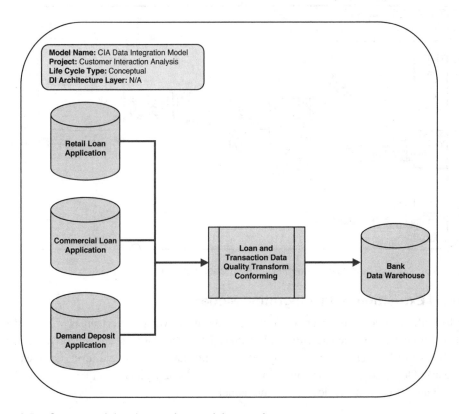

Figure 3.5   Conceptual data integration model example

Logical Data Integration Models

A logical data integration model produces a set of detailed representations of the data integration requirements that captures the first-cut source mappings, business rules, and target data sets (table/file). These models portray the logical extract, data quality, transform, and load requirements for the intended data integration application. These models are still considered to be technology-independent. The following sections discuss the various logical data integration models.

High-Level Logical Data Integration Model

A high-level logical data integration model defines the scope and the boundaries for the project and the system, usually derived and augmented from the conceptual data integration model. A high-level data integration diagram provides the same guidelines as a context diagram does for a data flow diagram.

The high-level logical data integration model in Figure 3.6 provides the structure for *what* will be needed for the data integration system, as well as provides the outline for the logical models, such as extract, data quality, transform, and load components.

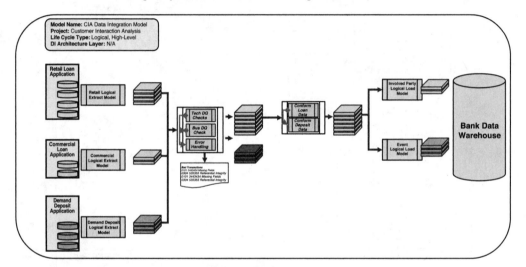

Figure 3.6   Logical high-level data integration model example

Logical Extraction Data Integration Models

The logical extraction data integration model determines what subject areas will need to be extracted from sources, such as *what* applications, databases, flat files, and unstructured sources.

Source file formats should be mapped to the attribute/column/field level. Once extracted, source data files should be loaded by default to the initial staging area.

Figure 3.7 depicts a logical extraction model.

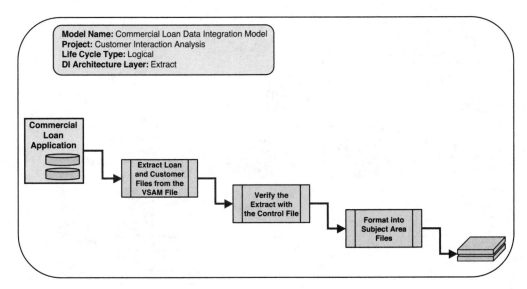

Figure 3.7 Logical extraction data integration model example

Extract data integration models consist of two discrete sub processes or components:

- **Getting the data out of the source system**—Whether the data is actually extracted from the source system or captured from a message queue or flat file, the network connectivity to the source must be determined, the number of tables\files must be reviewed, and the files to extract and in what order to extract them in must be determined.

- **Formatting the data to a subject area file**—As discussed in Chapter 2, "An Architecture for Data Integration," subject area files provide a layer of encapsulation from the source to the final target area. The second major component of an extract data integration model is to rationalize the data from the source format to a common subject area file format, for example mapping a set of Siebel Customer Relationship Management Software tables to a customer subject area file.

Logical Data Quality Data Integration Models

The logical data quality data integration model contains the business and technical data quality checkpoints for the intended data integration process, as demonstrated in Figure 3.8.

Regardless of the technical or business data quality requirements, each data quality data integration model should contain the ability to produce a clean file, reject file, and reject report that would be instantiated in a selected data integration technology.

Also the error handling for the entire data integration process should be designed as a reusable component.

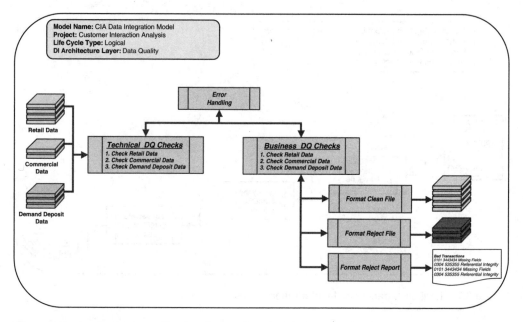

Figure 3.8   Logical data quality data integration model example

As discussed in the data quality architectural process in Chapter 2, a clear data quality process will produce a clean file, reject file, and reject report. Based on an organization's data governance procedures, the reject file can be leveraged for manual or automatic reprocessing.

Logical Transform Data Integration Models

The logical transform data integration model identifies at a logical level what transformations (in terms of calculations, splits, processing, and enrichment) are needed to be performed on the extracted data to meet the business intelligence requirements in terms of aggregation, calculation, and structure, which is demonstrated in Figure 3.9.

Transform types as defined in the transformation processes are determined on the business requirements for conforming, calculating, and aggregating data into enterprise information, as discussed in the transformation architectural process in Chapter 2.

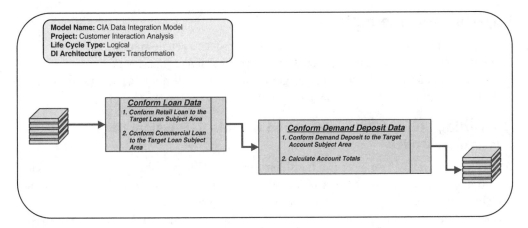

Figure 3.9   Logical transformation data integration model example

Logical Load Data Integration Models

Logical load data integration models determine at a logical level what is needed to load the transformed and cleansed data into the target data repositories by subject area, which is portrayed in Figure 3.10.

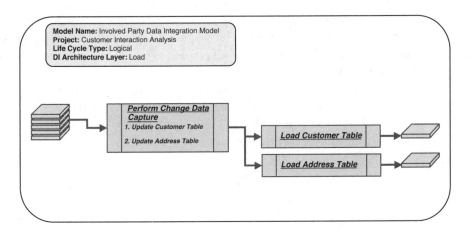

Figure 3.10   Logical load data integration model example

Designing load processes by target and the subject areas within the defined target databases allows sub-processes to be defined, which further encapsulates changes in the target from source data, preventing significant maintenance. An example is when changes to the physical database schema occur, only the subject area load job needs to change, with little impact to the extract and transform processes.

Physical Data Integration Models

The purpose of a physical data integration model is to produce a detailed representation of the data integration specifications at the component level *within* the targeted data integration technology.

A major concept in physical data integration modeling is determining how to best take the logical design and apply design techniques that will optimize performance.

Converting Logical Data Integration Models to Physical Data Integration Models

As in data modeling where there is a transition from logical to physical data models, the same transition occurs in data integration modeling. Logical data integration modeling determines *what* extracts, data quality, transformations, and loads. Physical data integration leverages a target-based design technique, which provides guidelines on how to design the "hows" in the physical data integration models to ensure that the various components will perform optimally in a data integration environment.

Target-Based Data Integration Design Technique Overview

The target-based data integration design technique is an approach that creates physical data integration components based on the subject area loads and the source systems that populate those subject areas. It groups logical functionality into reusable components based on the data movement patterns of local versus enterprise usage within each data integration model type.

For example, in most data integration processes, there are source system-level and enterprise-level data quality checks. The target-based technique places that functionality either close to the process that will use it (in this case, the extract process) or groups enterprise capabilities in common component models.

For example, for source system-specific data quality checks, the target-based technique simply moves that logic to the extract processes while local transformations are moved to load processes and while grouping enterprise-level data quality and transformations are grouped at the common component level. This is displayed in Figure 3.11.

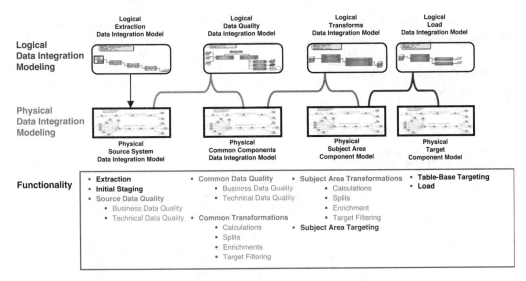

Figure 3.11   Distributing logical functionality between the "whats" and "hows"

The target-based data integration design technique is not a new concept: Coupling and cohesion, modularity, objects, and components. are all techniques used to group "stuff" into understandable and highly functional units of work. The target-based technique is simply a method of modularizing core functionality within the data integration models.

Physical Source System Data Integration Models

A source system extract data integration model extracts the data from a source system, performs source system data quality checks, and then conforms that data into the specific subject area file formats, as shown in Figure 3.12.

The major difference in a logical extract model from a physical source system data integration model is a focus on the final design considerations needed to extract data from the specified source system.

Designing an Extract Verification Process

The data from the source system files is extracted and verified with a *control file*. A control file is a data quality check that verifies the number of rows of data and a control total (such as loan amounts that are totaled for verification for a specific source extract as an example).

It is here where data quality rules that are source system-specific are applied. The rationale for applying source system-specific data quality rules at the particular source system rather than in one overall data quality job is to facilitate maintenance and performance. One giant data quality job becomes a maintenance nightmare. It also requires an unnecessary amount of system memory to load all data quality processes and variables that will slow the time for overall job processing.

Cross-system dependencies should be processed in this model. For example, associative relationships for connecting agreements together should be processed here.

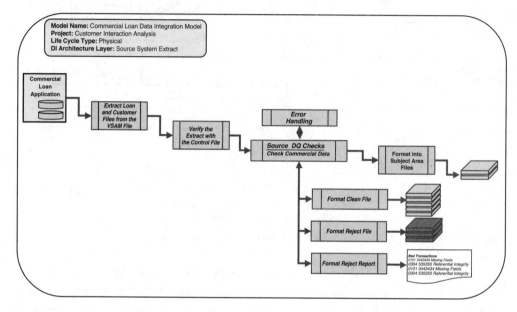

Figure 3.12   Physical source system extract data integration model example

Physical Common Component Data Integration Models

The physical common component data integration model contains the enterprise-level business data quality rules and common transformations that will be leveraged by multiple data integration applications. This layer of the architecture is a critical focal point for reusability in the overall data integration process flow, with particular emphasis on leveraging existing transformation components. Any new components must meet the criteria for reusability.

Finally, in designing common component data integration models, the process flow is examined on where parallelism can be built in to the design based on expected data volumes and within the constraints of the current data integration technology.

Common Component Data Quality Data Integration Models

Common component data quality data integration models are generally very "thin" (less functionality) process models, with enterprise-level data quality rules. Generally, source system-specific data quality rules are technical in nature, whereas business data quality rules tend to be applied at the enterprise level.

For example, gender or postal codes are considered business rules that can be applied as data quality rules against all data being processed. Figure 3.13 illustrates an example of a common data quality data integration model.

Note that the source-specific data quality rules have been moved to the physical source system extract data integration model and a thinner data quality process is at the common component level. Less data ensures that the data flow is not unnecessarily constrained and overall processing performance will be improved.

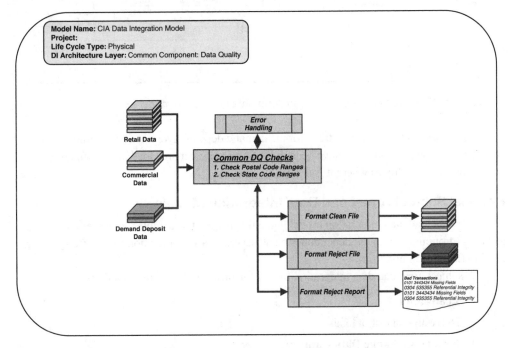

Figure 3.13   Common components—data quality data integration model example

Common Component Transformation Data Integration Models

Most common transforms are those that conform data to an enterprise data model. Transformations needed for specific aggregations and calculations are moved to the subject area loads, or where they are needed, which is in the subject areas that the data is being transformed.

In terms of enterprise-level aggregations and calculations, there are usually very few; most transformations are subject-area-specific. An example of a common component-transformation data integration subject area model is depicted in Figure 3.14.

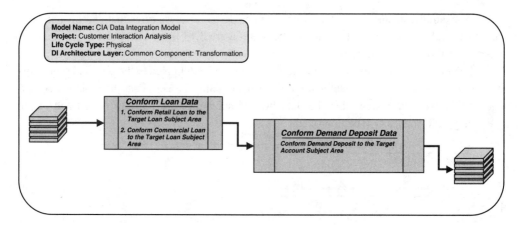

Figure 3.14   Common components—transform data integration model example

Please note that the aggregations for the demand deposit layer have been removed from the common component model and have been moved to the subject area load in line with the concept of moving functionality to where it is needed.

Physical Subject Area Load Data Integration Models

A subject area load data integration model logically groups "target tables" together based on subject area (grouping of targets) dependencies and serves as a simplification for source system processing (layer of indirection).

A subject area load data integration model performs the following functions:

- **Loads data**
- **Refreshes** snapshot loads
- **Performs Change Data Capture**

It is in the subject area load data integration models where primary and foreign keys will be generated, referential integrity is confirmed, and Change Data Capture is processed.

In addition to the simplicity of grouping data by subject area for understandability and maintenance, grouping data by subject area logically limits the amount of data carried per process because it is important to carry as little data as possible through these processes to minimize performance issues. An example of a physical data integration subject area model is shown in Figure 3.15.

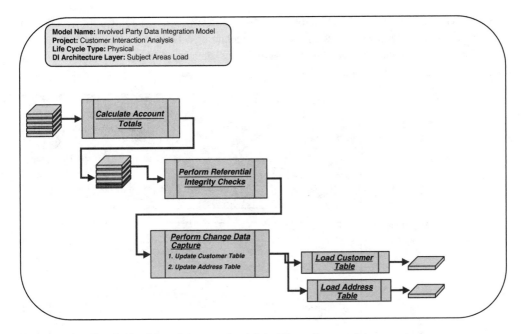

Figure 3.15 Physical subject data area load data integration model example

Logical Versus Physical Data Integration Models

One question that always arises in these efforts is, "Is there a need to have one set of logical data integration models and another set of physical data integration models?"

The answer for data integration models is the same as for data models, "It depends." It depends on the maturity of the data management organization that will create, manage, and own the models in terms of their management of metadata, and it depends on other data management artifacts (such as logical and physical data models).

Tools for Developing Data Integration Models

One of the first questions about data integration modeling is, "What do you build them in?" Although diagramming tools such as Microsoft Visio® and even Microsoft PowerPoint® can be used (as displayed throughout the book), we advocate the use of one of the commercial data integration packages to design and build data integration models.

Diagramming tools such as Visio require manual creation and maintenance to ensure that they are kept in sync with source code and Excel spreadsheets. The overhead of the maintenance often outweighs the benefit of the manually created models. By using a data integration package, existing data integration designs (e.g., an extract data integration model) can be reviewed for potential reuse in other data integration models, and when leveraged, the maintenance to the actual data integration job is performed when the model is updated. Also by using a data integration package such as Ab Initio, IBM Data Stage®, or Informatica to create data integration models, an organization will further leverage the investment in technology it has.

Figure 3.16 provides examples of high-level logical data integration models built in Ab Initio, IBM Data Stage, and Informatica.

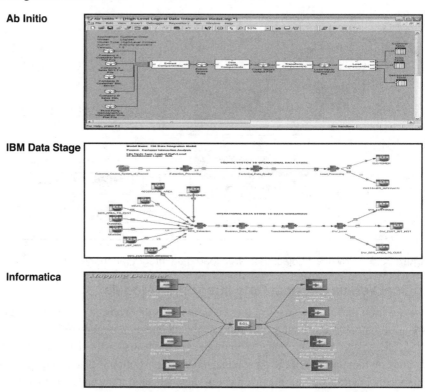

Figure 3.16   Data integration models by technology

Experience in using data integration packages for data integration modeling has shown that data integration projects and Centers of Excellence have seen the benefits of increased extract, transform and load code standardization, and quality. Key benefits from leveraging a data integration package include the following:

- **End-to-end communications**—Using a data integration package facilitates faster transfer of requirements from a data integration designer to a data integration developer by using the same common data integration metadata. Moving from a logical design to a physical design using the same metadata in the same package speeds up the transfer process and cuts down on transfer issues and errors. For example, source-to-target data definitions and mapping rules do not have to be transferred between technologies, thereby reducing mapping errors. This same benefit has been found in data modeling tools that transition from logical data models to physical data models.

- **Development of leveragable enterprise models**—Capturing data integration requirements as logical and physical data integration models provides an organization an opportunity to combine these data integration models into enterprise data integration models, which further matures the Information Management environment and increases overall reuse. It also provides the ability to reuse source extracts, target data loads, and common transformations that are in the data integration software package's metadata engine. These physical data integration jobs are stored in the same metadata engine and can be linked to each other. They can also be linked to other existing metadata objects such as logical data models and business functions.

- **Capture of navigational metadata earlier in the process**—By storing logical and physical data integration model metadata in a data integration software package, an organization is provided with the ability to perform a more thorough impact analysis of a single source or target job. The capture of source-to-target mapping metadata with transformation requirements earlier in the process also increases the probability of catching mapping errors in unit and systems testing. In addition, because metadata capture is automated, it is more likely to be captured and managed.

Industry-Based Data Integration Models

To reduce risk and expedite design efforts in data warehousing projects, prebuilt data models for data warehousing have been developed by IBM, Oracle, Microsoft, and Teradata.

As the concept of data integration modeling has matured, prebuilt data integration models are being developed in support of those industry data warehouse data models.

Prebuilt data integration models use the industry data warehouse models as the targets and known commercial source systems for extracts. Having industry-based source systems and targets, it is easy to develop data integration models with prebuilt source-to-target mappings. For example, in banking, there are common source systems, such as the following:

- **Commercial and** retail loan systems
- **Demand** deposit systems
- **Enterprise** resource systems such as SAP and Oracle

These known applications can be premapped to the industry-based data warehouse data models. Based on actual project experience, the use of industry-based data integration models can significantly cut the time and cost of a data integration project. An example of an industry-based data integration model is illustrated in Figure 3.17.

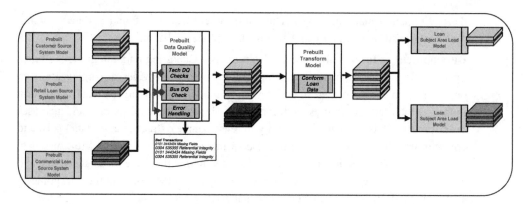

Figure 3.17   Industry-based data integration model example

In the preceding example, the industry data integration model provides the following:

- Prebuilt extract processes from the customer, retail loan, and commercial loan systems
- Prebuilt data quality processes based on known data quality requirements in the target data model
- Prebuilt load processes based on the target data model subject areas

Starting with existing designs based on a known data integration architecture, source systems, and target data models, provides a framework for accelerating the development of a data integration application.

Summary

Data modeling is a graphical design technique for data. In data integration, data integration modeling is a technique for designing data integration processes using a graphical process modeling technique against the data integration reference architecture.

This chapter detailed the types of data integration models—conceptual, logical, and physical—and the approach for subdividing the models based on the process layers of the data integration reference architecture. This chapter also provided examples of each of the different logical and physical data integration model types.

It covered the transition from logical data integration models to physical data integration models, which might be better stated as how to move from the "whats" to the "hows."

Finally, the chapter discussed how this maturing technique can be used to create prebuilt, industry-based data integration models.

The next chapter is a case study for a bank that is building a set of data integration processes and uses data integration modeling to design the planned data integration jobs.

End-of-Chapter Questions

Question 1.
Data integration modeling is based on what other modeling paradigm?

Question 2.
List and describe the types of logical data integration models.

Question 3.
List and describe the types of physical data integration models.

Question 4.
Using the target-based design technique, document where the logical data quality logic is moved to and why in the physical data integration model layers.

Question 5.
Using the target-based design technique, document where the logical transformation logic is moved to and why in the physical data integration model layers.

Case Study: Customer Loan Data Warehouse Project

This chapter presents a case study that will be used to demonstrate the life cycle of data integration modeling. For this exercise, we have been tasked with defining, designing, and developing the data integration processes needed to populate a customer loan data warehouse and its associated customer loan reporting data mart tables.

Case Study Overview

Due to new regulatory reporting requirements, a small regional bank known as the Wheeler Bank needs to better understand its overall loan portfolio exposure. Currently, it has disparate customer, commercial loan, and retail source systems that would provide the data needed for the loan reporting requirements. New federal credit loan reporting regulations require that all banks loans are aggregated by customer on a monthly basis. To provide this ability to view all loans by customer, a data warehouse will be needed for reporting and analysis of a combined loan portfolio.

This case study revolves around the design of the data integration processes necessary to populate a customer loan data warehouse and data mart for a bank to analyze loan performance.

Because the target data model drives the sources, extracts, and business rules (data quality and transforms), it is important to first understand the customer loan data warehouse and data mart data models.

Figures 4.1 and 4.2 illustrate the case studies' data models (entity-relationship diagrams) for the customer loan data warehouse and data mart.

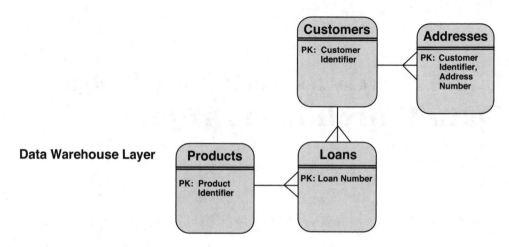

Figure 4.1   Customer loan data warehouse data model

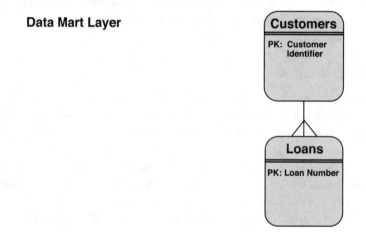

Figure 4.2   Case Study 1: Customer loan reporting dimensional model

These two databases will be the targets that require extracting, checking, conforming, and loading data from the following source systems of the Wheeler Bank, as displayed in Figure 4.3:

- A commercial banking loan system
- A retail banking loan system
- A customer hub system

For the rest of this chapter, we use data integration modeling techniques to develop conceptual, logical, and physical data integration models for both the customer loan data warehouse and data mart. Further information on the case studies' entity-attribute reports, subject area files, and data mapping documents can be found in Appendix D, "Case Study Models," which is available online.

Current Banking Reporting Environment

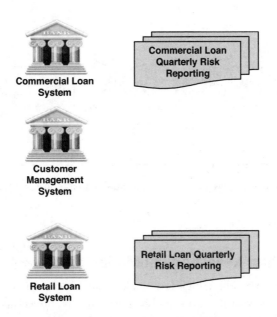

Figure 4.3   Case Study 1: Current bank reporting environment

Step 1: Build a Conceptual Data Integration Model

Because a conceptual data integration model is a representation of the data integration requirements for the loan data warehouse, let us start with creating a "view" or diagram of the three systems and two targets for the envisioned system, as portrayed in Figure 4.4.

At this stage, the purpose of a conceptual data integration model is to only identify the major conceptual data store sources, targets, and processes to fully understand the ramifications of the users' requirements for data integration in terms of the feasibility of the proposed project.

The conceptual data integration model should drive out all the important "*what*" questions, such as the following:

- What are the subject areas of the target databases?
- How many files are there for the identified source systems?
- What are the high-level data quality and transformation requirements for the intended system?

All these questions are typically addressed in the analysis and logical design.

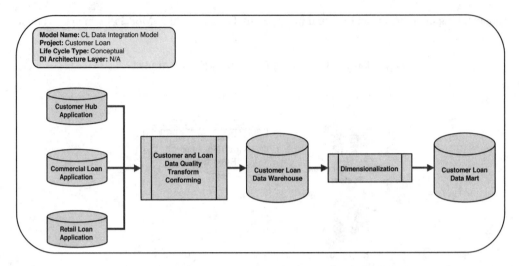

Figure 4.4   Customer loan data warehouse conceptual data integration model

Step 2: Build a High-Level Logical Model Data Integration Model

The next thing we need to build is a high-level logical data integration model. This provides the next-level, big-picture view of the scope and boundary for the project and the system. It is a refined and better detailed conceptual data integration model.

To build the customer loan data warehouse high-level logical data integration model, we need to ask the following questions:

- **What is the logical extraction data integration model?**
  - The customer hub with the following files:
    - Header
    - Detail
  - The commercial loan system with the following files:
    - COM 010
    - COM 200
  - The retail loan system with the following files:
    - RETL 010
    - RETL 020
- **What is the logical data quality data integration model?**
  - Business: Name and Address Checking

- **What is the logical transform data integration model?**
  - Data Warehouse: Not Yet
  - Data Mart: Some level of dimensionalization ("flattening" out the tables for reporting and query)
- **What is the logical load data integration model (if known)?**
  - For both the data warehouse and the data mart, the following subject areas:
  - Customer
  - Loan

With this information, we extend the conceptual data integration model into a high-level logical data integration model, as illustrated in Figure 4.5.

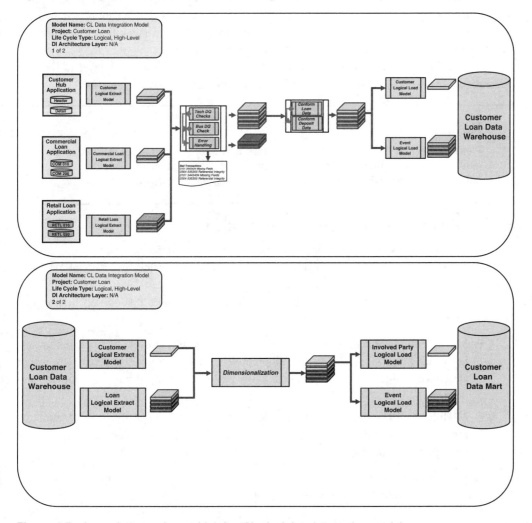

Figure 4.5   Loan data warehouse high-level logical data integration model

For readability, the model was broken into two views: Source to Data Warehouse and Data Warehouse to Data Mart.

Do you need both a conceptual data integration model and high-level data integration model?

It is the same as to whether a project needs a conceptual and logical data model. Projects need to go through the process of defining a conceptual data model, defining the core subject areas and primary key structures, then completing the attribution and relationships to complete a logical data model so that at a point in the project, there will be a conceptual data model and then a logical data model.

Whether a project and/or organization plans to keep and use a separate conceptual data integration model along with a high-level logical integration data model depends on the level of data management maturity within an organization and the intended uses for both models.

If it is envisioned within an organization that there will be enterprise data integration models similar to enterprise data models, then there will be great benefit. These enterprise data integration models can be built from the project-based conceptual data integration models, again depending on the maturity and intentions of the organization.

Now, the focus is on designing logical data integration models for each layer of the data integration reference architecture (e.g., extract, data quality, transformation, and load).

NOTE

Please note that *source-to-subject area files* and *subject area-to-target* mappings must be completed before logical data integration modeling can occur. Techniques on data mapping are reviewed in Chapter 5, "Data Integration Analysis."

Step 3: Build the Logical Extract DI Models

The first question is how we structure the logical extract data integration model or models, one or many. For our case study, there are only three sources: the customer hub, commercial loan, and retail loan.

It is best to put all three sources on the same diagram for the sake of simplicity. In practice, however, there are some things to consider:

- **Multiple data sources**—Most projects have many, many sources. In a new data warehouse build-out, a typical data integration project can have from 20 to 30 sources, which at a conceptual and high level can potentially be displayed on one page, but not with any detail.

- **Modularity 101**—Following the development technique of one function per process, focusing on one source per extract data integration model will be refined from analysis through design into building one data integration job per source system.

In addition, we will need to build three logical extract data integration models, one per source system. These activities include the following:

- Confirming the subject area focus from the data mapping document
- Reviewing whether the existing data integration environment can fulfill the requirements
- Determining the business extraction rules

Confirm the Subject Area Focus from the Data Mapping Document

Confirm the target database subject areas. Subject is defined as a logical grouping or "super type" of entities/tables surrounding a business concept. An example is the **Party** concept, which may have multiple entities such as Party, which includes the following entities:

- Customer
- Employee
- Individual

By grouping the entities/tables from subject areas such as Party into a target subject area, a common target is created that multiple source systems can be mapped in such a way to be conformed into a common format, as shown in Figure 4.6 from our earlier example.

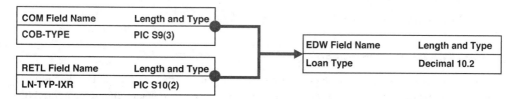

Figure 4.6   Subject area mappings

So what are the subject areas for the data warehouse and data mart? By reviewing the data models, a pattern can be determined for logical groupings for subject areas. In the tables defined for both models, a clear grouping can be observed:

- **Customer**
  - Customers
  - Addresses
- **Loan**
  - Loans
  - Products

So for our logical data integration models, the following subject area files will be used:

- CUST.dat
- LOAN.dat

Review Whether the Existing Data Integration Environment Can Fulfill the Requirements

One of the major tenets of building data integration models and components from the models is reuse. It is our nature to build first and then look for reuse opportunities! So to break that bad habit, let's look first, especially in a maturing data integration environment if a model exists and *then* build new if necessary.

Determine the Business Extraction Rules

Determine what needs to occur to extract or capture the data from the source system.

For batch, determine when and how the files need to be captured:

- From the source system?
- From an extract directory?
- When (e.g., 3:00 a.m.)?

For real time, determine when and how the transactional packets need to be captured:

- From a message queue?
- From the source system log?

Control File Check Processing

An important aspect of extraction is confirming that the data extract is correct. The best practice used to verify file extracts is *control file check*, which is a method to ensure that the captured files meet predefined quality criteria, as shown in Figure 4.7.

Loan File

Loan Number	Loan Amount
111	$90,000
112	$11,000
113	$120,000
114	$45,000
115	$38,000
	$304,000

Loan File Control File

Total Loans	Loan Amount
5	$304,000

Figure 4.7   Sample control files

Complete the Logical Extract Data Integration Models

The final step is to assemble the requirements into the logical extract data integration models. Figures 4.8, 4.9, and 4.10 illustrate the customer hub logical extract data integration model, the commercial loan logical extract data integration model, and the retail loan logical extract data integration model.

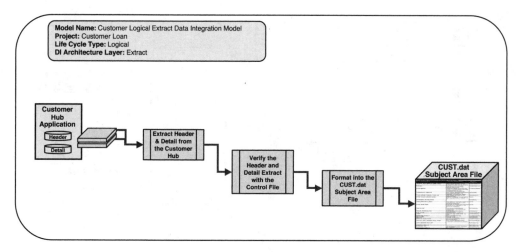

Figure 4.8   Customer logical extract data integration model

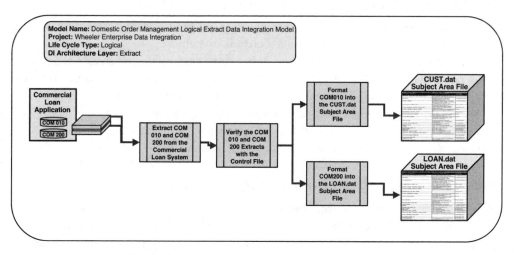

Figure 4.9   Commercial loan logical extract data integration model

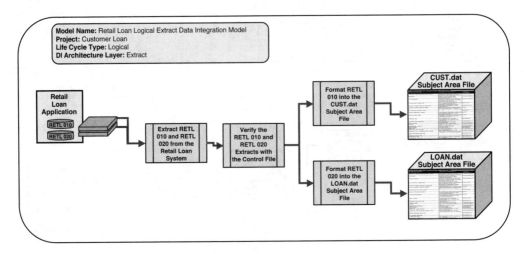

Figure 4.10   Retail loan logical extract data integration model

Final Thoughts on Designing a Logical Extract DI Model

One of the key themes is to get the "big" picture before design; it is best practice to first identify *all* the sources then evaluate each of the data sources in its entirety.

In addition, to leverage the "read once, write many" best practice, when extracting from a source, rather than only extracting the data elements needed for a specific target, it is best to extract the entire file for both current and potentially future sourcing needs.

When extracting a limited set of data for a single application or database, it is highly probable that there will be the need to extend the application, or rewrite the application, or in the worst case, write another extract from the same source system.

Step 4: Define a Logical Data Quality DI Model

Let's first review the purpose of a data quality data integration model. Data quality processes are those data integration processes that qualify and cleanse the data, based on technical and business process rules. These rules or data quality criteria are built in to the data integration jobs as data quality criteria or "checks."

First are *technical data quality checks*, which define the data quality criteria often found in both the entity integrity and referential integrity relational rules.

Second are *business data quality checks*, which confirm the understanding of the key data quality elements in terms of what the business definition and ranges for a data quality element are and what business rules are associated with that element.

Design a Logical Data Quality Data Integration Model

The data quality process in the data integration reference architecture provides us the basic blueprint for a logical design.

The data quality design framework in Figure 4.11 has separated the data quality functionality into technical and business components for both ease of maintenance and ease of converting the logical model to a physical model where source-specific and enterprise-level data quality can be distributed for system performance.

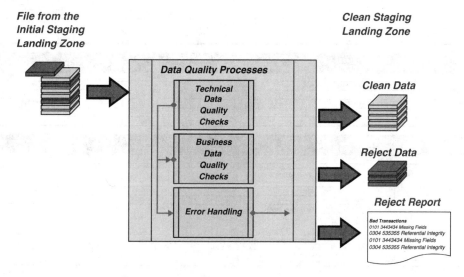

Figure 4.11   Data quality design framework

Because the data model is the target and contains the key data elements that we want to base our data quality on, let's use the customer loan data warehouse data model to determine the technical data quality criteria.

Identify Technical and Business Data Quality Criteria

The data model contains attributes for which maintaining data quality is critical to ensure the level of data integrity. In reviewing the customer loan data warehouse data model, the following attributes that are either key structures or mandatory fields meet that critical attribute requirement, thereby becoming candidates for technical data quality criteria. At the same time, the business requirements and data mapping business-specific data quality checks should be reviewed as candidates. The Customer Loan Data Warehouse Entity-Attribute Report in Figure 4.12 illustrates the source of data quality criteria.

Note that those data quality checks in the shading in Figure 4.12 are noted as business data quality checks.

Customer

Attribute Name	Attribute Definition	Column Name	Domain	Manditory	Key	Data Quality Check
Customer Identifier	The unique identifier assigned to a customer.	Cust_Id	INTEGER(10)	Yes	Primary	Must be unique and not null
Customer Name	Customer Name: specifies the primary current name, (normally the legal name for the customer),as used by the Financial	Cust_Name	VARCHAR(64)	Yes		Must be Not Null
Gender	Gender of the customer. Data Quality Criteria: Male, Female, Unknown	Gender	VARCHAR(10)	Yes		It must be "Male", "Female", or "Unknown"
Source System Unique Key Text	The unique identifier of the customer in the source system.	Source_Sys_Unique_Key_Text	VARCHAR(32)	Yes		Must be Not Null
Source System Code	The unique identifier of the source system.	Source_Sys_Code	VARCHAR(20)	Yes		Must be Not Null
Customer Type Identifier	The unique identifier assigned to the customer type. For example, Commercial, Retail	Customer_Type_Id	SMALLINT	Yes		Must be Not Null
Customer Effective Date	The date on which the customer first became relevant to the financial institution.	Cust_Effective_Date	DATE	Yes		Must be Not Null and a Date Field
Customer End Date	The date on which the customer ceased to be relevant to the financial institution.	Cust_End_Date	DATE	Yes		Must be Not Null and a Date Field
Last Update Run Identifier		Last_Update_Run_Id	INTEGER(10)	Yes		Must be Not Null
Created Run Identifier		Created_Run_Id	INTEGER(10)	Yes		Must be Not Null
Customer Legal Status Type Identifier	The unique identifier of the classification.	Cust_Legal_Status_Type_Id	INTEGER(10)	Yes		Must be Not Null

Addresses

Attribute Name	Attribute Definition	Column Name	Domain	Manditory	Key	Data Quality Check
Customer Identifier	The unique identifier assigned to a customer.	Cust_Id	INTEGER(10)	Yes	Primary	Must be unique and not null
Address Number	The unique identifier assigned an address	Address_No	INTEGER(10)	Yes	Primary	Must be unique and not null
Address Line 1	The first address line	Address_Line_1	VARCHAR(20)	Yes		Must be Not Null
City Code	The city of the customer	City_Code	VARCHAR(20)	Yes		Must be Not Null
State	The two digit state code, e.g. "NY"	State	VARCHAR(2)	Yes		Must be Not Null
Zip Code	The Zip code	Zip_Code	INTEGER(5)	Yes		Must be Not Null

Loans

Attribute Name	Entity Definition Attribute Definition	Column Name	Domain	Manditory	Key	Data Quality Check
Loan Number	The unique identifier of a loan between two or more	Loan_No	INTEGER(10)	Yes	Primary	Must be unique and not null
Customer Name	Customer Name: specifies the primary current name (normally the legal name for the customer), as used by the financial	Cust_Name	VARCHAR(64)	Yes	Foreign	Must be unique and not null
Source System Code	The unique identifier of the source system.	Source_System_Code	VARCHAR(20)	Yes		Must be Not Null
Source System Unique Key Text	The unique identifier of the loan in the source system.	Source_System_Unique_Key_Text	VARCHAR(32)	Yes		Must be Not Null
Loan Name	The primary name assigned to the loan .This name is used in	Loan_Name	CHAR(36)	Yes		Must be Not Null
Loan Type Identifier	The unique identifier of the loan type.	Loan_Type_Id	INTEGER(10)	Yes		Must be Not Null
Loan Term Type Identifier	The unique identifier of the loan term type.This indicates	Loan_Term_Type_Id	NTEGER(10)	Yes		Must be Not Null
Loan Effective Date	The calendar date on which the Loan became relevant to the financial institution. This can be extracted from the appropriate instance of the entity recording 'Accepted Loan Financial Status'	Loan_Effective_Date	DATE	Yes		Must be Not Null

Products

Attribute Name	Attribute Definition	Column Name	Domain	Manditory	Key	Data Quality Check
Product Identifier	The unique identifier of a product.	Product_Id	INTEGER(10)	Yes	Primary	Must be unique and not null
Source System Code	The unique identifier of the application or system from which the information last used to update the entity instance was populated.	Source_System_Code	VARCHAR(20)	Yes		In must be the unique identifier of the application or system from which the information last used to update the entity instance was populated.

Figure 4.12   Business data quality checks

With the data quality design blueprint and the data quality criteria information, we can design a logical data quality data integration model that is portrayed in Figure 4.13.

Figures 4.14 and 4.15 illustrate the data quality data integration model detail for the technical data quality checks and business data quality checks.

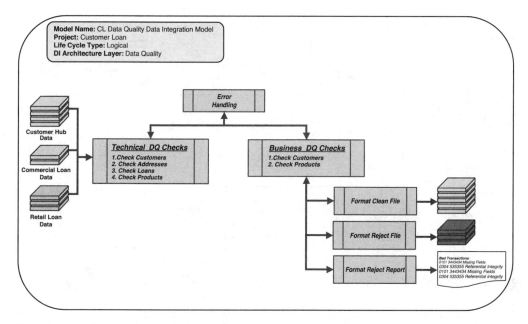

Figure 4.13 Customer logical data quality data integration model

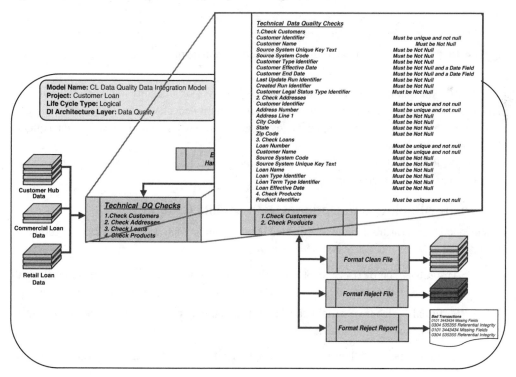

Figure 4.14 Customer loan logical data quality data integration model—technical data quality view

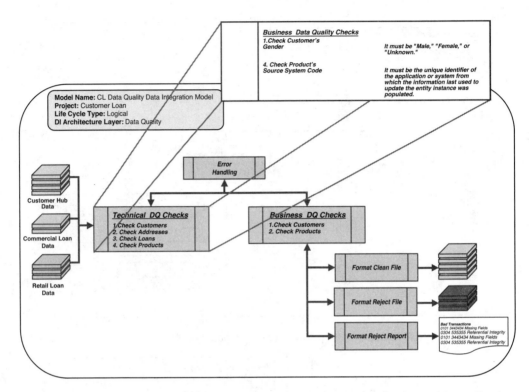

Figure 4.15　Customer loan logical data quality data integration model—business data quality view

Please note that it is typical on initial projects to have a significantly higher number of technical data quality checks compared with business data quality checks. As an organization matures in both Information Management and data governance processes, so will the business data quality checks in the data quality data integration model.

As the logical data quality data integration model is defined, further considerations should be determined, as discussed in the next section.

Determine Absolute and Optional Data Quality Criteria

As data quality criteria are defined for selected data attributes, each data quality criteria should be evaluated on whether it needs to be *absolute* or *optional*:

- **Absolute**—There exists a set of enterprise-wide, nonnegotiable data quality rules. Records that fail such tests should not be used for any purpose. Such rules are deemed "Absolute."

- **Optional**—There are certain checks of data that may be important for certain data uses but may not invalidate the data for other uses.

There is additional detail on absolute and optional in Chapter 5, "Data Integration Analysis."

Step 5: Define the Logical Transform DI Model

One of the most difficult aspects of any data integration project is the identification, definition, design, and build of the transformations needed to re-craft the data from a source system format to a subject area based on a conformed data model used for reporting and analytics.

To approach the complexity of transformations, we segment the transforms needed for the data integration model by the "types" of transforms as reviewed in the data integration reference architecture transformation process.

In the high-level logical data integration model, transforms are broken into two subject areas—customer and loan—as portrayed in Figure 4.16.

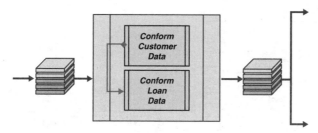

Figure 4.16   High-level transformation data integration model view

The customer and loan subject areas provide an opportunity to segment the source systems for transformation types, as follows:

- **Customer subject area**
  - Customer hub
  - Commercial loan customer data
  - Retail loan customer data
- **Loan subject area**
  - Commercial loan data
  - Retail loan data

We can now build the high-level structure for the transformations. This "componentization" will also facilitate the "physicalization" of the transformation data integration model.

Each data mapping rule should be reviewed in context of the following transformation types:

- **Determine conforming requirements.**

  What mapping rules require fields to change data types? Trimmed? Padded?

- **Determine calculation and split requirements.**

  What fields need calculations? Splits? Address fields are often split or merged due to table layouts and the Zip+4 requirements.

- **Determine processing and enrichment requirements.**

  What fields need to be the results of a join, lookup, or aggregation?

- **Determine any additional business transformation rules.**

  What other considerations should be reviewed for the target data model?

The logical transformation data integration model for the customer loan data warehouse is shown in Figure 4.17, which has the transformation logic segmented by subject area.

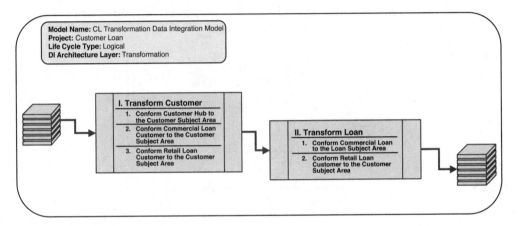

Figure 4.17   Customer loan logical transformation data integration model

Figures 4.18 and 4.19 provide the detail of the types of transformations needed for the Transform Customer and Transform Loan components.

As discussed in the Transform Types section of Chapter 2, "An Architecture for Data Integration," there are several types of transforms patterns or types, several of which are demonstrated in the transformation data integration model case study. They include conforming, calculation, splits, and lookup. Examples of each are shown in Figure 4.20.

Although the focus of this book is data integration, there are data warehouse modeling architectural patterns that impact the design and architecture of data integration processes. One is that most transforms from source to EDW (enterprise data warehouse) are simple conforms, whereas from the EDW to the data mart, they are mostly calculations and aggregations.

There are two types of transformations between databases:

- **Source to EDW**—Typically conform transformation types

- **EDW to data mart**—Typically dimensionalization business rules, which requires calculations and aggregations

I. Transform Customer

1. Conform Customer Hub to the Customer Subject Area

Source File/ Table	Source Field	Source Domain	Transformation	Column Name	Target Domain
HEADER	Cust_Id	INTEGER(10)	Translate Integer to Varchar	Source_Sys_Unique_Key_Text	VARCHAR(32)
HEADER	Name	VARCHAR(10)	Pad to 64	Cust_Name	VARCHAR(64)
HEADER	Customer_Type	VARCHAR(10)	Translate Varchar to Smallint	Customer_Type_Id	SMALLINT
HEADER	Legal_Status	Date	Translate Date to Integer	Cust_Legal_Status_Type_Id	INTEGER(10)
HEADER	Legal_Status_Date	VARCHAR(10)	Reformat field to YYYYMMDD and move	Cust_Legal_Status_Date	DATE
HEADER	Employee_ID	VARCHAR(10)	Translate VarChar to Char, truncate the last 2 digits	Employer_Id_No_Text	CHAR(12)
HEADER	End_Date	VARCHAR(10)	Translate Varchar to Date	Cust_End_Date	DATE
HEADER	Tax_ID_Number	VARCHAR(10)	Translate Varchar to Integer, Truncate last digit	Tax_Id_No	INTEGER(9)
HEADER	Ind_Soc_Security_Number	VARCHAR(10)	Translate Varchar to Integer, Truncate last digit	Social_Security_No	INTEGER(9)
DETAIL	Postal_Barcode	VARCHAR()	1. Translate Varchar to Integer 2. Populate the first 5 into "Zip_Code", the final 4 into	Zip_Code	INTEGER(5)
				Zip_Ext	INTEGER(4)
Calculated Customer Transforms for the Customer Hub					
			Must be Assigned "001"	Source_Sys_Code	VARCHAR(20)
			Must be Assigned "CUSTOMER HUB"	Source_Sys_Unique_Key_Text	VARCHAR(32)
			Must be Assigned "SYSTEM DATE"	Last_Update_Run_Id	INTEGER(10)
			Must be Assigned "SYSTEM DATE"	Created_Run_Id	INTEGER(10)
			Must be System Generated by Customer Number	Address_No	INTEGER(10)

2. Conform Commercial Loan Customer to the Customer Subject Area

Source File/ Table	Source Field	Source Domain	Transformation	Column Name	Target Domain
COM010	OIN-BANK OIN-APPL OIN-OBLIG-NO	PIC XX PIC 9 PIC 9(10)	Concatenate OIN-BANK & OIN-APPL & OIN-OBLIG-NO	Cust_Id	INTEGER(10)
COM010	MN100-FULL MN100-CONTINUATION	PIC X(30) PIC X(30)	Concatenate MN100-FULL & MN100-CONTINUATION	Cust_Name	VARCHAR(64)
COM010	MN100-TAXID	PIC X(9)	If MN100-TAXID > 0, move "Commercial", else move	Customer_Type_Id	SMALLINT
COM010	COB-LEGAL-STATUS-DT	PIC S9(7)	Reformat field to YYYYMMDD and move	Cust_Effective_Date	DATE
COM010	MN100-TAXID MN100-BIRTH-INC-DATE	PIC S9(7) PIC S9(7)	If MN100-TAXID > 0, Reformat MN100-BIRTH-INC-DATE to YYYYMMDD and move, else leave blank	Employer_Id_No_Text	CHAR(12)
COM010	MA100-ZIP	PIC X(9)	Split first 5	Zip_Code	INTEGER(5)
			Load second 4	Zip_Ext	INTEGER(4)
Calculated Customer Transforms for Commercial Loans					
			Transformation	**Column Name**	**Target Domain**
			Match the Customer Id of the Customer Table to the Customer Id of the Commercial Loan Customer Id and derive the Gender from the Customer	Gender	VARCHAR(10)
			Match the Customer Id of the Customer Table to the Customer Id of the Commercial Loan Customer Id and derive the Cust End Date from the	Cust_End_Date	DATE
			From the current Loan Id derive the Created_Run_Id, populate it into the Last_Update_Run_Id	Last_Update_Run_Id	INTEGER(10)
			Populate the Created_Run_Id from the current system date	Created_Run_Id	INTEGER(10)
			Match the Customer Id of the Customer Table to the Customer Id of the Commercial Loan Customer Id and derive the Cust_End_Date from the	Cust_Legal_Status_Type_Id	INTEGER(10)
			Match the Customer Id of the Customer Table to the Customer Id of the Commercial Loan Customer Id and derive the Cust_Legal_Status_Date from the Customer Table	Cust_Legal_Status_Date	DATE
			Match the Customer Id of the Customer Table to the Customer Id of the Commercial Loan Customer Id and derive the Address_No from the	Address_No	INTEGER(10)

3. Conform Retail Loan Customer to the Customer Subject Area

Source File/ Table	Source Field	Source Domain	Transformation	Column Name	Target Domain
RETL 10	LEGAL-LOAN-STATUS	PIC X(20)	Convert to Integer and truncate the first 10 fields	Cust_Legal_Status_Type_Id	INTEGER(10)
RETL 10	PRIMARY-LOAN-APPLICANT	PIC X(9)	Reformat field to YYYYMMDD and move	Cust_Legal_Status_Date	DATE
RETL 10	PRIMARY-TAX-ID-NUM	PIC X(9)	Reformat field to Chair and Pad the last 3	Employer_Id_No_Text	CHAR(12)
RETL 10	LOAN-EFFECTIVE-DATE	PIC S9(08)	Reformat field to YYYYMMDD and move	Cust_Effective_Date	DATE
RETL 10	LOAN-END-DATE	PIC S9(08)	Reformat field to YYYYMMDD and move	Cust_End_Date	DATE
RETL 10	MAIL-STREET-NUM	PIC X(20)	Convert to Varchar, then move	Address_Line_1	VARCHAR(20)
RETL 10	MAIL-STREET-NAME	PIC X(20)	Convert to Varchar, then move	Address_Line_2	VARCHAR(20)
RETL 10	MAIL-ZIP-CODE	PIC X(09)	Split first 5	Zip_Code	INTEGER(5)
			Load second 4	Zip_Ext	INTEGER(4)
RETL 10	MAIL-STATE-NAME	PIC X(20)	Map to the State Table, find the match then populate the 2 digit value (e.g. "NY" or "CA")	State	VARCHAR(2)
Calculated Customer Table Attributes for Retail Loans					
			Transformation	**Column Name**	**Target Domain**
			Match the Customer Id of the Customer Table to the Customer Id of the Retail Loan Customer Id and derive the Gender from the Customer	Gender	VARCHAR(10)
			Move "Retail" to the field	Customer_Type_Id	VARCHAR(10)
			Match the Customer Id of the Customer Table to the Customer Id of the Retail Loan Customer Id and derive the Address_No from the Customer	Address_No	INTEGER(10)
			Match the Customer Id of the Customer Table to the Customer Id of the Retail Loan Customer Id and derive the Source_Sys_Code from the	Source_Sys_Code	VARCHAR(20)
			Match the Customer Id of the Customer Table to the Customer Id of the Retail Loan Customer Id and derive the Source_Sys_Unique_Key_Text from the Customer Table	Source_Sys_Unique_Key_Text	VARCHAR(32)
			Must be Assigned "SYSTEM DATE"	Last_Update_Run_Id	INTEGER(10)
			Must be Assigned "SYSTEM DATE"	Created_Run_Id	INTEGER(10)

Figure 4.18 Customer transforms

II. Transform Loan

1. Conform Commercial Loan to the Loan Subject Area

Source File/ Table	Source Field	Source Domain	Transformation	Column Name	Target Domain
COM200	COM-BANK COM-APPL-CODE COM-OBLIGOR COM-OBLIGATION	PIC 9(2) PIC 9 PIC 9(10) PIC S9(11)	1. Concatenate COB-BANK & COB-APPL-CODE & COB-OBLIGOR & COB-OBLIGATION 2.Map the COM-BANK, COM-APPL-CODE, last 9 of COM-OBLIGOR to Source System Code	Source_System_Code	VARCHAR(20)
COM200	COM-PRIME-NO-9	PIC S9(5)	Determine if code is "1", "2", or "3", else flag as reject	Loan_Type_Id	INTEGER(10)
COM200	COM-TYPE	PIC S9(5)	Determine if code is "Fixed" or "Revolving", else flag as reject	Loan_Term_Type_Id	INTEGER(10)
	MBS-METHOD-COLL	PIC X(2)	Reformat field to Integer and pad the first 8 fields with zeroes, then load the	Loan_Payment_Type_Id	INTEGER(10)
COM200	PURPOSE_NO	PIC 9(5)	Reformat field to Integer and pad the first 5 fields with zeroes, then load the	Loan_Purpose_Type_Id	INTEGER(10)
COM200	COM-POSTED-DT	PIC S9(7)	Reformat field to YYYYMMDD and	Last_Transaction_Date	DATE
COM200	COM-EFFECTIVE-DT	PIC S9(7)	Reformat field to YYYYMMDD and	Loan_Effective_Date	DATE
COM200	COM-LGL-MATUR-DT	PIC S9(7)	Reformat field to YYYYMMDD and	Loan_End_Date	DATE
COM200	COM-RENEWAL-DATE	PIC S9(7)	Reformat field to YYYYMMDD and	Renewal_Date	DATE
COM200	COM-MAT-DT	PIC S9(7)	Reformat field to YYYYMMDD and	Maturity_Date	DATE
COM200	COM-EST-MAT-DT	PIC S9(7)	Reformat field to YYYYMMDD and	Est_Maturity_Date	DATE
COM200	ACT_STAT-ID	PIC X(2)	1. Truncate the first fiend and reformat to char. 2. The remaining field must either be "A" for Active, or "I" for	Active_Status_Indicator	CHAR(1)
COM200	ACT-STAT-DT	PIC S9(7)	Reformat field to YYYYMMDD and	Active_Status_Date	DATE
COM200	COM-LAST_STMT-DATE	PIC S9(7)	Reformat field to YYYYMMDD and	Last_Statement_Date	DATE
COM200	BRCH_NO	PIC 9(5)	Reformat field to Varchar and pad the last 27 digits with spaces <20>.	Branch_No_Text	VARCHAR(32)
Calculated Loan Table Attributes for Commercial Loans					
			Match the Source_Sys_Unique_Key_Text of the Loan Table to the Source_Sys_Unique_Key_Text of the Commercial Loan Tabled and derive the	Source_Sys_Unique_Key_Text	VARCHAR(32)
			Map as = "Commercial Loan"	Source_Sys_Code	VARCHAR(20)
			Match the Customer Id of the Customer Table to the Customer Id of the Commercial Loan Customer Id and derive the Description Text from the	Description_Text	VARCHAR(256)
			Match the Product_Id of the Commercial Loan System to the Product Table Product_Id and derive	Product_Id	INTEGER(10)
			Match the Product_Id of the Commercial Loan System to the Product Table Product_Id and derive	Product_Type_Id	INTEGER(10)
			Match the Product_Id of the Commercial Loan System to the Product Table Product_Id and derive	Product_Code	VARCHAR(20)
			Match the Product_Id of the Commercial Loan System to the Product Table Product_Id and derive	Product_Name	CHAR(36)

2. Conform Retail Loan Customer to the Customer Subject Area

Source File/ Table	Source Field	Source Domain	Transformation	Column Name	Target Domain
RETL20	LOAN-LAST-NAME	PIC X(25)	Convert to Char and move to the field,pad the last 11 with spaces	Loan_Name	CHAR(36)
RETL20	TERM-ID	PIC X(9)	Move to the field, pad the last digit with a space	Loan_Term_Type_Id	INTEGER(10)
RETL20	PAY-TYPE	PIC X(15)	Move to the field, truncate the first 5	Loan_Payment_Type_Id	INTEGER(10)
RETL20	LOAN-RECORD-TYPE-CODE	PIC X(15)	Move to the field, truncate the first 5	Loan_Purpose_Type_Id	INTEGER(10)
RETL20	ACTIVE-LOAN-TYPE	PIC X(5)	Move to the field, truncate the last 4	Active_Status_Indicator	CHAR(1)
RETL20	ACTIVE-LOAN-DATE	PIC S9(08)	Reformat field to YYYYMMDD and	Active_Status_Date	DATE
RETL20	STMT-DATE	PIC S9(08)	Reformat field to YYYYMMDD and	Last_Statement_Date	DATE
RETL20	LOAN-RECEIVED-DATE	PIC S9(08)	Reformat field to YYYYMMDD and	Loan_Effective_Date	DATE
RETL20	LOAN-DATE-SENT-INACTIVE	PIC S9(08)	Reformat field to YYYYMMDD and	Loan_End_Date	DATE
RETL20	LOAN-UPDATE-DATE	PIC S9(08)	Reformat field to YYYYMMDD and	Renewal_Date	DATE
RETL20	BRANCH-CODE	PIC X(05)	Reformat field to VarChar, move to field pad 27 digits with spaces	Branch_No_Text	VARCHAR(32)
RETL20	RET-LOAN-APPL-DESC	PIC X(100)	Reformat field to VarChar, move to field pad 156 digits with spaces	Description_Text	VARCHAR(256)
RETL20	LOAN-MATURITY-DATE	PIC S9(08)	Reformat field to YYYYMMDD and	Maturity_Date	DATE
RETL20	LOAN-EXPECTED-MATURITY DATE	PIC S9(08)	Reformat field to YYYYMMDD and move	Est_Maturity_Date	DATE
RETL20	LAST-UPDATE-DATE	PIC S9(08)	Reformat field to YYYYMMDD and	Last_Transaction_Date	DATE
RETL20	LOAN-PRODUCT-CODE	PIC X(05)	Match the Product_Id of the Retail Loan System to the Product Table Product_Id and derive the Product_Code	Product_Code	VARCHAR(20)
Calculated Loan Table Attributes for Retail Loans					
			Map as = "Retail Loan"	Source_System_Code	VARCHAR(20)
			Match the Source_Sys_Unique_Key_Text of the Loan Table to the Source_Sys_Unique_Key_Text of the Retail Loan Tabled and derive the	Source_System_Unique_Key_Text	VARCHAR(32)
			Match the Product_Id of the Retail Loan System to the Product Table Product_Id and derive the Product_Id	Product_Id	INTEGER(10)
			Match the Product_Id of the Retail Loan System to the Product Table Product_Id and derive the Product_Type_Id	Product_Type_Id	INTEGER(10)
			Match the Product_Id of the Retail Loan System to the Product Table Product_Id and derive the Product_Name	Product_Name	CHAR(36)

Figure 4.19　Loan transforms

Conforming Transform Types

Source File/ Table	Source Field	Source Domain	Transformation	Column Name	Target Domain
HEADER	Cust_Id	INTEGER(10)	Translate Integer to Varchar	Source_Sys_Unique_Key_Text	VARCHAR(32)
HEADER	Name	VARCHAR(10)	Pad to 64	Cust_Name	VARCHAR(64)

Calculation Transform Types

			=Sum(Loan Numbers by Customer Name)	**Total Number of Loans**	VARCHAR(256)
			= Total Daily Loan Balances/Total Number of Loans	**Average Daily Loan Balance**	VARCHAR(256)

Splits Transform Types

2. Conform Commercial Loan Customer to the Customer Subject Area

Source File/ Table	Source Field	Source Domain	Transformation	Column Name	Target Domain
COM010	MA100-ZIP	PIC X(9)	Split first 5	Zip_Code	INTEGER(5)
			Load second 4	Zip_Ext	INTEGER(4)

Lookup Transform Types

			Transformation	Column Name	Target Domain
			Match the Customer Id of the Customer Table to the Customer Id of the Commercial Loan Customer Id and derive the Gender from the Customer Table	Gender	VARCHAR(10)

Figure 4.20   Types of transformations

The rationale is that at the data warehouse level, it is an architectural principle to keep clean, conformed data for all possible analytic uses, while at the data mart level, application-specific business rules such as calculations are applied.

Step 6: Define the Logical Load DI Model

The loads will be determined first by the target database and then by subject area within that database. For this case study, it would be as follows:

- **Data warehouse**
  - Customers
  - Loans

- **Customer loan reporting data mart**
  - Customers
  - Loans

The data warehouse subject areas would contain the following tables:

- **Customer**
  - Customers
  - Addresses
- **Loan**
  - Loans
  - Products

The data warehouse subject area loads are defined in the logical load data integration model portrayed in Figure 4.21.

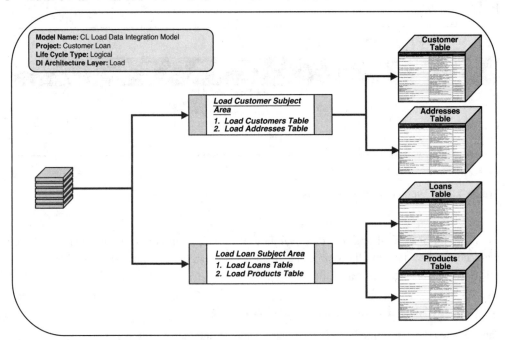

Figure 4.21   Customer loan logical load data integration model

Step 7: Determine the Physicalization Strategy

With all the "whats" determined in the logical data integration models, each data integration model needs to be evaluated for the "hows." This means how to maximize the processing performance. There is a technique used to simplify the design and ensure that there is a smaller end code base that is both flexible and scalable.

Extending the concept of subject areas into an entire target (a group of subject areas) provides a basis for a data integration model technical design technique that we call target-based design. The core concept of the target-based design technique is to place functionality where it is needed and will perform the best. The target-based design technique is applied against logical data integration models to determine whether functionality such as data quality checks and transforms are source-specific or common, often called enterprise, and from this design investigation, align the business rules with the appropriate processing function.

When the target-based design technique is applied to the case study data integration models in Figure 4.22, observe how certain business rule functionality is moved from one data integration model and closer to where the actual processing needs to occur, which will again increase performance and throughput when executed.

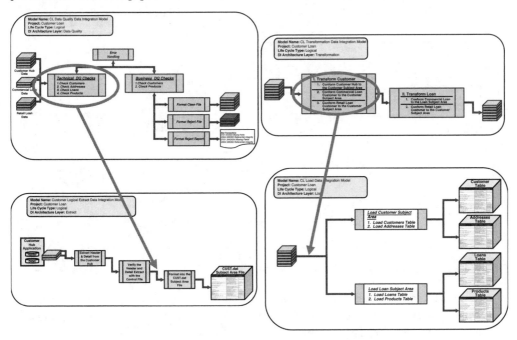

Figure 4.22 Logical to physical data integration model transformations

Observe in particular how the data quality and transformation logic is segmented between local and common requirements in Step 10.

Step 8: Convert the Logical Extract Models into Physical Source System Extract DI Models

Converting the customer hub extract from logical to physical requires moving the following data quality business rules from the logical data quality data integration model to the physical data quality data integration model, as shown in Figure 4.23. These changes include the following:

- **Customer technical data quality checkpoints**
  - "Customer" technical data quality checkpoints
  - "Address" (location) technical data quality checkpoints

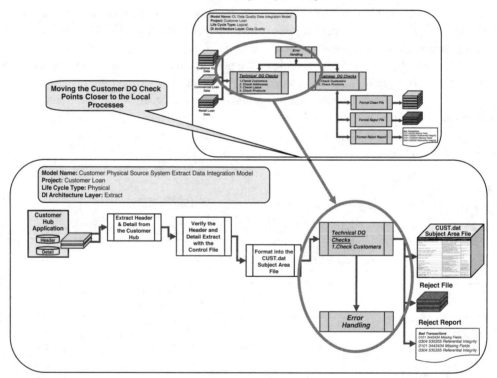

Figure 4.23   Customer loan physical source system extract data integration model example

For the commercial loan extract data integration model, the following data quality business rules from the data quality logical data integration model in Figure 4.24 to the physical data integration model were moved. These changes include the following:

- **Commercial loan customer technical data quality checkpoints**
- **Commercial loan technical data quality checkpoints**
  - Commercial loan customer technical data quality checkpoints
  - Commercial product address technical data quality checkpoints

These changes are reflected in the commercial loan physical data integration model in Figure 4.24.

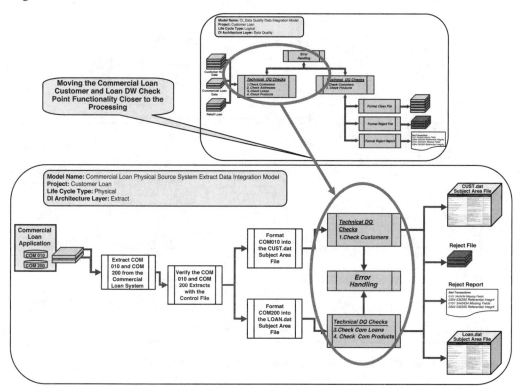

Figure 4.24   Commercial loan physical source system data integration model

Finally, for the retail loan extract data integration model, the following data quality business rules from the data quality logical data integration model to the physical data integration model were moved. These changes include the following:

- **Retail loan customer technical data quality checkpoints**
- **Retail loan technical data quality checkpoints**
  - Retail loan technical data quality checkpoints
  - Retail product address technical data quality checkpoints

These changes are also reflected in the commercial loan physical data integration model in Figure 4.25.

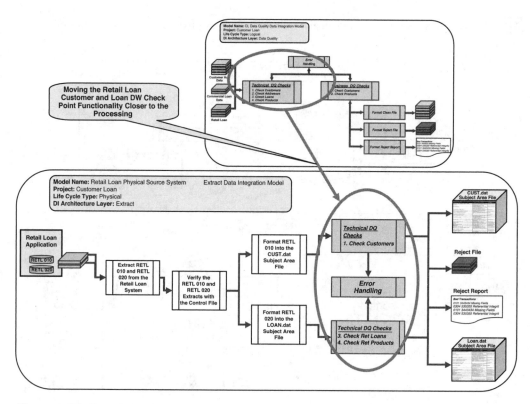

Figure 4.25   Retail physical source system data integration model

At this point, the three physical source system extract data integration models are ready to be completed with any final development changes in a commercial data integration development package, such as Ab Initio, Data Stage, or Informatica.

Step 9: Refine the Logical Load Models into Physical Source System Subject Area Load DI Models

After the data quality business rule functionality has been distributed with the local data quality checkpoints being moved to the source system extract, and the enterprise data quality checkpoints consolidated into a common component data integration model, the focus shifts to the physicalization of the logical load data integration models.

The change from the logical load data integration models to subject area load data integration models is where the transformation business rules are evaluated and distributed between subject area and enterprise processing. Subject area-specific transformations are placed in the load data integration models, and enterprise-level transformations are moved to a common component model, as displayed in Figure 4.26.

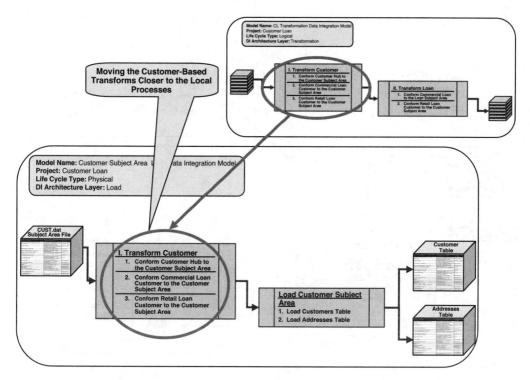

Figure 4.26   Customer physical subject area load data integration model

The transformation business rules are placed first in the model to complete all changes to the data before any preparation for loading, as demonstrated in Figure 4.27.

The load order of the tables needs to account for referential integrity rules, for example, first lookup tables, second master data, then finally detail data. Close collaboration with the data modeling and database administration team on defining the correct load order to ensure referential integrity within the database is critical.

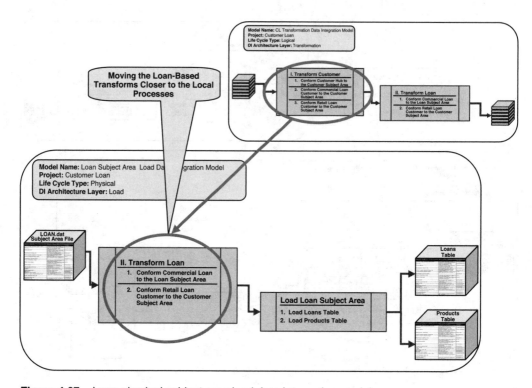

Figure 4.27   Loan physical subject area load data integration model

With the distribution of functionality between the physical source system extract and subject area load models, any remaining enterprise-level business rules are built in to common component data integration models, which are the next steps.

Step 10: Package the Enterprise Business Rules into Common Component Models

This case study mirrors what is found in most projects and mature data integration environments in terms of common components, which are a very thin layer of enterprise data quality and transformation business rules that are commonly used. The steps for developing common component data integration models include the following:

1. **Packaging enterprise-level data quality checkpoints into a common component model**

    - Glean any enterprise data quality checkpoints from the logical data quality data integration model that were not picked up in the physical source system extract data integration model.

- For the case study, we have the one enterprise-level data quality checkpoint, which is the Gender checkpoint, shown in Figure 4.28, and the data quality common component data integration model, shown in Figure 4.29.

Attribute Name	Attribute Definition	Column Name	Domain	Data Quality Check
Gender	Gender of the customer. Data Qualiy Criteria: Male, Female, Unknown	Gender	VARCHAR(10)	It must be "Male," "Female," or "Unknown"

Figure 4.28   Enterprise-level data quality checkpoint

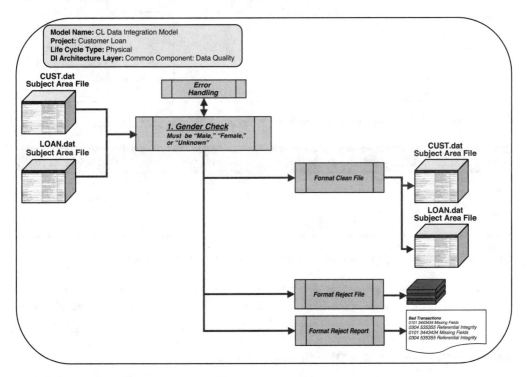

Figure 4.29   Physical data quality common components data integration model

2. **Packaging enterprise-level transformation business rules into a common component model**

- Glean any enterprise transformation business rules from the logical transformation data integration model that were not picked up in the physical subject area load data integration model, shown in Figure 4.30.

- For the case study, we also have the one enterprise-level transformation, which is the matching logic for Customer Source System Code, shown in Figure 4.31.

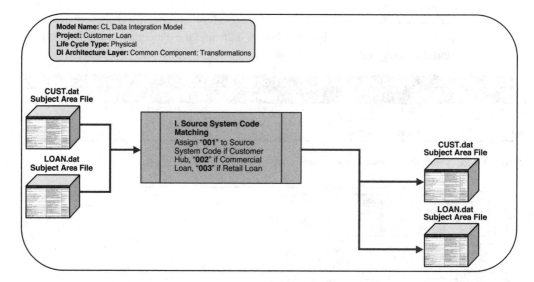

Figure 4.30   Physical transformation common components data integration model

Transform	Subject Area File	Column Name	Column Definition	Target Domain
Must be Assigned "001" if Customer Hub, "002 if Commercial Loan, "003" if Retail Loan	CUST.dat	Source_Sys_Code	The unique identifier of the Source System.	VARCHAR(20)

Figure 4.31   Enterprise-level customer source system code transformation

The two common component data integration models can be developed either as separate physical code models or built in to a component library for use by multiple other processes.

Step 11: Sequence the Physical DI Models

Once the data integration models have been converted into physical functional modules and are ready for final instantiation into source code, then all the data integration models should be reviewed for job sequencing and scheduling, as depicted in Figure 4.32.

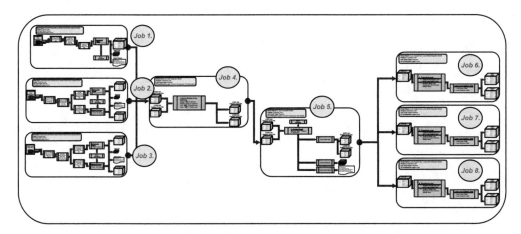

Figure 4.32 The physical data integration model job flow

More details on the tasks and steps to making these data integration processes "production ready" are reviewed in Chapter 7, "Data Integration Logical Design."

Summary

This case study presents all the tasks and activities and techniques needed to build a scalable application and a foundation for a component-based data integration environment.

Although the case study is not at a large scale, for example of integrating 30 systems into an enterprise data warehouse, it does demonstrate what is needed to represent that level of integration using a graphical diagramming approach.

It used three sources to demonstrate how to consolidate data into a single target using the subject area approach; it demonstrated how to apply the target-based design technique in moving data quality business rules to the sources and transformation business rules to the targeted subject areas.

The next part of the book focuses on all the phases, tasks, activities, and deliverables in the data integration Systems Development Life Cycle.

PART 2

The Data Integration Systems Development Life Cycle

Data Integration Analysis

This chapter reviews the initial tasks for analyzing the requirements for a data integration solution, with the focus on the following:

- Scoping the target solution
- Confirming the source system information
- Determining the quality of the source data
- Developing the data mappings from source to target

This chapter also discusses how data integration analysis fits into an overall Systems Development Life Cycle (see Figure 5.1). The next several chapters detail how the data integration architecture and modeling techniques are integrated with analysis, logical design, technical design, build activities, tasks, and deliverables in addition to other key data integration analysis techniques and principles.

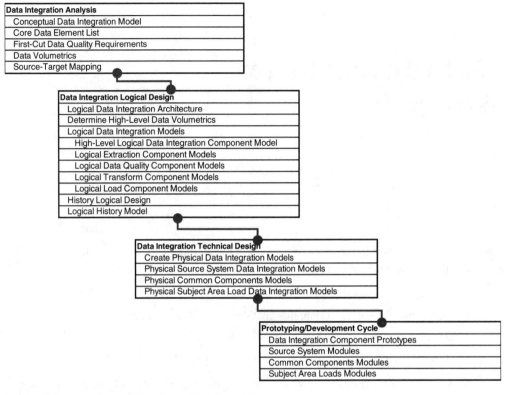

Figure 5.1   Data integration life cycle deliverables

Analyzing Data Integration Requirements

Traditional Systems Development Life Cycles define *analysis* as the phase that investigates a key business area or business problem as defined by the end-user community. It discerns the "whats" of a business problem.

The data integration analysis project phase scopes and defines the "logical whats" of the intended data integration processes or application.

That first step in a data integration project is also the same step performed for any Information Technology project, which is defining the scope of the efforts and providing answers to the question "What do we need to do?" These activities are then aligned, sequenced, timed, and integrated into an overall project plan.

For a data integration project, defining scope means determining the following:

- *What* are the sources?
- *What* is the target (or targets)?
- *What* are the data requirements (fulfill business requirements if any)?

- *What* are the business rules needed to restructure the data to meet the requirements of the intended target(s)?

Once the scope is defined, understood, and agreed to, the data integration project team will need to analyze the sources of the data for the targets, investigate their data quality and volumes, and then map the source data fields to the intended target to produce deliverables, as illustrated in Figure 5.2.

Analysis Deliverable   Analysis Deliverable   Analysis Deliverable

Figure 5.2   Sample data integration analysis deliverables

To define the project scope for the data integration project and determine the requirements needed for the intended data integration processes, the following data integration solution requirements tasks must be performed:

1. Build a conceptual data integration model.
2. Perform source system profiling.
3. Review/assess source data quality.
4. Perform data mapping to source systems.

Building a Conceptual Data Integration Model

The first task in data integration analysis is to define the scope of the intended data integration process. The best scope management "tool" is a visual representation of the sources and targets. That visual representation is the conceptual data integration model.

How does a conceptual data integration model help define scope? A conceptual data integration model provides a high-level representation of how the data integration requirements will be met for the proposed system. It also provides that visual representation of how those requirements will be satisfied.

At this stage, it is only necessary to identify the planned source and target data stores and potential processes needed to fully understand the ramifications of the users' requirements for data integration in terms of the feasibility for the project. Things to review in developing a conceptual data integration model include the following:

- Identifying existing source system extractions that could be leveraged as potential sources

- Determining if existing data quality checkpoints in the environment could be reused
- Identifying existing target data stores for the target database

Figure 5.3 is the conceptual data integration model from the banking case study as sample output of the conceptual data integration modeling task that was developed in Chapter 4, "Case Study: Customer Loan Data Warehouse Project."

Please notice the differences and similarities in the models when the conceptual data integration model is developed for the Wheeler Bank case study in Chapter 4.

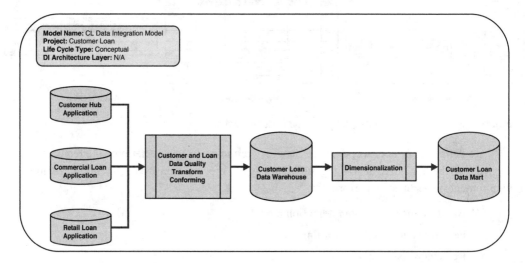

Figure 5.3   Data integration life-cycle deliverables

Again, a conceptual data integration model simply documents the scope of the proposed data integration application in terms of the high-level sources, targets, and business rules.

Key Conceptual Data Integration Modeling Task Steps

Building a conceptual data integration model requires these steps:

1. **Identify the major source data stores**—What are the expected systems that the data will be extracted from? How many files/tables are expected to be sourced from these systems? How wide are the files/tables (e.g., the number of columns)?

2. **Document initial volumetrics by source system**—What is the high-level estimate on the frequency and volumes of data from each source system?

3. **Review the data integration environment for reusable components**—If this is an existing data integration environment, are there extract components/jobs for the needed source system in place? Are there loads in place that can be extended and/or leveraged? Are there common data quality or transformation components/jobs that can be used?

4. **Define initial business rules**—What are the business rules in terms of data quality business rules and transformation business rules that can be documented at a high level?

5. **Identify the major target data stores**—What is the intended data store(s)? What are their subject areas, such as customer and product?

With the scope defined as well as the source systems and high-level business rules identified, it is critical to discover as much as possible about the sources' underlying data structures, data quality, frequency, and volumes. The next three tasks focus on that source system data discovery.

Why Is Source System Data Discovery So Difficult?

It used to be a foregone conclusion that a project manager would have to significantly pad their development and unit testing estimates due to data mapping issues. Those issues were due to a lack of understanding of underlying format and the data rules of the source systems, as well as the lack of rigor attached to the time and effort in performing source systems data discovery. This task was often overlooked due to the sheer magnitude of the difficulty.

Why is source systems data discovery so difficult? There are several reasons, including the following:

- **Undocumented and complex source formats**—Documentation for many systems are either out of date or undocumented. For example, many systems use old flat-file formats with unstructured file layouts with nested logic (hierarchies) built in with no easy method of understanding the number of layers. Documentation if it does exist is typically not kept up to date and has led to significant misunderstandings of the actual format of source systems.

- **Data formatting differences**—Often, data goes through an undocumented process that converts a field from one type to another while en route from one system to the source system being examined. For example, a calculation field defined as Packed Decimal is really Integer based on an undocumented transformation. This incorrect data formatting can cause an incorrect data mapping error, incorrect calculation, or even the data integration job to terminate.

- **Lack of client subject matter knowledge**—Often, the designers and developers of older transactional data systems are no longer available, leaving little to no documentation to aid in understanding the underlying data format and processing rules.

- **Bad data quality**—Often in source systems analysis, mapping issues can be a result of bad data quality, for example, a lack of primary or foreign keys. Referential integrity is often not enforced in the database, but in the ETL logic, which occurs for a multitude of reasons (e.g., performance). However, when these keys are not checked in the ETL logic or missed, leaving the mandatory key fields null, there are significant downstream technical data quality issues.

A series of data discovery techniques have been developed over time to analyze the data structures of the source systems to aid in discovering the underlying format and data rules of the source systems. The first of these techniques is data profiling.

Performing Source System Data Profiling

The first source system discovery task, data profiling, uncovers source systems' structural information, such as the data elements (fields or database columns), their format, dependencies between those data elements, relationships between the tables (if they exist via primary and foreign keys), data redundancies both known and unknown, and technical data quality issues (such as missing or unmatched key fields).

Data profiling as a formal data integration technique has evolved into a more formal and integrated function within the data integration discipline. It is simply impossible to build highly reliable data integration processes without a thorough understanding of the source data. In the past, data profiling was performed sporadically on data projects, often where a database administrator would run a series of SQL queries to look for data gaps. Both the technique and tools for data profiling have matured greatly in the past five years.

The following sections provide a brief overview of techniques and the tasks for performing data profiling.

Overview of Data Profiling

Data profiling uncovers critical source system information through the following:

- **Reviewing the data elements (fields or database columns) and their actual formats**—As discussed earlier, existing system documentation on the formats of the data is either inaccurate or outdated. Determining that a field is *Integer 7* rather than *VarChar 6* is invaluable in preventing mapping, coding, and testing issues.

- **Determining data dependencies and their actual relationships between the tables (if they exist via primary and foreign keys)**—For a host of reasons (performance for one), referential integrity is not enforced in most source systems. Determining and verifying that the data in the lookup tables matches the data in the main tables and that the primary key cascades into the detail tables is critical in maintaining referential integrity.

Figure 5.4 provides an example of the types of data quality issues uncovered in data profiling.

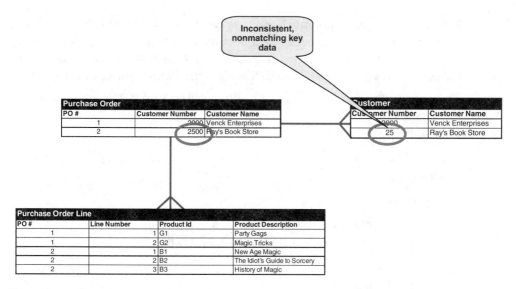

Figure 5.4   Example of an issue found in source system data profiling

- **Reviewing industry-specific data rules and anomalies**—Data profiling is simply not a technical exercise that only requires technical data understanding. When the source system's data elements and their relationships are analyzed, a "picture" emerges of the use and purpose of that data that follows some business purpose often based on industry.

Although data profiling is a time-intensive technical activity, it also requires a level of business knowledge of the source data. For example, the use, purpose, and business rules associated with product data are very different between manufacturing and banking organizations. It is best to have data profilers with industry expertise or at the least access to data stewards or subject matter experts while performing profiling tasks.

Key Source System Data Profiling Task Steps

Source system data profiling includes the following steps:

1. **Identify the data elements**—The first task of data profiling is to determine what files and tables are needed for the data integration project or process. Data elements should be identified and documented. This also includes reviewing

   - File formats
   - Database DDL
   - System documentation (if any exists)

   The objective is to confirm what is really in the source data (files\tables).

The data element level information that is gathered through the profiling efforts should be consolidated into a document called the Core Data Element List, which is a very simple listing of the data elements, its actual data type and size, whether it is nullable, and any business or technical rules (such as referential integrity) that may exist.

The source system data elements in the report should be listed and sorted by the following criteria:

- File/table name

- Data element name

- Subject area

- Business definition (if exists)

- Domain (e.g., Integer, VarChar)

- Data quality criteria, which might include the following:

  - Null

  - Key value

  - Valid ranges

Figure 5.5 provides an example of the output of a data profiling exercise.

2. **Prioritize critical data elements**—From the Core Data Elements List, identify and prioritize the critical data elements needed for the intended target and ensure that the right data elements are being focused on in the correct sequential order. Critical data elements are those that have either technical or business importance to the target database. For example, those columns that are used for primary or foreign keys are considered critical. Columns such as Comment fields are usually not critical.

Core Data Element List								
Source File/ Table Name	Data Element Name	Subject Area	Business Definition	Domain	Data Quality Criteria			
					Null	Key	Ranges	
HEADER	Cust_Id	Customer	The unique identifier of the customer in the source system.	INTEGER(10)	No	PK		
HEADER	Name	Customer	Customer name: specifies the primary current name (normally the legal name for the customer) as used by the bank	VARCHAR(10)	No			
HEADER	Gender	Customer	Gender of the customer.	VARCHAR(10)	No		Data Quality Criteria: Male, Female, Unknown	
HEADER	Customer_Type	Customer	The unique identifier assigned to the customer type. For example, commercial, retail	VARCHAR(10)	No			
HEADER	Legal_Status	Customer	The unique identifier of the classification.	Date	No			
HEADER	Legal_Status_Date	Customer	Date of a change in legal status such as bankruptcy Chapter 11, 7	VARCHAR(10)				
HEADER	Effective_Date	Customer	The date on which the customer first became relevant to the financial institution.	Date				
HEADER	End_Date	Customer	The date on which the customer ceased to be relevant to the financial institution.	VARCHAR(10)				
HEADER	Tax_ID_Number	Customer	The government-issued identification for commercial customers.	VARCHAR(10)				
HEADER	Ind_Soc_Security_Number	Customer	The government-issued identification.	VARCHAR(10)				
DETAIL	Address ID	Customer	The unique identifier of the customer in the source system.	INTEGER(10)	No	PK		
DETAIL	Cust_Id	Customer	The unique identifier of the customer in the source system.	INTEGER(10)	No	PK		
DETAIL	Address_Line_1	Customer	The first address line	VARCHAR()	No			
DETAIL	Address_Line_2	Customer	The second address line	VARCHAR()				
DETAIL	City_Name	Customer	The city of the customer	VARCHAR()	No	FK		
DETAIL	State_Code	Customer	The two-digit state code, e.g. "NY"	VARCHAR()	No			
DETAIL	Postal_Barcode	Customer	The Zip code	VARCHAR()	No			
		Customer	The Zip extension		No			

Figure 5.5 Core data element list example

3. **Perform column analysis**—The purpose of this task is to analyze the table/file columns and examine all values of the same column of data to determine that column's technical definition and other properties, such as domain values, ranges, and minimum/maximum values. During column analysis, each available column of each table of source data should be individually examined in depth on

- Minimum, maximum, and average length
- Precision and scale for numeric values

- Basic data types encountered, including different date/time formats
- Minimum, maximum, and average numeric values
- Count of empty values, null values, and non-null/empty values
- Count of distinct values or cardinality

4. **Perform foreign key analysis**—In this task, the foreign keys of the columns are evaluated by comparing all columns in selected tables against the primary keys in those same tables. The objective is to confirm that there is an actual foreign key relationship between two tables based on the overlap of values between each specified column and the identified primary key. Where these pairings are a match, the foreign key analysis process identifies overlapping data, from which the user can review and designate the primary key and corresponding columns as a foreign key relationship, as shown in Figure 5.6.

Core Data Element List

Source File/ Table Name	Data Element Name	Subject Area	Business Definition	Domain	Data Quality Criteria		
					Null	Key	Ranges
HEADER	Cust_Id	Customer	The unique identifier of the customer in the source system.	INTEGER(10)	No	PK	
HEADER	Name	Customer	Customer name: specifies the primary current name (normally the legal name for the customer) as used by the bank	VARCHAR(10)	No		
HEADER	Gender	Customer	Gender of the customer.	VARCHAR(10)	No		Data Quality Criteria: Male, Female, Unknown
DETAIL	Address ID	Customer	The unique identifier of the customer in the source system.	INTEGER(10)	No	PK	
DETAIL	Cust_Id	Customer	The unique identifier of the customer in the source system.	INTEGER(10)	No	PK	
DETAIL	Address_Line_1	Customer	The first address line	VARCHAR()	No		
DETAIL	Address_Line_2	Customer	The second address line	VARCHAR()			
DETAIL	City_Name	Customer	The city of the customer	VARCHAR()	No	FK	
DETAIL	State_Code	Customer	The two-digit state code, e.g. "NY"	VARCHAR()	No		
DETAIL	Postal_Barcode	Customer	Zip_Code	VARCHAR()	No		
		Customer	The Zip extension		No		

Figure 5.6   Foreign key analysis example

5. **Perform cross-domain analysis**—Cross-domain analysis is the process of comparing all columns in each selected table against all columns in the other selected tables. The goal is to detect columns that share a common data type. If a pair of columns is found to share a common data type, this might indicate a relationship between the data stored in the two tables, such as consistent use of state or country codes, or it might simply indicate unnecessary duplicate data. Commonality is observed from the viewpoint of both columns; that is, the user can review the association in either direction from either column. If the data is found to be redundant, users can mark it accordingly. This type of analysis can be performed repeatedly over time, both in the same sources or in new sources that are added to a project to continuously build out the knowledge of cross-domain relationships.

Reviewing/Assessing Source Data Quality

This task reviews the profile results in the context of the critical data elements and develops the first-cut technical and business data quality checkpoints for the data quality process layer in the data integration environment.

Its focus is on the checkpoints that will be needed per source system, as illustrated in Figure 5.7. Data quality checkpoints for the target are the focus in Chapter 7, "Data Integration Logical Design."

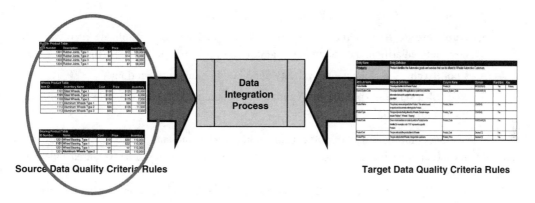

Figure 5.7 Data quality analysis focus

Validation Checks to Assess the Data

Data elements should be confirmed against the following types of data quality validations. Those that fail should be documented as a data quality checkpoint. These validations include **record-level checks**, which test individual records to confirm record validity. These checks are performed against each row of data. There are two types of record-level validations: data validation checks and error threshold checks.

Data Validation Checks

The following is a partial list of the types of data validation checks used in assessing data:

- **Data type validation**—Ensures that numeric data is placed in numeric fields, alpha data in alpha fields, and valid dates in date fields. This validation prevents accidental loading of nonsequenced data.

- **Date format checks**—Checks date fields for valid formats (i.e., YYYYMMDD, YYMMDD).

- **Numeric value range check**—Checks upper and lower limits of numeric fields for validity.

  Example: Employee salary should not be greater than 999999 or less than 0.

- **Date range validation**—Checks date ranges to catch data errors.

  Example: Date of Birth (DOB) check should ensure that the DOB of active customers is within 100–110 years range.

- **Percentage range check**—Verifies that a percent field is between 0% and 100%.

- **Null check**—Checks for null values in mandatory columns/fields.

- **Duplicate key/field checks**—Prevents accidental loading of duplicate records, business-defined critical data elements, and key columns (primary, foreign, unique).

- **Lookup checks**—Checks for validity and/or code mapping/decoding.

- **Record-level lookup checks**—Validates the contents of a selected field by comparing them with a list/table of values.

Fields that commonly use lookup checks include codes, indicators, and those with distinct sets of values. Examples include state code, country code, product code, Zip code, area code, past due indicator.

Figure 5.8 provides an example of records that have failed data quality checkpoints and have been rejected into the Reject Record Log.

Record Number	Date	Transaction Amount	Status	Customer Name				Reject Record Log	
				001	06/02/3005	$15,000	New	Mr. Brown	Failed Data Range Check
				002	06/02/2005	$AAA	Open	Mr. Corpe	Failed Numeric Check
003	06/02/2005	$27,000	Open	Mr. Green					
				<null>	06/07/2005	$29,000	Edit	Mr. Green	Failed Null/Key Check
005	06/07/2005	$40,000	New	Mr. Fargo					
006	06/07/2005	$35,000	Del	Mr. Corpe					

Figure 5.8   Reject Record Log example

Error Threshold Checks

Error threshold checks manage processing based on defined tolerances, for example, the failure of the processing of an entire file as a result of too many row failures for a given data file. In another threshold testing condition, examine if a given record fails a test, only the row is rejected. Error threshold checks track the percentage of failures for the entire source. The aggregate number of row failures can be used to fail the whole file.

If the threshold is exceeded, it causes the whole source to be rejected. Even though some individual rows from the source might have passed the test, they would not be passed to the clean staging area because the file has been rejected.

Key Review/Assess Source Data Quality Task Steps

Reviewing and assessing source data quality requires the following steps:

1. **Review the profile results in the context of the critical data elements**—Review the Core Data Element List.

2. **Verify completeness of values (not nulls, required fields)**—Check the expected or intended primary key, foreign key, and mandatory fields for values and redundancies.

3. **Verify conformance and validity checking for valid values and ranges**—Check data ranges and domain range fields (e.g., gender ["M", "F", "U"] fields).

4. **Determine first-cut data technical data quality checkpoints**—Document missing requirements into data quality checkpoints, as portrayed in Figure 5.9.

Customer						
Attribute Name	Attribute Definition	Column Name	Domain	Mandatory	Key	Data Quality Check
Customer Identifier	The unique identifier assigned to a customer.	Cust_Id	INTEGER(10)	Yes	Primary	Must be unique and not null
Customer Name	Customer name: specifies the primary current name (normally the legal name for the customer) as used by the financial	Cust_Name	VARCHAR(64)	Yes		Must be not null
Gender	Gender of the customer. Data Quality Criteria: Male, Female, Unknown	Gender	VARCHAR(10)	Yes		It must be "Male," "Female," or "Unknown"
Source System Unique Key Text	The unique identifier of the customer in the source system.	Source_Sys_Unique_Key_Text	VARCHAR(32)	Yes		Must be not null
Source System Code	The unique identifier of the source system.	Source_Sys_Code	VARCHAR(20)	Yes		Must be not null
Customer Type Identifier	The unique identifier assigned to the customer type. For example, commercial, retail	Customer_Type_Id	SMALLINT	Yes		Must be not null
Customer Effective Date	The date on which the customer first became relevant to the financial institution.	Cust_Effective_Date	DATE	Yes		Must be not null and a date field
Customer End Date	The date on which the customer ceased to be relevant to the financial institution.	Cust_End_Date	DATE	Yes		Must be not null and a date field
Last Update Run Identifier		Last_Update_Run_Id	INTEGER(10)	Yes		Must be not null
Created Run Identifier		Created_Run_Id	INTEGER(10)	Yes		Must be not null
Customer Legal Status Type Identifier	The unique identifier of the classification.	Cust_Legal_Status_Type_Id	INTEGER(10)	Yes		Must be not null

Figure 5.9 Data quality checkpoint definition example

Performing Source\Target Data Mappings

This task maps *each* source system data element's technical and business definition to the intended target element (or data elements). For example, for every expected derived or transactional data element, it needs to be mapped from each source system, in terms of reconciling technical metadata, business definitions, and calculations.

Overview of Data Mapping

Data mapping, one of the most critical aspects of data integration, is the process of conforming data elements between one or (usually) more sources to a target data model. Data mapping is used as a first step for a wide variety of data integration tasks, including the following:

- Data transformation or data mediation between a data source and a destination, which includes the identification of *all* data relationships as part of this data lineage analysis
- The discovery of hidden sensitive data, for example, the last four digits of a Social Security number hidden in another user ID as part of a data masking or de-identification project for multiple databases into a single database

For example, a company that would like to transmit and receive purchases and invoices with other companies might use data mapping to create data maps from a company's data to standardized ANSI ASC X12 messages for items such as purchase orders and invoices. Figure 5.10 illustrates a typical data mapping example where three system primary keys, Customer #, Customer Number (using Social Security number), and Customer #, are used to build an overall customer key, Involved Party.

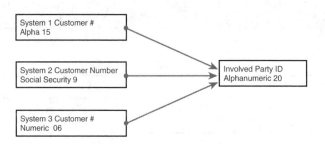

Figure 5.10   Typical data mapping example

Data mapping is *not* a technical task; it is a business analysis task and is one of the most important tasks in any data integration project.

Data mapping is also not a ***one-to-one*** concept. It requires both "horizontal" and "vertical" analysis of the one-to-many sources to (usually) one target, as demonstrated in Figure 5.11; it requires deep business knowledge of the particular industry.

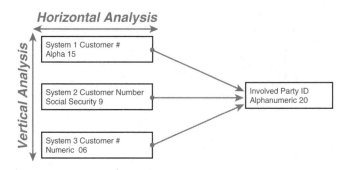

Figure 5.11   The multidimensional analysis aspect of data mapping

For example, for integration loans from multiple loan systems, a data integration analyst with knowledge of banking is needed. For the integration of multiple product masters for automotive parts, a data integration analyst with knowledge of manufacturing would be needed to explain the business rules and relationships of their particular data.

Types of Data Mapping

Data mapping is a series of design patterns or "types" that requires the different types of analysis, as follows:

- **One-to-one data mapping**—The simplest type of data mapping is a one-to-one (see Figure 5.12). Even in this scenario, there is a level of transformation that is needed. In this mapping, the data elements need to be translated from Integer to VarChar to not have data mapping errors in the data integration jobs.

Source File/ Table	Source Field	Source Domain	Mapping Rule	Column Name	Target Domain	Mandatory	Key
CS1001	SOC-SEC-#	INTEGER (09)	Translate Integer to Varchar	Social_Sec_Number	VARCHAR(09)	Yes	Yes

Figure 5.12   One-to-one data mapping scenario

- **One-to-many data mapping**—One-to-many scenarios often occur when data is being mapped from a second normal form data model to a third normal form data model, as displayed in Figure 5.13. In this example, the Customer File data elements are mapped to a normalized relational database. The data mapper will need to analyze what data elements map to what table. For example:

    CUST_ID maps to Customer Number in the Customer_Table and to the Address_Table.

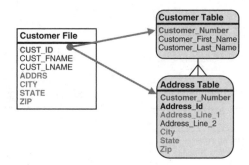

Figure 5.13   One-to-many data mapping example: one file to two tables

The mapping to perform this normalization creates the one-to-many mapping shown in Figure 5.14.

Source File/ Table	Source Field	Source Domain	Mapping Rule	Target Table	Column Name	Target Domain	Mandatory	Key
CUST FILE	CUST_ID	CHAR (15)	None.	Customer	Customer Number	VARCHAR(15)	Yes	Yes
CUST FILE	CUST_FNAME	CHAR (20)	None.	Customer	Customer First Name	VARCHAR(20)	Yes	No
CUST FILE	CUST_LNAME			Customer	Customer Last Name			No
			Increment from 1	Address	Address Id		Yes	Yes	Yes
CUST FILE	CUST_ID	CHAR (15)	None.	Address	Customer Number	VARCHAR(15)	Yes	No
CUST FILE		CHAR (20)	None.	Address	Address Line 1		Yes	No
				Address	Address Line 2	VARCHAR(20)		
CUST FILE	CITY	CHAR (20)	None.	Address	City	VARCHAR(20)	Yes	No
CUST FILE	STATE	CHAR (20)	None.	Address	State	VARCHAR(20)	Yes	No
CUST FILE	ZIP	CHAR (09)	None.	Address	Zip	VARCHAR(09)	Yes	No

Figure 5.14   One-to-many data mapping example

- **Many-to-one data mapping**—The next mapping scenario, shown in Figure 5.15, requires a horizontal mapping view and is a typical mapping situation that rationalizes multiple source customer keys to one new customer key, in this example the Customer_Number attribute.

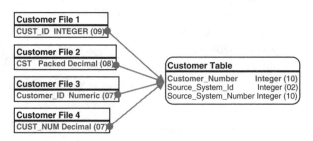

Figure 5.15   Many-to-one data mapping example: four files to one table

This mapping is illustrated in Figure 5.16 as each of the source customer IDs are mapped to the target customer ID.

Source File/ Table	Source Field	Source Domain	Mapping Rule	Target Table	Column Name	Target Domain	Mandatory	Key
			System generated key	Customer	Customer_Number	Integer (10)	Yes	Yes
			If source system 1, then move "1" to the field, else if source system 2, then move "2" to the field, else if source system 3, then move "3" to the field, else if source system 4, then move "4" to the field, else if "U".	Customer	Source_System_Id	Integer (02)	Yes	Yes
CUSTOMER FILE 1	CUST_ID	INTEGER (09)	Pad last digit	Customer	Source_System_Number	Integer (10)	Yes	No
CUSTOMER FILE 2	CST	Packed Decimal (08)	Translate pad Decimal to Integer. Pad last two digits	Customer	Source_System_Number	Integer (10)		No
CUSTOMER FILE 3	Customer_ID	Numeric (07)	Translate pad Numeric to Integer. Pad last three digits	Address	Source_System_Number	Integer (10)	Yes	No
CUSTOMER FILE 4	CUST_NUM	Decimal (07)	Translate pad Decimal to Integer. Pad last three digits	Address	Source_System_Number	Integer (10)	Yes	No

Figure 5.16 Many-to-one data mapping example

Key Source\Target Data Mapping Task Steps

Key source-to-target data mapping steps include the following:

1. **Determine the target subject areas**—If applicable, review the target data model to group the target tables into logical subject areas.

2. **Identify the target data element or elements by subject area**—For each of the subject areas (such as customer or product), determine what data elements fit within that grouping.

3. **Review all the source systems for candidate data elements**—Review the other sources for potential one-to-many source data elements for the target data element.

4. **Map the candidate data element or elements to the target data element**—Map the identified source data element to target data element. For this deliverable, document differences in technical metadata such as format (e.g., VarChar versus Char) and length.

5. **Review each source and target data element for one-to-many or many-to-one requirements**—Perform both a vertical and horizontal review of the sources against the target data element.

6. **Map technical mapping requirements to each target's subject area data element**—Build in any mapping business rules, which may be as simple as padding or trimming the field, to aggregating and/or calculating amounts.

7. **Reconcile definitional (data governance) issues between source systems**—Resolve any data element (attribute)–level definitional differences between the different sources and the target data element.

Summary

This chapter covered the data integration analysis tasks, steps, and techniques necessary to determine the requirements for a data integration solution.

The first task is to graphically scope the project by building a "picture" of the intended data integration processes in a conceptual data integration diagram. Once documented and the scope is identified and confirmed, attention is moved to the source systems.

Much of the time spent in difficult downstream development phase errors are a result of a lack of knowledge of the source systems (not the target); therefore, a significant amount of time and effort needs to be spent on determining the structures, the content, and the explicit and implicit business rules of the data.

Gaining an understanding of this data requires an iterative approach of profiling and analyzing the data first within the file or table (e.g., columnar profiling) and then across the data files or tables.

We reviewed the fact that data mapping is *not* a one-to-one exercise but requires both a horizontal and vertical view of the sources to target.

The key theme of iterative design was embedded in all the tasks in this chapter. For example, the understanding of the data sources and how to map those sources to the target usually requires more than one pass to get it right.

The next chapter begins the next of a multichapter case study that goes through the entire data integration life cycle. Chapter 6, "Data Integration Analysis Case Study," focuses on applying the analysis techniques in this chapter to the Wheeler Automotive Company.

End-of-Chapter Questions

Question 1.
How does a conceptual data integration model help define scope?
Question 2.
What are the reasons why source system data discovery is so difficult?
Question 3.
Define data profiling.
Question 4.
Define data mapping.
Question 5.
Using the following diagram, what type of data mapping scenario is this?

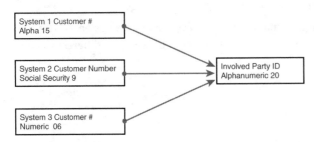

CHAPTER 6

Data Integration Analysis Case Study

This chapter begins our second case study with the emphasis on working through the entire data integration life cycle tasks and deliverables. Subsequent chapters cover the phases of the data integration life cycle and provide case studies for each phase. This case study is based on integrating three order management systems for the Wheeler Automotive Company into an enterprise data warehouse and product line profitability data mart.

For the analysis case study, we focus on developing project scope, source systems analysis, and data mapping deliverables.

Case Study Overview

The Wheeler Automotive Company is a fictional midsized auto parts supplier to the automotive industry and has been fairly successful since the company's inception back in the mid-1960s. Due to the recent recession, there has been increased focus on cost and profitability at a level of detail that is not currently available in its current plant-level reporting, as shown in Figure 6.1.

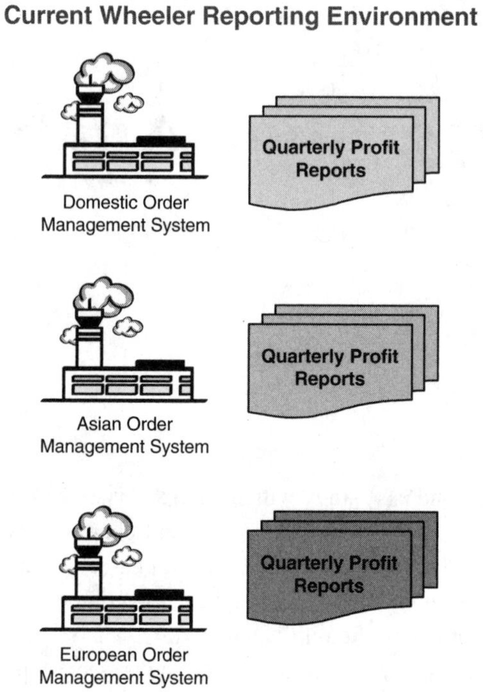

Current Wheeler Reporting Environment

Figure 6.1   Case study 2: Wheeler source systems

For Wheeler to perform the types of analysis needed to answer these profitability questions, it needs an environment where the disparate order information is consolidated, conformed by subject areas, aggregated by time, and displayed at a transaction level that provides management information about what product lines are selling and showing a profit.

Envisioned Wheeler Data Warehouse Environment

To meet the profitability reporting requirements as well as other future analytic and reporting needed, the Wheeler Information Technology Department has planned to define, design, and build an enterprise data warehouse and product line profitability data mart, as shown in Figure 6.2.

To date, the data warehousing team has completed a logical and physical data model for the data warehouse and product line data mart, as shown in Figure 6.3.

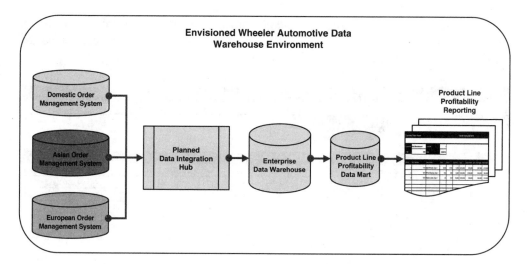

Figure 6.2   Envisioned Wheeler data warehouse environment

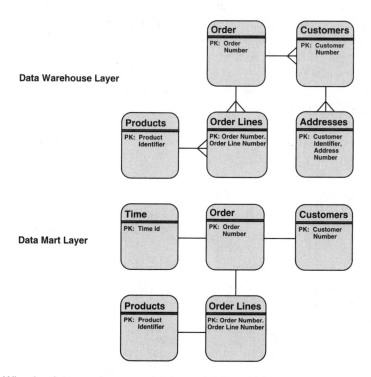

Figure 6.3   Wheeler data warehouse and data mart data models

The Wheeler data warehousing team has also produced a sample report layout portrayed in Figure 6.4 for the product line profitability reporting that includes the known aggregations and calculations.

Customer Order Report							Month Ending 02/27/2010			
Customer	Auto Manufacturer 1	Location			1					
Order		1001	Date		2/2/2010					
Line #	Item Number	Description		Cost	Price	Quantity	Total	Gross Profit	30% Overhead	Net Profit
1		1101	Steel Wheels, Type 1	$100	$125	1,000	$125,000	$25,000	$37,500	-$12,500
2		1201	Wheel Bearing, Type 1	$10	$30	5,000	$150,000	$100,000	$45,000	$55,000
3		1301	Rubber Joints, Type 1	$7	$12	10,000	$120,000	$50,000	$36,000	$14,000

Figure 6.4   Wheeler sample report layout

Aggregations in a Data Warehouse Environment

To meet all the requirements of this case study, we need to deal with aggregations, and where they occur for this effort. Although this text is primarily focused on data integration, it is important to take a moment to discuss a general data warehousing best practice. The "when" and "where" of data aggregation and calculation can be performed in all the layers of a data warehouse. In what layer the aggregation or calculation is performed should be evaluated based on potential performance and static nature of the aggregation or calculation, for example, Pre-Query or On-Query.

Figure 6.5 illustrates the possible data warehouse layers where an aggregation or calculation transform could occur.

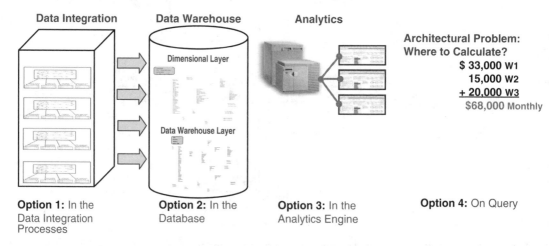

Figure 6.5   Architectural options on where to perform a transform

Option 1: In the data integration layer—Where the aggregation is performed in the transformation layer of a data integration process. This option is preferred for large volumes of static data that needs to be aggregated.

Advantages:

- Faster performance on query, no in-memory calculations. By having the data pre-calculated, the report query simply needs to return a value and the processing load is placed on the data integration environment, rather than on the data warehouse database or analytics engine. In this scenario, there is no query wait time for calculations to perform.

Disadvantages:

- Inflexibility in recalculation is required. In business intelligence environments where recalculations are required (for example, what-if scenarios), precalculated query results will not meet the business requirements.

Option 2: In the data warehouse database layer—Where the aggregation or calculation is performed as a stored procedure in the data warehouse or data mart based upon a trigger from a query (e.g., the ON QUERY SQL function). This option provides a little more flexibility than in the data integration layer and pushes the processing requirements on the database server rather than on the analytics engine.

Advantages:

- Faster performance on query, no in-memory calculations. In this scenario, the only wait time is for the database engine to perform the aggregation or calculation.

Disadvantages:

- Inflexible for recalculations when recalculating the query is required; the stored procedure will need to re-execute, causing query wait time.

- Poor metadata management and loss of metadata on the transformations. Store procedures are notoriously poorly documented and their metadata is typically not managed in a metadata tool unlike data integration packages.

Option 3: In the analytics layer—Most business intelligence software packages, such as MicroStrategy, Cognos®, and Business Objects, have the ability to perform query calculations and aggregations within their core engine. In this scenario, the BI engine performs the query to the data warehouse/mart database for the raw information, and then performs the calculation/aggregation in the BI server engine, thereby serving the results to the query requester.

Advantages:

- Faster performance on query, no in-memory calculations.

- Simplifies the data integration processes into more straight loads and allows the data warehouse to be simply common, and conformed raw data "pure" from a business rule transformation perspective. It moves the reporting aggregation and calculation transformations to the analytic layer.

Disadvantages:

- Inflexible when recalculations are required. Although similar to the issues of inflexibility in the data integration and data warehouse database layers, by having the aggregations/calculations in the BI engine, the query results are closer (on the network) to where the results need to be delivered, providing some level of faster performance.

- Requires recalculation, which can affect overall BI server performance. When the BI server engine is processing large resultsets for aggregations and calculations, other queries and requests will be placed in a wait state.

Option 4: During the database query—Where the aggregation or calculation is performed in memory of the analytics server or even the requestor's PC or Internet device. In this scenario, the speed of the aggregation or calculation is dependent on the SQL request to the database for the raw data, the network's speed and throughput of serving the raw results to the requestor's machine, and the time it takes on that machine to aggregate or calculate the resultset.

Advantages:

- Creates dynamic aggregations and calculations on the fly. This is the most flexible approach. This approach is most often observed in budgeting and forecasting analytic applications.

Disadvantages:

- Dynamic calculations are not scalable. This approach impacts the requestor's machine and can be constrained by a much smaller PC or Internet devices CPU memory than in server environments.

The best practice is to aggregate or calculate as far back as possible into the data warehouse layers and store the result in the data warehouse or data mart, thereby pushing the workload on the data integration server and managing the metadata in the data integration processes. However, there are exceptions to each rule. For each potential aggregation or calculation, an architectural review is needed for each of the business rules in the user requirements and logical data integration models. In addition, other documentation is required to determine the types of transforms, and where the transformation would best occur.

For the Wheeler Automotive case study, the aggregations in the report will be performed as transformations in the data integration processes and stored in the product line profitability data mart.

The first step is to scope and "visualize" the intended solution by developing a conceptual data integration model for the Wheeler project.

Data Integration Analysis Phase

The tasks of the Wheeler data integration analysis project phase is to define the project by building a conceptual data integration model, profile the data in the three Wheeler order management source systems, and map that data into the Wheeler enterprise data warehouse.

Step 1: Build a Conceptual Data Integration Model

Recall that a conceptual data integration model is a representation of the data integration scope for a project or environment. For the Wheeler project, the visual representation of the scope is represented by answering the following questions:

- What are the subject areas of the target databases? Customer, Order, and Product
- How many files are there for the identified source systems? Three for each source

Figure 6.6 shows the three sources and two targets for the intended Wheeler data warehouse environment.

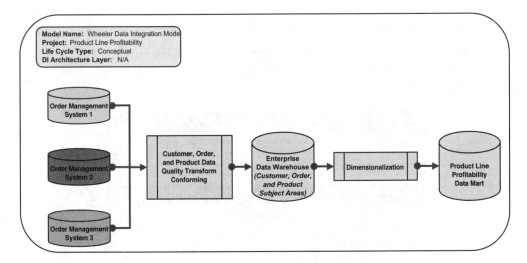

Figure 6.6   The Wheeler loan data warehouse conceptual data integration model

With a conceptual view of the intended project, our attention can be turned to the source system discovery tasks, beginning with performing source system data profiling.

Step 2: Perform Source System Data Profiling

For this case study, the best approach is to first review each file individually, then review them by subject area types, as shown in Figure 6.7.

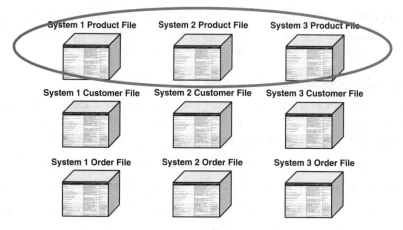

Figure 6.7   Profiling the Wheeler sources by subject area

By grouping the files, the ability to perform cross-domain analysis is significantly easier:

1. **Identify the data elements**—By grouping by subject areas, each set of data elements can be isolated and grouped for a first-cut profiling activity, which is illustrated in Figures 6.8 through Figure 6.10.

System 1 Rubber Product File

Item Number	Description	Cost	Price	Inventory
1301	Rubber Joints, Type 1	$7	$12	100,000
1302	Rubber Joints, Type 2	$8	$14	76,000
1303	Rubber Joints, Type 3	$10	$15	46,000
1304	Rubber Joints, Type 1	$5	$7	58,000

System 2 Wheels Product File

Item ID	Inventory Name	Cost	Price	Inventory
1101	Steel Wheels, Type 1	$100	$125	20,000
1101	Steel Wheels, Type 2	$120	$147	6,000
1103	Steel Wheels, Type 3	$150	$175	7,500
1111	Alum Wheels, Type 1	$70	$90	12,000
<null>	Alum Wheels, Type 2	$90	$135	11,500
1113	Alum Wheels, Type 3	$65	$89	8,900

System 3 Bearing Product File

ID Number	Description	Cost	Price	Inventory
1201	Wheel Bearing, Type 1	$10	$60	110,000
1101	Wheel Bearing, Type 2	$14	$32	110,000
1203	Wheel Bearing, Type 3	<null>	<null>	110,000
1204	Alum Wheels, Type 2	$7	$25	110,000

Figure 6.8   Product data elements

System 1 Customer File

CUST_#	ORG	CUST_NAME	ADDRESS	CITY	STATE	ZIP
410	General Motors	Mr. Jones	1230 Main Street	Warren	Michigan	48010
520	Toyota	Ms. Smith	444 Elm Street	Pontiac	Michigan	48120
660	Ford Motor	Mr. Cartwright	510 Amber St	Detroit	Michigan	48434
200	Nissan	Ms. Wheelright	626 Anderson	Lansing	Michigan	48232

System 2 Customer File

ID	O_NAME	F_NAME	L_NAME	ADDRSS 1	ADDRSS 2	CITY	STATE	ZIP
11100011	General Motors	Jasper	Jones	1230 Main St		Warren	Michigan	48010
11100012	Chrysler	Katie	Harvey	03 Daimler	Gate 2	Pontiac	Michigan	48120
<null>	Ford Motor	Mr. Cartwright	Mr. Cartwright	510 Amber St		Dearborn	Michigan	48012
1110001A	Nissan	Kelsie	Harvey	626 Anderson		Lansing	Michigan	48232

System 3 Customer File

CUST_ID	ORGANIZATION	FRST	LAST	ADDR 1	ADDR 2	ADDR 3	CITY	STATE	ZIP	EXT
310001	Ford Motor	Mr. Cartwright	Mr. Cartwright	510 Amber St			Dearborn	Michigan	48012	1234
310002	Chrysler	June	Jones	03 Daimler	Gate 2	Dock 1	Pontiac	Michigan	48120	4321
310003	General Motors	Jasper	Jones	1230 Main St		Warren	Michigan	Michigan	48012	1232
310004	Nissan	Kelsie	Harvey	626 Anders			Lansing	Michigan	48232	2331

Figure 6.9 Customer data elements

System 1 Order File

ORDER_NO	STATUS	DATE	CUST_#	TERMS_CD	ITEM_NO	PROD_PRICE	AMNT_ORDR
10001	Shipped	03032010	410	Fixd	1302	$14	2,000
10002	Ordered	03112010	520	Open	1303	$15	5,000
10003	Ordered	03122010	660	Open	1303	$15	3,000
10004	Shipped	03122010	200	Fixd	1301	$12	20,000

System 2 Order File

ORD_NUM	STATUS	DATE	CUST_#	LINE_1	TERMS_CD	ITEM_ID	PROD_PRICE	AMNT_ORDR	LINE_2	TERMS_CD	ITEM_ID	PROD_PRICE	AMNT_ORDR
22221	Shipped	03042010	11100011	1	02/10, net 30	1101	$125	100	2	02/10, net 30	1111	$135	550
22222	Ordered	03222010	11100012	1	02/10, net 30	1101	$147	230	2	02/10, net 30	1103	$175	400
22223	Ordered	03142010	<null>	1	02/10, net 30	1111	$135	1,000	2	02/10, net 30	<null>	$135	400
22224	Shipped	03212010	1110001A	1	02/10, net 30	1113	$89	2,000	2	02/10, net 30	1101	$125	200

System 3 Order File

ORD_#	STS	DTE	CUST_#	LN_1	ID_NUMBER	PROD_PRICE	AMNT_ORDR	LN_2	ID_NUMBER	PROD_PRICE	AMNT_ORDR	LN_3	ID_NUM	PROD_PRICE	AMNT_ORDR
30010	Ordered	03302010	310001	1	1201	$30	500	2	1204	$25	3,500				
30020	Ordered	03152010	310002	1	1101	$32	320								
30030	Ordered	03222010	310003	1	1203	<null>	2,000	2	1204	$25	5,000	3	1201	$30	300
30040	Ordered	03232010	310004	1	1204	$25	4,000	2	1101	$32	500				

Figure 6.10 Order data elements

Each column represents a data element with a technical definition, business definition, a set of business rules, and relationships. As the data elements are analyzed, they are grouped by subject area and cataloged into the Core Data Element List.

> **NOTE**
>
> This analysis is prone to rework and is highly iterative. Expect to take three to four passes in source system profiling as the entire "scheme" of the data begins to emerge. Source system profiling very much follows the "80/20" rule, where the first pass provides a majority of the expected profiling results. Keep in mind the next several passes will unearth the irregularities in the data (such as missing keys). It is important to verify the data with those users of the information who can confirm the findings.

2. **Prioritize critical data elements**—As the list is created, critical data elements such as potential keys should be identified and marked as "**Not Null**" and "**Key**," as demonstrated in Figure 6.11.

Wheeler Source System Core Data Element List						
Source File/ Table Name	Data Element Name	Subject Area	Domain	Data Quality Criteria		
				Not Null	Key	Ranges
System 1 Customer File						
	CUST_#	Customer	Varchar(04)	Y	Y	
	ORG	Customer	Varchar(40)	N	N	
	CUST_NAME	Customer	Varchar(40)	N	N	
	ADDRESS	Customer	Varchar(20)	N	N	
	CITY	Customer	Varchar(20)	N	N	
	STATE	Customer	Varchar(20)	N	N	
	ZIP	Customer	Varchar(09)	N	N	
System 2 Customer File						
	ID	Customer	Decimal(10)	Y	Y	
	O_NAME	Customer	Char(15)	Y	N	
	F_NAME	Customer	Char(15)	Y	N	
	L_NAME	Customer	Char(15)	Y	N	
	ADDRSS 1	Customer	Char(20)	Y	N	
	ADDRSS 2	Customer	Char(20)	N	N	
	CITY	Customer	Char(15)	N	N	
	STATE	Customer	Char(02)	N	N	
	ZIP	Customer	Decimal(09)	N	N	
System 3 Customer File						
	CUST_ID	Customer	Decimal(10)	Y	Y	
	ORGANIZATION	Customer	Varchar(20)	Y	N	
	FRST	Customer	Varchar(20)	Y	N	
	LAST	Customer	Varchar(20)	Y	N	
	ADDR 1	Customer	Char(20)	Y	N	
	ADDR 2	Customer	Char(20)	N	N	
	ADDR 3	Customer	Char(20)	N	N	
	CITY	Customer	Char(15)	N	N	
	STATE	Customer	Varchar(2)	N	N	
	ZIP	Customer	Integer(05)	N	N	
	EXT	Customer	Integer(04)	N	N	

Figure 6.11   Wheeler source system Core Data Element List—customer files

Figure 6.11 also shows the first-cut set of customer elements on the Core Data Element List from the three customer files.

The determination on whether a data element is critical or not is solely based on observational analysis, industry experience, and existing documentation, usually performed by a data integration analysis in conjunction with a data steward.

An additional task in profiling is finding and analyzing usage patterns of the data. This information can be found in SQL Explain Plans and database monitoring tools (if the sources are relational).

3. **Perform foreign key analysis**—It appears that only the order file has candidate foreign keys, which are:

- Customer numbers

- Product numbers

These are derived from the customer and product files.

4. **Perform column analysis**—As we review the columns of the source data, we find that there are null fields in the data, as shown in Figure 6.12.

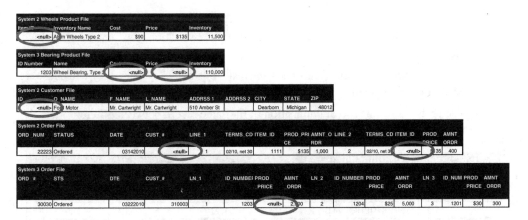

Figure 6.12 Null data found in column analysis data profiling

Our analysis reveals a significant lack of referential integrity in the data as evidenced in the following:

- **System 2 Wheels Product File**

- The Item_Id data element (the probable primary key) is null.

- **System 3 Bearing Product File**

- The Cost data element is null.

- The Price data element is null, which will impact downstream cost calculations.

- **System 2 Customer File**
  - The ID data element (the probable primary key) is null.
- **System 2 Order File**
  - The CUST data element (a probable foreign key) is null.
  - The ITEM_ID data element (another probable foreign key) is null.
- **System 3 Order File**
  - The PROD_PRICE data element is null.

The profiling column analysis also reveals potential duplication of data within the System 1 Rubber Product File, as shown in Figure 6.13.

System 1 Rubber Product File				
Item Number Description		Cost	Price	Inventory
1301 Rubber Joints, Type 1		$7	$12	100,000
1301 Rubber Joints, Type 1		$5	$7	58,000

Figure 6.13   Duplicated keys and descriptions found in column analysis data profiling

It appears that Record 1301 Rubber Joints, Type 1 is found twice with different costs and price, which indicates a suspected primary key violation (the nonrepeat rule) with the System 2 Wheels Product File.

Although these errors are often simply the result of sloppy key entry, they will cause significant issues in loading and using the data warehouse.

The profiling results reveal duplication of the same record between different files, System 2 and System 3, as shown in Figure 6.14.

System 2 Wheels Product File				
Item ID Inventory Name		Cost	Price	Inventory
1101 Steel Wheels, Type 1		$100	$125	20,000
1101 Steel Wheels, Type 2		$120	$147	6,000

System 3 Bearing Product File				
ID Number Name		Cost	Price	Inventory
1201 Wheel Bearing, Type 1		$10	$30	110,000
1101 Wheel Bearing, Type 2		$14	$32	110,000

Figure 6.14   Duplicated primary keys between tables in column analysis data profiling

The column profiling analysis has also found that there is the same product record; 1101 Steel Wheels, Type 2 is found both in System 2's Item_ID column and System 3's ID_Number column.

This data anomaly should be resolved in the source systems prior to the initial load of the data warehouse, else a fairly complicated data quality checkpoint will need to be developed to capture and report on the anomaly.

A preliminary assessment of the Wheeler data is that referential integrity is not present and will need to be designed and built in the technical data quality data integration model.

It is also important to pass this information to the system owners in order to fix it in the source system.

5. **Perform cross-domain analysis**—A review of cross-domain analysis states that it is the process of comparing all columns in each selected table against all columns in the other selected tables. The goal is to detect columns that share a common data type.

Performing cross-domain analysis against the Wheeler data files, we find both customer and product numbers that are common data elements that will most likely need to be conformed into a common key, as shown in Figure 6.15.

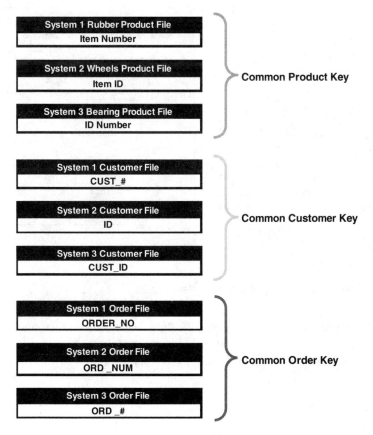

Figure 6.15 Rationalizing common keys

Data modelers will often use source system profile data analysis to design or confirm their data model key structure designs.

Once the source system profiling is complete (usually one to three iterations), the Core Data Element List is evaluated for data quality anomalies.

Step 3: Review/Assess Source Data Quality

This step further refines the Wheeler Core Data Element List for data quality issues and develops the first-cut set of data quality checkpoints.

Although it appears that there are redundancies in the source system profiling and data quality assessment tasks, profiling gathers the information and provides a first set of data quality issues. The review\assess source data quality task confirms those findings, performs further root cause analysis, and, finally, develops the first-cut technical and business data quality checkpoints for the data quality process layer in the data integration environment, as shown in Figure 6.16.

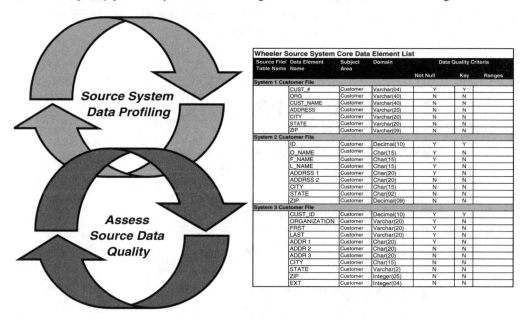

Figure 6.16   The iterative nature of source system analysis

1. **Perform validation checks to assess the data**—Using the Wheeler source system Core Data Element List, review and determine the types of checks that would be needed in the data quality layer of the proposed data integration process:

- **Data format checks**—A secondary review of the data elements does not reveal any errors in terms of format, for example VarChar in Integer.

- **Date format checks**—Not only does it appear that there are no inconsistencies in the date formats of each of the order systems, they are also in the same format of two-digit month, two-digit day, four-digit year (e.g., 03122010.) It would be wise to work with the data modeler, ensure that the target Wheeler data warehouse data model has the same format, and reduce an unnecessary data format transformation unless there is a desire to standardize to the relational DATE format.

- **Numeric value range check**—Review the source data for numeric upper and lower limits in the numeric fields in the Wheeler order system source data. For example, a rule could be placed on the order numeric fields, such as cost and price that prevents them from being negative, thereby preventing downstream incorrect calculations.

> **NOTE**
>
> Before such a business data quality rule is created, it is important to verify with an appropriate business user that this is an appropriate rule and there are not legitimate reasons for negatives in such columns.

- **Null checks**—When performing a secondary check for null values in mandatory columns/fields, the null key field in System 3 was captured in the prior analysis. It is good to double-check that a rule had been put in place in ensuring key rules are enforced.

- **Duplicate key/field checks**—When reviewing the Wheeler data for the prevention of the accidental loading of duplicate records, business-defined critical data elements, and key columns (primary, foreign, unique), we should review and ensure that the duplication error found between the Wheeler System 2 Product File and System 3 Product File has been communicated to prevent any future issues in the online systems.

2. **Review any other observed anomalies**—In this secondary review, we find that order file 3 does not contain a Terms field, as illustrated in Figure 6.17. This can cause significant data governance issues and merits further research with both the source system IT and business users.

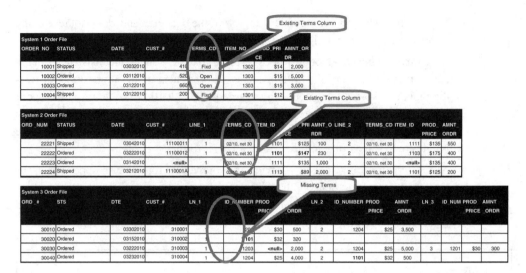

Figure 6.17 Missing columns

Often in the first review of the data, the focus is so intense on the anomalies within a column, broader data anomalies or missing critical data is overlooked. Only after the "picture" data and its structure becomes clearer will less obvious issues be observed, which is another reason for a secondary review task.

We have now reviewed and documented the actual structure of the source data, the data itself, and the anomalies within the data.

The source system discovery tasks have provided a good understanding of the source system data in terms of its structure, its data, and its anomalies. With this body of knowledge, we can move on to the next task of data mapping.

Figure 6.18 provides the completed version of the Wheeler Core Data Element List that will be used for the complex task of data mapping.

Wheeler Source System Core Data Element List

Source File/ Table	Data Element Name	Subject Area	Domain	Not Null	Key	Ranges/Rules
						Data Quality Criteria
System 1 Customer File						
	CUST_#	Customer	Varchar(04)	Y	Y	Should be Primary Key
	ORG	Customer	Varchar(40)	N	N	
	CUST_NAME	Customer	Varchar(40)	N	N	
	ADDRESS	Customer	Varchar(20)	N	N	
	CITY	Customer	Varchar(20)	N	N	
	STATE	Customer	Varchar(20)	N	N	
	ZIP	Customer	Varchar(09)	N	N	
System 2 Customer File						
	ID	Customer	Decimal(10)	Y	Y	Should be Primary Key
	O_NAME	Customer	Char(15)	Y	N	
	F_NAME	Customer	Char(15)	Y	N	
	L_NAME	Customer	Char(15)	Y	N	
	ADDRSS 1	Customer	Char(20)	Y	N	
	ADDRSS 2	Customer	Char(20)	N	N	
	CITY	Customer	Char(15)	N	N	
	STATE	Customer	Char(02)	N	N	
	ZIP	Customer	Decimal(09)	N	N	
System 3 Customer File						
	CUST_ID	Customer	Decimal(10)	Y	Y	Should be Primary Key
	ORGANIZATION	Customer	Varchar(20)	Y	N	
	FRST	Customer	Varchar(20)	Y	N	
	LAST	Customer	Varchar(20)	Y	N	
	ADDR 1	Customer	Char(20)	Y	N	
	ADDR 2	Customer	Char(20)	N	N	
	ADDR 3	Customer	Char(20)	N	N	
	CITY	Customer	Char(15)	N	N	
	STATE	Customer	Varchar(2)	N	N	
	ZIP	Customer	Integer(05)	N	N	
	EXT	Customer	Integer(04)	N	N	

Source File/ Table	Data Element Name	Subject Area	Domain	Not Null	Key	Ranges/Rules
						Data Quality Criteria
System 1 Rubber Product File						
	Item Number	Product	Varchar(04)	Y	Y	Should be Primary Key
	Description	Product	Char(30)	Y	N	Non Repeating
	Cost	Product	Decimal(12,2)	N	N	**Cannot be negative**
	Price	Product	Decimal(12,2)	N	N	**Cannot be negative**
	Inventory	Product	Decimal(12,2)	N	N	
System 2 Wheels Product File						
	Item ID	Product	Integer(06)	N	N	Should be Primary Key
	Inventory Name	Product	Char(30)	N	N	
	Cost	Product	Decimal(12,2)	N	N	**Cannot be negative**
	Price	Product	Decimal(12,2)	N	N	**Cannot be negative**
	Inventory	Product	Decimal(12,2)	N	N	
System 3 Bearing Product File						
	ID Number	Product	Integer(06)	N	N	Should be Primary Key
	Name	Product	Char(30)	Y	N	
	Cost	Product	Decimal(12,2)	N	N	**Cannot be negative**
	Price	Product	Decimal(12,2)	N	N	**Cannot be negative**
	Inventory	Product	Decimal(12,2)	N	N	

Additional fields from the data quality exercise task. Need to be verified with the business.

Figure 6.18 The completed Wheeler source system Core Data Element List

Wheeler Source System Core Data Element List

Source File/ Table Name	Data Element Name	Subject Area	Domain	Not Null	Key	Ranges/Rules
						Data Quality Criteria
System 1 Order File						
	ORDER_NO	Order	Decimal(05,2)	Y	Y	Should be Primary Key
	STATUS	Order	Char(11)	N	N	
	DATE	Order	Integer(08)	N	N	
	CUST_#	Order	Varchar(04)	Y	N	Should be Foreign Key
	TERMS_CD	Order	Char(05)	Y	N	
	ITEM_NO	Order	Varchar(04)	Y	Y	Should be Foreign Key
	PROD_PRICE	Order	Decimal(05,2)	Y	N	
	AMNT_ORDR	Order	Decimal(08,2)	Y	N	
System 2 Order File						
	ORD _NUM	Order	Decimal(05,2)	Y	Y	Should be Primary Key
	STATUS	Order	Char(08)	N	N	
	DATE	Order	Integer(08)	N	N	
	CUST_#	Order	Varchar(04)	Y	N	Should be Foreign Key
	LINE_1	Order	Decimal(2,2)	Y	N	
	TERMS_CD	Order	Char(05)	Y	Y	
	ITEM_ID	Order	Integer(06)	Y	N	Should be Foreign Key
	PROD_PRICE	Order	Decimal(05,2)	Y	N	
	AMNT_ORDR	Order	Decimal(08,2)	N	N	
	LINE_2	Order	Decimal(2,2)	N	N	
	TERMS_CD	Order	Char(05)	N	N	
	ITEM_ID	Order	Integer(06)	Y	N	Should be Foreign Key
	PROD_PRICE	Order	Decimal(05,2)	N	N	
	AMNT_ORDR	Order	Decimal(08,2)	N	N	
System 3 Order File						
	ORD _#	Order	Decimal(05,2)	Y	Y	Should be Primary Key
	STS	Order	Char(07)	N	N	
	DTE	Order	Integer(08)	N	N	
	CUST_#	Order	Varchar(04)	Y	Y	Should be Foreign Key
	LN_1	Order	Decimal(2,2)	Y	N	
	ID_NUMBER	Order	Integer(06)	N	N	Should be Foreign Key
	PROD_PRICE	Order	Decimal(05,2)	Y	N	
	AMNT_ORDR	Order	Decimal(08,2)	Y	N	
	LN_2	Order	Decimal(2,2)	Y	N	
	ID_NUMBER	Order	Integer(06)	N	N	Should be Foreign Key
	PROD_PRICE	Order	Decimal(05,2)	Y	N	
	AMNT_ORDR	Order	Decimal(08,2)	Y	N	
	LN_3	Order	Decimal(2,2)	Y	N	
	ID_NUMBER	Order	Integer(06)	N	N	Should be Foreign Key
	PROD_PRICE	Order	Decimal(05,2)	Y	N	
	AMNT_ORDR	Order	Decimal(08,2)	Y	N	

Figure 6.18   The completed Wheeler source system Core Data Element List

Step 4: Perform Source\Target Data Mappings

Data mapping is the final task in analyzing the requirements for the intended data integration environment. Both the conceptual data integration model and the Core Data Element List are used to map the data elements from the source systems to the intended Wheeler enterprise data warehouse and product line profitability dimensional model.

Referring to the Wheeler conceptual data integration model, the first step is to determine the mapping task plan, as shown in Figure 6.19.

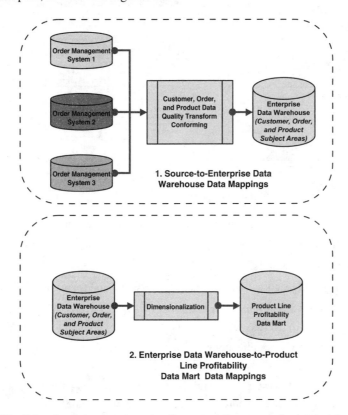

Figure 6.19   The Wheeler data mapping plan (based on the conceptual data integration model)

There are two target databases in this plan, the enterprise data warehouse and the product line dimensional model, so there should be two sets of data mappings:

- Source-to-enterprise data warehouse data mappings
- Enterprise data warehouse-to-product line profitability dimensional model data mappings

The activities needed to perform these source-to-target data mappings include the following:

1. **Determine the target subject areas**—If applicable, review the target data model to group the target tables into logical subject areas. The enterprise data warehouse model provides the logical subject areas (e.g., order, product, customer) so that we can focus our target mappings, which include the customer subject area, as shown in Figure 6.20.

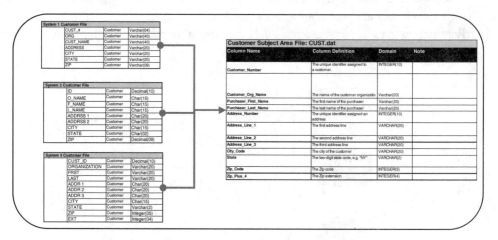

Figure 6.20   Customer data mapping subject area

For the Wheeler data integration project, the subject area files include the following:

- Product subject area file
- Order subject area file

These target subject area files help narrow the scope and focus of the data mapping task.

2. **Identify target data element or elements by subject area**—Confirm that the data elements from the Wheeler source systems are properly aligned to the target subject areas.

This is normally a simple double-check to ensure that elements are aligned to the intended target subject areas properly.

3. **Review all source systems for candidate data elements**—Based on a target data element, review the current source system, then review the other sources for potential one-to-many source data elements for the target data element. It is also appropriate to review the sources for source system candidate keys.

As shown in Figure 6.21, candidate source system keys have been collected from the Wheeler Core Data Element List and are organized by subject area.

Customer Subject Area Keys		
SYS 1 CUST FILE	CUST_#	Varchar(04)
SYS 2 CUST FILE	ID	Decimal(10)
SYS 3 CUST FILE	CUST_ID	Decimal(10)
Product Subject Area Keys		
SYS 1 PROD FILE	Item Number	Varchar(04)
SYS 2 PROD FILE	Item ID	Integer(06)
SYS 3 PROD FILE	ID Number	Integer(06)
Order Subject Area Keys		
SYS 1 ORDR FILE	ORDER_NO	Decimal(05,2)
SYS 2 ORDR FILE	ORD _NUM	Decimal(05,2)
SYS 3 ORDR FILE	ORD _#	Decimal(05,2)

Figure 6.21   Common keys organized by subject area

4. **Review each data element for one-to-many or many-to-one requirements**—This is the step that completes the definition of the candidate key structure. For the Wheeler enterprise data warehouse data model, the primary key will be a compound key that consists of the following attributes:

   <EDW Table Unique Identifier>.<Source Identifier>.<Original Key>

   An example of this compound key is the following compound customer key, which is also an example of a many-to-one data mapping:

   <Customer_Number> .<Source_System_Identifier>. <Source_System_Code>

5. **Map the data element or elements to the target data element**—First map the element or elements to the target element, then working with a data modeler, a data integration analyst would create mappings for the three core key structures that followed the customer key example shown in Figure 6.22.

1. Source-to-Enterprise Data Warehouse Data Mappings

Source File/ Table	Source Field	Source Domain	Mapping Rule	Subject Area File	Column Name	Column Definition	Target Domain	Mandatory	Key
Customer Subject Area									
			Create a system-generated ID	CUST.dat	Customer_Number	The unique identifier assigned to a customer.	INTEGER(10)	Yes	Primary
			Must be assigned "SYS1"	CUST.dat	Source_System_Identifier	The identifier of the source system that the data was sourced.	VARCHAR(4)	Yes	Primary
SYS 1 CUST FILE	CUST_#	Varchar(04)	Pad last 6 digits	CUST.dat	Source_System_Code	The unique identifier of the application or system from which the information last used to update the entity instance was populated.	VARCHAR(10)	Yes	Primary
			Create a system-generated ID	CUST.dat	Customer_Number	The unique identifier assigned to a customer.	INTEGER(10)	Yes	Primary
			Must be assigned "SYS2"	CUST.dat	Source_System_Identifier	The identifier of the source system that the data was sourced.	VARCHAR(4)	Yes	Primary
SYS 2 CUST FILE	ID	Decimal(10)	Translate decimal to Varchar	CUST.dat	Source_System_Code	The unique identifier of the application or system from which the information last used to update the entity instance was populated.	VARCHAR(10)	Yes	Primary
			Create a system-generated ID	CUST.dat	Customer_Number	The unique identifier assigned to a customer.	INTEGER(10)	Yes	Primary
			Must be assigned "SYS3"	CUST.dat	Source_System_Identifier	The identifier of the source system that the data was sourced.	VARCHAR(4)	Yes	Primary
SYS 3 CUST FILE	CUST_ID	Decimal(10)	Translate Decimal to Varchar	CUST.dat	Source_System_Code	The unique identifier of the application or system from which the information last used to update the entity instance was populated.	VARCHAR(10)	Yes	Primary

Figure 6.22   Common customer key

6. **Map technical mapping requirements to each target's subject area data element**—Build in any mapping business rules, which may be as simple as padding or trimming the field, to aggregating and/or calculating amounts.

This mapping from the Wheeler customer subject area provides a simple padding example, as shown in Figure 6.23.

1. Source-to-Enterprise Data Warehouse Data Mappings

Source File/ Table	Source Field	Source Domain	Mapping Rule	Subject Area File	Column Name	Column Definition	Target Domain	Mandatory	Key
Customer Subject Area									
SYS 2 CUST FILE	F_NAME	Char(15)	Pad last 5 digits	CUST.dat	Purchaser_First_Name	The first name of the purchaser	Varchar(20)	Yes	No
SYS 2 CUST FILE	L_NAME	Char(15)	Pad last 5 digits	CUST.dat	Purchaser_Last_Name	The last name of the purchaser	Varchar(20)	Yes	No

Figure 6.23   Applying technical requirement: padding data elements

7. **Reconcile definitional (data governance) issues between source systems**—Resolve any data element (attribute)–level definitional differences between the different sources and the target data element.

This task addresses the very first point in the book. Addressing the technical challenges of data integration are difficult enough; determining the correct interpretation of a data element, whether it is simply two fields being merged into one, or a calculation, requires attention from the data integration analyst performing the mapping, the data modeler that created the target element and target definition, and the business subject matter experts that understand *each* of the source data element definitions that are being mapped to the target.

The completed Wheeler data warehouse source-to-EDW mapping document is illustrated in Figure 6.24.

Source File/ Table	Source Field	Source Domain	Mapping Rule	Subject Area File	Column Name	Target Domain
Customer Subject Area						
			Create a system-generated ID	CUST.dat	Customer_Number	INTEGER(10)
			Must be Assigned "SYS1"	CUST.dat	Source_System_Identifier	VARCHAR(4)
SYS 1 CUST FILE	CUST_#	Varchar(04)	Pad last 6 digits	CUST.dat	Source_System_Code	VARCHAR(10)
SYS 1 CUST FILE	ORG	Varchar(40)	Populate the first 20 digits only	CUST.dat	Customer_Org_Name	Varchar(20)
SYS 1 CUST FILE	CUST_NAME	Varchar(40)	Populate the first 20 digits only	CUST.dat	Purchaser_First_Name	Varchar(20)
SYS 1 CUST FILE	CUST_NAME	Varchar(40)	Populate the last 20 digits only	CUST.dat	Purchaser_Last_Name	Varchar(20)
			Increment by 1	CUST.dat	Address_Number	INTEGER(10)
SYS 1 CUST FILE	ADDRESS	Varchar(20)	Straight move	CUST.dat	Address_Line_1	VARCHAR(20)
			Insert 20 blanks	CUST.dat	Address_Line_2	VARCHAR(20)
			Insert 20 blanks	CUST.dat	Address_Line_3	VARCHAR(20)
SYS 1 CUST FILE	CITY	Varchar(20)	Straight move	CUST.dat	City_Code	VARCHAR(20)
SYS 1 CUST FILE	STATE	Varchar(20)	Straight move	CUST.dat	State	VARCHAR(2)
SYS 1 CUST FILE	ZIP	Varchar(09)	1. Translate Varchar to Integer 2. Populate the first 5 into "Zip_Code,"the final 4 into "Zip_Ext."	CUST.dat	Zip_Code	INTEGER(5)
					Zip_Plus_4	INTEGER(4)
			Create a system-generated ID	CUST.dat	Customer_Number	INTEGER(10)
			Must be Assigned "SYS2"	CUST.dat	Source_System_Identifier	VARCHAR(4)
SYS 2 CUST FILE	ID	Decimal(10)	Translate Decimal to Varchar	CUST.dat	Source_System_Code	VARCHAR(10)
SYS 2 CUST FILE	O_NAME	Char(15)	1. Translate Char to Varchar. 2. Pad the last 5 digits	CUST.dat	Customer_Org_Name	Varchar(20)
SYS 2 CUST FILE	F_NAME	Char(15)	Pad last 5 digits	CUST.dat	Purchaser_First_Name	Varchar(20)
SYS 2 CUST FILE	L_NAME	Char(15)	Pad last 5 digits	CUST.dat	Purchaser_Last_Name	Varchar(20)
			Increment by 1	CUST.dat	Address_Number	INTEGER(10)
SYS 2 CUST FILE	ADDRSS 1	Char(20)	1. Translate Char to Varchar. 2. Pad the last 5 digits	CUST.dat	Address_Line_1	VARCHAR(20)
SYS 2 CUST FILE	ADDRSS 2	Char(20)	1. Translate Char to Varchar. 2. Pad the last 5 digits	CUST.dat	Address_Line_2	VARCHAR(20)
SYS 2 CUST FILE	CITY	Char(15)	1. Translate Char to Varchar. 2. Pad the last 5 digits	CUST.dat	City_Code	VARCHAR(20)
SYS 2 CUST FILE	STATE	Char(02)	Translate Char to Varchar.	CUST.dat	State	VARCHAR(2)
SYS 2 CUST FILE	ZIP	Decimal(09)	1. Translate Decimal to Integer 2. Populate the first 5 into "Zip_Code,"the final 4 into "Zip_Ext."	CUST.dat	Zip_Code	INTEGER(5)
					Zip_Plus_4	INTEGER(4)
			Create a system-generated ID	CUST.dat	Customer_Number	INTEGER(10)
			Must be assigned "SYS3"	CUST.dat	Source_System_Identifier	VARCHAR(4)
SYS 3 CUST FILE	CUST_ID	Decimal(10)	Translate decimal to Varchar	CUST.dat	Source_System_Code	VARCHAR(10)
SYS 3 CUST FILE	ORGANIZATION	Varchar(20)	Translate Char to Varchar.	CUST.dat	Customer_Org_Name	Varchar(20)
SYS 3 CUST FILE	FRST	Varchar(20)	Straight move	CUST.dat	Purchaser_First_Name	Varchar(20)
SYS 3 CUST FILE	LAST	Varchar(20)	Straight move	CUST.dat	Purchaser_Last_Name	Varchar(20)
			Increment by 1	CUST.dat	Address_Number	INTEGER(10)
SYS 3 CUST FILE	ADDR 1	Char(20)	Translate Char to Varchar.	CUST.dat	Address_Line_1	VARCHAR(20)
SYS 3 CUST FILE	ADDR 2	Char(20)	Translate Char to Varchar.	CUST.dat	Address_Line_2	VARCHAR(20)
SYS 3 CUST FILE	ADDR 3	Char(20)	Translate Char to Varchar.	CUST.dat	Address_Line_3	VARCHAR(20)
SYS 3 CUST FILE	CITY	Char(15)	1. Translate Char to Varchar. 2. Pad the last 5 digits	CUST.dat	City_Code	VARCHAR(20)
SYS 3 CUST FILE	STATE	Varchar(2)	Straight move	CUST.dat	State	VARCHAR(2)
SYS 3 CUST FILE	ZIP	Integer(05)	Straight move	CUST.dat	Zip_Code	INTEGER(5)
SYS 3 CUST FILE	EXT	Integer(04)	Straight move	CUST.dat	Zip_Plus_4	INTEGER(4)

Source File/ Table	Source Field	Source Domain	Mapping Rule	Subject Area File	Column Name	Target Domain
Product Subject Area						
			Create a system-generated ID	PROD.dat	**Product_Id**	INTEGER(10)
			Must be assigned "SYS1"	PROD.dat	**Source_System_Identifier**	VARCHAR(4)
SYS 1 PROD FILE	Item Number	Varchar(04)	1.Translate Varchar to integer. 2. Pad last 6 digits.	PROD.dat	**Source_System_Code**	INTEGER(10)
SYS 1 PROD FILE	Description	Char(30)	Pad last 10 digits.	PROD.dat	**Product_Name**	CHAR(40)
			Must be either "Rubber," "Wheels," or "Bearings."		**Product_Type**	CHAR(40)
			Insert "No Source System Value"		**Product_Code**	VARCHAR(20)
SYS 1 PROD FILE	Cost	Decimal(12,2)	Trim first 5 digits.	PROD.dat	**Product_Cost**	Decimal 7,2
SYS 1 PROD FILE	Price	Decimal(12,2)	Trim first 5 digits.	PROD.dat	**Product_Price**	Decimal 7,2
SYS 1 PROD FILE	Inventory	Decimal(12,2)	Trim first 5 digits.	PROD.dat	**Inventory**	Decimal 7,2
			Create a system-generated ID	PROD.dat	**Product_Id**	INTEGER(10)
			Must be assigned "SYS1"	PROD.dat	**Source_System_Identifier**	VARCHAR(4)
SYS 2 PROD FILE	Item ID	Integer(06)	1.Translate Integer to Varchar. 2. Pad last 4 digits.	PROD.dat	**Source_System_Code**	VARCHAR(10)
SYS 2 PROD FILE	Inventory Name	Char(30)	1. Pad last 10 digits.	PROD.dat	**Product_Name**	CHAR(40)
			Must be either "Rubber," "Wheels," or "Bearings."		**Product_Type**	CHAR(40)
			Insert "No Source System Value"		**Product_Code**	VARCHAR(20)
SYS 2 PROD FILE	Cost	Decimal(12,2)	Trim first 5 digits.	PROD.dat	**Product_Cost**	Decimal 7,2
SYS 2 PROD FILE	Price	Decimal(12,2)	Trim first 5 digits.	PROD.dat	**Product_Price**	Decimal 7,2
SYS 2 PROD FILE	Inventory	Decimal(12,2)	Trim first 5 digits.	PROD.dat	**Inventory**	Decimal 7,2
			Create a system-generated ID	PROD.dat	**Product_Id**	INTEGER(10)
			Must be assigned "SYS1"	PROD.dat	**Source_System_Identifier**	VARCHAR(4)
SYS 3 PROD FILE	ID Number	Integer(06)	1.Translate Integer to Varchar. 2. Pad last 4 digits.	PROD.dat	**Source_System_Code**	VARCHAR(10)
SYS 3 PROD FILE	Name	Char(30)	1. Pad last 10 digits.	PROD.dat	**Product_Name**	CHAR(40)
			Must be either "Rubber," "Wheels," or "Bearings."		**Product_Type**	CHAR(40)
			Insert "No Source System Value"		**Product_Code**	VARCHAR(20)
SYS 3 PROD FILE	Cost	Decimal(12,2)	Trim first 5 digits.	PROD.dat	**Product_Cost**	Decimal 7,2
SYS 3 PROD FILE	Price	Decimal(12,2)	Trim first 5 digits.	PROD.dat	**Product_Price**	Decimal 7,2
SYS 3 PROD FILE	Inventory	Decimal(12,2)	Trim first 5 digits.	PROD.dat	**Inventory**	Decimal 7,2

Figure 6.24   Wheeler source-to-data warehouse data mapping

Source File/ Table	Source Field	Source Domain	Mapping Rule	Subject Area File	Column Name	Target Domain
Order Subject Area						
			Create a system-generated ID	PROD.dat	Order_Number	INTEGER(07
			Must be assigned "SYS1"	PROD.dat	Source_System_Identifier	VARCHAR(4
SYS 1 ORDR FILE	ORDER_NO	Decimal(05,2)	Translate Decimal to Varchar	ORDR.dat	Source_System_Code	VARCHAR(1
SYS 1 ORDR FILE	STATUS	Char(11)	1. Translate Char to VarChar. 2. Trim the last digit	ORDR.dat	Status_Code	VARCHAR(1
SYS 1 ORDR FILE	DATE	Integer(08)	Translate Integer to Date	ORDR.dat	Order_Date	Date
			Insert "00/00/0000"	ORDR.dat	Effective_Date	Date
SYS 1 ORDR FILE	CUST_#	Varchar(04)	1. Translate Varchar to integer. 2. Perform a lookup and match the "Cust_#" with the customer table "Cust_ID," once matched insert the "Cust_ID" value from that row.	ORDR.dat	Cust_Id	INTEGER(10
SYS 1 ORDR FILE	TERMS_CD	Char(05)	1. Translate char to VarChar. 2. Pad the last 25 digits	ORDR.dat	Terms	VARCHAR(3
			use	PROD.dat	Order_Number	INTEGER(07
			Use the same system-generated ID		Order_Line_Number	INTEGER(04
SYS 1 ORDR FILE	ITEM_NO	Varchar(04)	1. Translate Varchar to Integer. 2. Perform a lookup and match the "Item_NO" with the product table "Source_System_Code" in the "Product_Id.Source_System_Identifier.Source_System_Code" primary key; once matched insert the "Product_ID" value from that row. 3. Pad the last 6 digits.	ORDR.dat	Product_Id	INTEGER(10
SYS 1 ORDR FILE	PROD_PRICE	Decimal(05,2)	Pad first 2 digits.	PROD.dat	Product_Price	Decimal 7,2
SYS 1 ORDR FILE	AMNT_ORDR	Decimal(08,2)	Translate Decimal to Integer	ORDR.dat	Quantity_Ordered	INTEGER(07
			Create a system-generated ID	PROD.dat	Order_Number	INTEGER(07
			Must be assigned "SYS1"	PROD.dat	Source_System_Identifier	VARCHAR(4
SYS 2 ORDR FILE	ORD _NUM	Decimal(05,2)	1.Translate Decimal to Varchar. 2. Trim the last 2 digits; pad the first 5.	ORDR.dat	Source_System_Code	VARCHAR(1
SYS 2 ORDR FILE	STATUS	Char(08)	1. Translate Char to VarChar. 2. Pad the first 2 digits.	ORDR.dat	Status_Code	VARCHAR(1
SYS 2 ORDR FILE	DATE	Integer(08)	Translate Integer to Date	ORDR.dat	Order_Date	Date
			Insert "00/00/0000"	ORDR.dat	Effective_Date	Date
SYS 2 ORDR FILE	CUST_#	Varchar(04)	1. Translate Varchar to Integer. 2. Perform a lookup and match the "Cust_#" with the customer Table "Cust_ID," once matched insert the "Cust_ID" value from that row.	ORDR.dat	Cust_Id	INTEGER(10
SYS 2 ORDR FILE	TERMS_CD	Char(05)	1. Translate Char to VarChar. 2. Pad the last 25 digits	ORDR.dat	Terms	VARCHAR(3

1. Source-to-Enterprise Data Warehouse Data Mappings

Source File/ Table	Source Field	Source Domain	Mapping Rule	Subject Area File	Column Name	Column Definition	Target Domain	Mandatory	Key	Note
Order Subject Area										
SYS 2 ORDR FILE	PROD_PRICE	Decimal(05,2)	1.Translate Decimal to Integer. 2. Trim the first digit.	PROD.dat	Product_Price	The per unit price that Wheeler charges their customers.	Decimal 7,2	Yes	No	
SYS 2 ORDR FILE	AMNT_ORDR	Decimal(08,2)	Translate Decimal to Integer	ORDR.dat	Quantity_Ordered	The per unit quantity of the product ordered	INTEGER(07)			
			Use the same system-generated ID	PROD.dat	Order_Number	This number represents a single occurrence of an order.	INTEGER(07)	Yes	Primary	
SYS 2 ORDR FILE	LINE_2	Decimal(2,2)	Insert "2" into the field.		Order_Line_Number	The unique identifier for one occurrence of a status code on a order.	INTEGER(04)	Yes	Primary	
SYS 2 ORDR FILE	ITEM_ID	Integer(06)	1. Pad the first 4 digits. 2. Perform a lookup and match the "Item_ID" with the product table "Source_System_Co de" in the "Product_Id.Source _System_Identifier.S ource_System_Cod e" primary key, once matched insert the "Product_ID" value from that row.	ORDR.dat	Product_Id	The unique identifier of a Wheeler product.	INTEGER(10)	Yes	Foreign	
SYS 2 ORDR FILE	PROD_PRICE	Decimal(05,2)	1.Translate Decimal to Integer. 2. Trim the first digit.	PROD.dat	Product_Price	The per unit price that Wheeler charges their customers.	Decimal 7,2	Yes	No	
SYS 2 ORDR FILE	AMNT_ORDR	Decimal(08,2)	Translate Decimal to Integer	ORDR.dat	Quantity_Ordered	The per unit quantity of the product ordered	INTEGER(07)			
			Create a system-generated ID	PROD.dat	Order_Number	This number represents a single occurrence of an order.	INTEGER(07)	Yes	Primary	
			Must be Assigned 'SYS1'	PROD.dat	Source_System_Identifier	The identifier of the source system that the data was sourced.	VARCHAR(4)	Yes	Primary	
SYS 3 ORDR FILE	ORD_#	Decimal(05,2)	1.Translate Decimal to Varchar. 2. Trim the last 2 digits, pad the first 5.	ORDR.dat	Source_System_Code	The unique identifier of the application or system from which the information last used to update the entity instance was populated.	VARCHAR(10)	Yes	Primary	
SYS 3 ORDR FILE	STS	Char(07)	1. Translate Char to VarChar. 2. Pad the last 25 digits	ORDR.dat	Terms	The terms of payment for the order.	VARCHAR(30)	Yes	No	
SYS 3 ORDR FILE	DTE	Integer(08)	Translate Integer to Date	ORDR.dat	Order_Date	The date that the order was placed.	Date	Yes	No	
			Insert "00/00/0000"	ORDR.dat	Effective_Date	The date that the order will take effect.	Date	No	No	
SYS 3 ORDR FILE	CUST_#	Varchar(04)	1. Translate Varchar to Integer. 2. Pad the first 6 digits. 3. Perform a lookup and match the "Cust_#" with the customer table " Cust_ID", once matched insert the "Cust_ID" value from that row	ORDR.dat	Cust_Id	The unique identifier assigned to a customer.	INTEGER(10)	Yes	Foreign	
			Use the same system-generated ID	PROD.dat	Order_Number	This number represents a single occurrence of a order.	INTEGER(07)	Yes	Primary	
SYS 3 ORDR FILE	LN_1	Decimal(2,2)	Insert "1" into the field.		Order_Line_Number	The unique identifier for one occurrence of a status code on a order.	INTEGER(04)	Yes	Primary	
SYS 3 ORDR FILE	ID_NUMBER	Integer(06)	1. Pad the first 4 digits. 2. Perform a lookup and match the "Item_ID" with the product table "Source_System_Co de" in the "Product_Id.Source _System_Identifier.S ource_System_Cod e" primary key, once matched insert the "Product_ID" value from that row.	ORDR.dat	Product_Id	The unique identifier of a Wheeler product.	INTEGER(10)	Yes	Foreign	
SYS 3 ORDR FILE	PROD_PRICE	Decimal(05,2)	1. Pad the first digit.	PROD.dat	Product_Price	The per unit price that Wheeler charges their customers.	Decimal 7,2	Yes	No	
SYS 3 ORDR FILE	AMNT_ORDR	Decimal(08,2)	1.Translate Decimal to Integer. 2. Trim the first digit, and the last 2 digits.	ORDR.dat	Quantity_Ordered	The per unit quantity of the product ordered	INTEGER(07)			
			Use the same system-generated ID	PROD.dat	Order_Number	This number represents a single occurrence of a order.	INTEGER(07)	Yes	Primary	
SYS 3 ORDR FILE	LN_2	Decimal(2,2)	Insert "2" into the field.		Order_Line_Number	The unique identifier for one occurrence of a status code on an order.	INTEGER(04)	Yes	Primary	
SYS 3 ORDR FILE	ID_NUMBER	Integer(06)	1. Pad the first 4 digits. 2. Perform a lookup and match the "Item_ID" with the product table "Source_System_Co de" in the "Product_Id.Source _System_Identifier.S ource_System_Cod e" primary key, once matched insert the "Product_ID" value from that row.	ORDR.dat	Product_Id	The unique identifier of a Wheeler product.	INTEGER(10)	Yes	Foreign	
SYS 3 ORDR FILE	PROD_PRICE	Decimal(05,2)	1. Pad the first digit.	PROD.dat	Product_Price	The per unit price that Wheeler charges their customers.	Decimal 7,2	Yes	No	
SYS 3 ORDR FILE	AMNT_ORDR	Decimal(08,2)	1.Translate Decimal to Integer. 2. Trim the first digit, and the last 2 digits.	ORDR.dat	Quantity_Ordered	The per unit quantity of the product ordered	INTEGER(07)			
			Use the same system-generated ID	PROD.dat	Order_Number	This number represents a single occurrence of a order.	INTEGER(07)	Yes	Primary	
SYS 3 ORDR FILE	LN_3	Decimal(2,2)	Insert "3" into the field.		Order_Line_Number	The unique identifier for one occurrence of a status code on a order.	INTEGER(04)	Yes	Primary	
SYS 3 ORDR FILE	ID_NUMBER	Integer(06)	1. Pad the first 4 digits. 2. Perform a lookup and match the "Item_ID" with the product table "Source_System_Co de" in the "Product_Id.Source _System_Identifier.S ource_System_Cod e" primary key, once matched insert the "Product_ID" value from that row.	ORDR.dat	Product_Id	The unique identifier of a Wheeler Product.	INTEGER(10)	Yes	Foreign	
SYS 3 ORDR FILE	PROD_PRICE	Decimal(05,2)	1. Pad the first digit.	PROD.dat	Product_Price	The per unit price that Wheeler charges their customers.	Decimal 7,2	Yes	No	
SYS 3 ORDR FILE	AMNT_ORDR	Decimal(08,2)	1.Translate Decimal to Integer. 2. Trim the first digit, and the last 2 digits.	ORDR.dat	Quantity_Ordered	The per unit quantity of the product ordered	INTEGER(07)			

Figure 6.24 Wheeler source-to-data warehouse data mapping

Once all the source fields have been mapped to the target data model, plan for two to three review (and renovation) sessions with the business stakeholders on confirming the completeness and accuracy of the data mappings.

Pay careful attention on calculations and key mapping confirmations.

Finally, it is a very good best practice to have an internal review session with formal checkpoints by peers or peer groups prior to a final sign-off on the data mappings with the end user.

Figure 6.25 provides an example of a formal sign-off sheet for data mapping.

Data Mapping Checkpoint

Version: 1.0 Released:	Content Owner: Dept Name:

Quality Control Process/Procedure/Task Review	Yes	No	N/A	Comments
Perform Data Mapping to Source Systems				
1. Were critical transaction-level data elements confirmed?				
2. Were key data aggregations and calculations confirmed?				
3. Were technical requirements mapped to each source system?				
1. Were definitional (data governance) issues between source systems reconciled?				

Roles and Responsibilities						
Key: R-Responsible, A-Approves, S-Supports, I-Informs, C-Consults	Project Manager	Data Steward	Business Analyst	Data Integration Architect	Data Integration Architect	Metadata Specialist
	A	A	A	B	S	A

The deliverables review on this checklist conforms to standards:

_____ Completely

_____ Partially

_____ Not at all

Comments

_____

_____

_____

_____

Figure 6.25   Data mapping sign-off form

Summary

In this chapter, we began our second case study with the emphasis on working through the entire data integration life cycle tasks and deliverables. In subsequent chapters, we cover phases of the data integration life cycle, and provide case studies for each phase. This case study was based on integrating three order management systems for the Wheeler Company into an enterprise data warehouse and product line profitability data mart.

Before starting the case study, the chapter first reviewed the important concept of where calculations and aggregations could go in the different layers of a data warehouse and the advantages and disadvantages of each approach.

The first task that the case study covered was how to graphically scope out the data integration project by building a "picture" of the intended Wheeler data integration processes in a conceptual data integration diagram. Once documented and the scope is identified and confirmed, attention is moved to the source systems.

Next, we performed source systems profiling and analysis to have a good understanding of the underlying Wheeler source system data.

Finally, we mapped the source data to the target database; in the Wheeler case study, it was the data warehouse data model. We reviewed the fact that data mapping is *not* a one-to-one exercise, but requires both a horizontal and vertical view of the sources to target.

Chapter 7, "Data Integration Logical Design," focuses on using the analysis phase deliverables such as the source-to-target mapping document and the Data Quality Criteria Work Book as sources for building out the logical design deliverables such as the logical data integration architecture and logical data integration models.

CHAPTER **7**

Data Integration Logical Design

In a data integration project, the logical design phase transforms the data integration requirements (e.g., the data mappings) into logical business designs. It segments those mappings into logical units of work, using the data integration modeling technique and reference architecture.

The logical design phase also completes the analysis on data quality by focusing on the target's data quality criteria, both technical and business.

It is also important to begin to determine the physical volume sizing of the proposed data integration application on the data integration environment.

The tasks for the data integration logical design phase include the following:

1. Determine high-level data volumetrics.
2. Establish the data integration architecture.
3. Identify data quality criteria.
4. Create logical data integration models.
5. Define one-time data conversion load logical design.

Determining High-Level Data Volumetrics

The first data integration logical design task determines the sizing of the expected production input files using a database sizing technique. Source systems volumetrics is the analysis of the potential size of the extract files coming from the source systems in terms of volume and frequency.

This is a critical task in determining the data integration production environment sizing and performance requirements.

Although there is much discussion on the integration of real-time data feeds that send either small batches or transactions, there will always be some level of large file processing based on the fact that there will always be systems that only run in batch (e.g., payroll processing). For batch systems, it is important that the files sizes are determined as soon as possible for the reasons discussed in the following sections.

Extract Sizing

How big are the extracts going to be in the context of potential network constraints? For example, if there are twenty 500GB files to move across a 30GB-per-second network channel and there is only a two-hour download window, then either the channel or the batch window will need to be expanded. Ordering and configuring network equipment requires extensive lead time, which must be taken into account as soon as possible. Communicating the requirements while still in the logical design phase may provide sufficient time for the project team to determine a solution.

Disk Space Sizing

How much space is needed for temp files during processing? Because each source system will have one-to-many files that may be perpetuated in several directories (see Figures 7.1 and 7.2), it is important to determine early in the development process how much disk space will be needed.

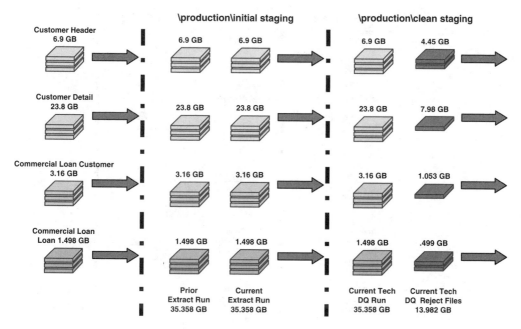

Figure 7.1   Sizing the initial and clean staging layers

As discussed in Chapter 2, "An Architecture for Data Integration," disk space sizing should also consider how many generations of these files should be kept based on rerun and disaster recovery requirements. For example, based on the organization's disaster recovery strategy, how many days back should the environment have data for potentially having to rerun production? If it is three days, then three days worth of files should be retained.

The second sizing task is dependent on the size of the intended target. Although this is a traditional database sizing task, it is also important in determining the sizing requirements for the subject area loads prior to the actual loads. Again, this staging area will be used to maintain generations of files for reruns and disaster recovery.

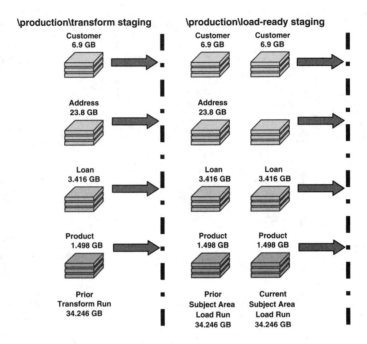

Figure 7.2   Sizing the transform and load-ready staging layers

File Size Impacts Component Design

Another reason to understand the size of the expected data files flowing through the environment is because it directly impacts how to optimally design the source system extracts and data movement using parallel processing techniques. The size of the files also has a direct relationship on how to partition the file within the data integration processes.

There will be a significant amount of time spent on outlining and defining the partitioning processes for data integration in Chapter 8, "Data Integration Logical Design Case Study."

Key Data Integration Volumetrics Task Steps

The two steps to determine source and target volumetrics are as follows:

1. **Determine source system extract data volumetrics**—The purpose of this step is to size the source system extract files into the Source System Extract Volumetrics Report format illustrated in Figure 7.3. Steps in this activity include the following:

    • Identify the system and number of files.

    • Determine the number of bytes per file.

    • Determine the number of records per file (average on a per-run basis).

- Multiply the number of bytes by the number of records to determine the size of each file.

- Determine the frequency and number of generations planned to be kept (e.g., reruns and disaster recovery).

Source System Extract Volumetrics Report								
System	Platform	Logical Name	Files	Number of Bytes	Number of Records	Extract File Size	Frequency	CDC Y/N
CUST_001	UNIX	Customer	Header	230	30,000,000	6,900,000,000	Daily	Y
			Detail	170	140,000,000	23,800,000,000	Daily	Y
COMM000	MVS	Commercial Loans	Customer File	244	14,000,000	3,416,000,000	Weekly	Y
			Loan File	107	14,000,000	1,498,000,000	Weekly	Y

Figure 7.3   Sample Source System Extract Volumetrics Report

2. **Determine subject area load data volumetrics**—The purpose of this step is to size the subject area load files into the Subject Area Load Volumetrics Report format illustrated in Figure 7.4. Steps in this activity include the following:

- Identify the target tables (files).

- Determine the number of bytes per file.

- Determine the number of records per file (average on a per-run basis).

- Multiply the number of bytes by the number of records to determine the size of each file.

- Determine the frequency and number of generations planned to be kept (e.g., reruns and disaster recovery).

Subject Area Load Volumetrics Report							
Subject Area	Table Name	Logical Name	Number of Bytes	Number of Records	Subject Area Load File Size	Frequency	CDC Y/N
Customer	cust	Customer	230	30,000,000	6,900,000,000	Daily	Y
	c_addrs	Address	170	140,000,000	23,800,000,000	Daily	Y
Loans	Loan	Loan	244	14,000,000	3,416,000,000	Weekly	Y
	Prod	Product	107	1,400	149,800	Weekly	Y

Figure 7.4   Subject Area Load Volumetrics Report

Establishing a Data Integration Architecture

The following data integration layers can be instantiated in the selected hardware environments once the baseline information on file sizing has been determined:

- Extract processing area
- Initial staging directory
- Data quality processing area

- Clean staging directory
- Transform processing area
- Load-ready staging directory
- Loading processing area

These directories and process areas should be designed and built out into the development, test, and production data integration environments.

It is important to have a functional data integration environment that will host the intended data integration application as early as possible in the Systems Development Life Cycle to allow for technical design tuning and prototyping.

A data integration architect must determine the potential frequency of the type and number of processes in each of the architectural layers in terms of infrastructure requirements (CPU/memory, storage, network bandwidth, etc.) to ensure that both the short- and long-term data integration requirements of the new data integration application are met.

Defining the logical data integration environment includes the following steps:

1. **Portray the logical data integration architectural framework**—The purpose of this step is to leverage an existing blueprint (e.g., the data integration reference architecture) or design one to provide the graphical diagram that will be used to build out or extend the intended data integration infrastructure (e.g., CPU, disk, network), as shown in Figure 7.5. Activities include the following:

   - Define the logical data integration architecture diagram.
   - Document the logical data integration architecture narrative.

2. **Define the logical data integration architecture**—Using the logical data integration architecture diagram, develop hardware, disk, and network specifications for each layer of the data integration environment. Activities include the following:

   - Determine the logical extract layer.
       - Determine probable source systems.
       - Determine potential real-time/EAI requirements.
       - Determine potential bulk extract requirements.
       - Determine frequency and volumes.
       - Establish retention requirements for landed files.
   - Determine the number of staging environments (e.g., initial, clean-staging, load-ready).
       - Determine the potential size and number of files in the staging environment.
   - Establish the data integration process (data quality and transform) architecture design.

- Estimate CPU and memory requirements based on expected processing types.
- Determine/develop the Reusable Components Library approach.

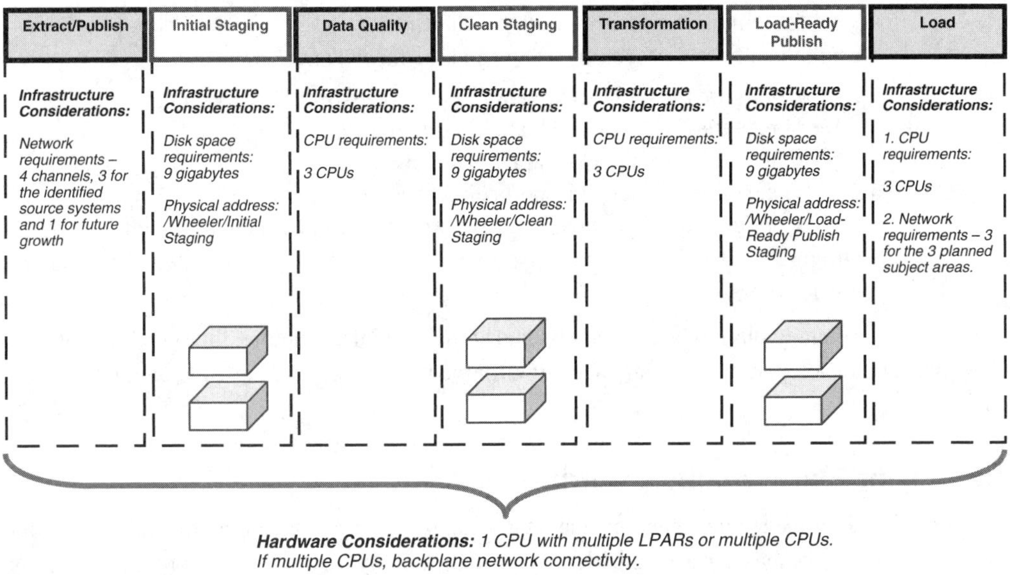

Extract/Publish	Initial Staging	Data Quality	Clean Staging	Transformation	Load-Ready Publish	Load
Infrastructure Considerations:	*Infrastructure Considerations:*	*Infrastructure Considerations:*	*Infrastructure Considerations:*	*Infrastructure Considerations:*	*Infrastructure Considerations:*	*Infrastructure Considerations:*
Network requirements – 4 channels, 3 for the identified source systems and 1 for future growth	*Disk space requirements: 9 gigabytes* *Physical address: /Wheeler/Initial Staging*	*CPU requirements: 3 CPUs*	*Disk space requirements: 9 gigabytes* *Physical address: /Wheeler/Clean Staging*	*CPU requirements: 3 CPUs*	*Disk space requirements: 9 gigabytes* *Physical address: /Wheeler/Load-Ready Publish Staging*	*1. CPU requirements: 3 CPUs* *2. Network requirements – 3 for the 3 planned subject areas.*

Hardware Considerations: 1 CPU with multiple LPARs or multiple CPUs. If multiple CPUs, backplane network connectivity.

Figure 7.5   Logical data integration architecture diagram example

3. **Configure the physical data integration environment**—Using the software, hardware, disk, and network specifications, configure the data integration environment for the organization's Information Technology platform. Steps include the following:

- Load and perform initial configuration of the data integration software.
- Design the overall physical data integration environment.
  - Determine the overall physical architecture (e.g., number of CPUs, multiple logical partitions [LPARs]).
  - Design the network backplane for throughput.
- Design the physical extract environment.
  - Determine the network connectivity to each of the target environments.
  - Determine the number and configuration of the CPU/processors.
  - Determine the amount of disk space based on storage requirements for landed files.
  - Configure the data integration software to the extract environment.

- Design the physical staging area environment.
  - Create the staging directories (e.g., initial, clean-staging, load-ready).
  - Instantiate and test the file retention roll-off process.
  - Instantiate the archiving approach/utility.
- Design the physical processing (DQ and transforms) environment.
  - Configure the CPU and memory based on expected processing types.
  - Create the DQ Cleansed Data Files directory.
  - Create the DQ Reject Data Files directory.
  - Create the DQ Reject Reports directory.
  - Configure the data integration software to the extract environment.
- Configure the data integration software metadata capability for the Reusable Components Library.

It is important to plan for time to assess and "tune" the infrastructure, thus ensuring that the designers and developers have an adequate environment to develop and test the data integration processes.

Identifying Data Quality Criteria

This task identifies the technical and business data quality criteria in the target logical data model for the intended database. Although identifying data quality issues in the source systems is important, the levels of data quality required should be defined in the target data warehouse data model. Unlike the source systems that will have varying levels of data quality, the data warehouse must have both consistent levels of data quality from all source systems for accurate reporting detail and reporting rollups.

The scope of the task is to identify the critical data elements, the domain values, and business rule ranges that will be used to extend the data quality checkpoints, as illustrated in Figure 7.6.

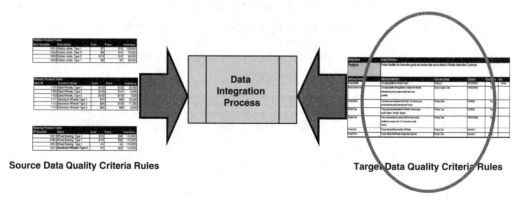

Source Data Quality Criteria Rules   **Target Data Quality Criteria Rules**

Figure 7.6   Target data quality focus

Examples of a target data quality checkpoint are primary key data quality checkpoints where primary key rules are enforced for query integrity in a data warehouse. Because most data warehouses do not enforce referential integrity at the constraint or database level, integrity would need to be enforced at the data integration layer. Therefore, a data quality checkpoint will need to be developed that will enforce that primary key rule.

Examples of Data Quality Criteria from a Target

The following two examples of developing technical and business data quality checkpoints from a data model are taken from Case Study 1:

- **Technical data quality criteria**—In Case Study 1, the Customer table's primary key attribute Cust_Id defined its primary key rules in the data quality checkpoint as a "not null" and must be a unique rule, as displayed in Figure 7.7.

Data Quality Criteria Workbook

Customer						
					Technical	Business
Column Name	Attribute Definition	Domain	Manditory	Key	Data Quality Check	Data Quality Check
Cust_Id	The unique identifier assigned to a customer.	INTEGER(10)	Yes	Primary	Must be unique and not null	

Figure 7.7   Technical data quality checkpoint

- **Business data quality criteria**—In the same table, there is a business data quality checkpoint needed that will ensure that the values in the Gender column are either "Male," "Female," or "Unknown," as shown in Figure 7.8.

Data Quality Criteria Workbook

Customer						
					Technical	Business
Column Name	Attribute Definition	Domain	Manditory	Key	Data Quality Check	Data Quality Check
Gender	Gender of the customer. Data Quality Criteria: Male, Female, Unknown	VARCHAR(10)	Yes			It must be "Male," "Female," or "Unknown"

Figure 7.8   Business data quality checkpoint

This task is usually performed by a data integration analyst in cooperation with the data modeler and a business domain subject matter expert.

Key Data Quality Criteria Identification Task Steps

Steps to identifying key data quality criteria for data quality checkpoints include the following:

1. **Identify critical entities and attributes for data quality requirements**—Using the target data model, identify the key entities and attributes for which it will be important to maintain a certain level of technical or business data quality.
   - Identify critical data entities in the logical data model.
   - Identify critical data attributes (e.g., mandatory attributes).

2. **Identify data quality criteria (domains, ranges, other DQ criteria)**—For the critical data attributes, identify the technical and business data quality "rules" that will require checkpoints.

    *   Identify data quality criteria for each critical data entity.
    *   Identify data quality criteria for each critical data attribute.

3. **Define data quality metrics and tolerances**—Many of the data quality checkpoints deal with ranges of acceptable values such as *"no numeric value less than zero or greater than 100"* or only *"Open," "Pending,"* or *"Closed."*

    *   Identify data quality metrics and tolerances for each critical data entity.
    *   Identify data quality metrics and tolerances for each critical data attribute.
    *   Capture any data quality criteria that are associated with the relationships in the data model.

Creating Logical Data Integration Models

The purpose of the logical data integration modeling task is to produce a detailed representation of the data integration requirements at the data set (table/file)-level. It leverages the source-to-target data mappings (source data format, data quality and transform business rules, and target data formats) and creates a graphical representation of the design components needed to meet the data integration requirements, as portrayed in Figure 7.9.

These logical data integration models are still considered to be technology independent.

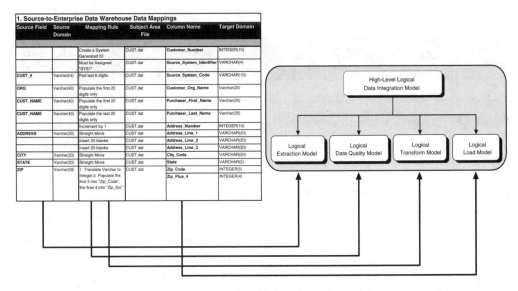

Figure 7.9   Mapping source-to-target functionality to a logical data integration model

Key Logical Data Integration Model Task Steps

Logical data integration modeling tasks design "logical units of data integration design" along the data integration reference architecture. By following this modeling approach, the overall model can be broken up into different work assignments, as portrayed in Figure 7.10.

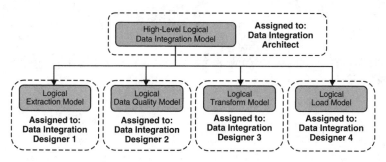

Figure 7.10   Assigning logical data integration model work

NOTE

For the following logical data integration modeling tasks, the banking logical data models from Case Study 1 will be used as examples of the task deliverables.

Logical data integration modeling requires very different approaches for each of the model types as well as different inputs. The following sections provide the detailed steps for logical data integration modeling.

Define the High-Level Logical Data Integration Component Model

The high-level logical data integration model task provides the structure for what will be needed for the data integration system, as well as providing the outline for the logical models, such as extract, data quality, transform, and load components, as portrayed from the banking customer loan high-level data integration model in [[AR x07fig11 I=D T=E]]Figure 7.11. Defining a high-level logical data integration model requires the following components:

1. Define logical extraction components.
2. Define logical data quality components.
3. Define logical transform components.
4. Define logical load components.

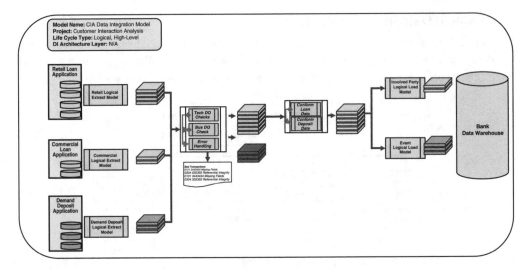

Figure 7.11   Logical high-level data integration model example

Define the Logical Extraction Data Integration Model

The logical extraction data integration model task determines what subject area data will need to be extracted from the scoped source systems. Extract data from such sources as applications, databases, flat files, and unstructured sources. The following steps are used to define a logical extract data integration model:

1. Confirm the subject area focus from the data mapping document.
2. Review whether the existing data integration environment can fulfill the requirements.
3. Determine/review existing applications/databases.
4. Determine/review existing data models and metadata repositories.
5. Determine the business extraction rules.
6. Estimate the data volumes for the production environment.
7. Map source file formats to the attribute level.

Figure 7.12 illustrates segmenting the customer subject area from the customer hub source-to-target data mapping document for the banking commercial loan logical extraction model.

Customer Hub to Subject Area File Mapping

Source File/ Table	Source Field	Source Domain	Mapping Rule	Subject Area File	Column Name	Column Definition	Target Domain	Mandatory	Key	Note
HEADER	Cust_Id	INTEGER(10)	Translate Integer to Varchar	CUST.dat	Source_Sys_Unique_Key_Text	The unique identifier of the customer in the source system.	VARCHAR(32)	Yes		
HEADER	Gender	VARCHAR(10)	Straight move	CUST.dat	Gender	Gender of the customer. Data Quality Criteria: Male, Female, Unknown	VARCHAR(10)	Yes		
HEADER	Name	VARCHAR(10)	Pad to 64	CUST.dat	Cust_Name	Customer name specifies the primary current name (normally the legal name for the customer) as used by the financial	VARCHAR(64)	Yes		
HEADER	Customer_Type	VARCHAR(10)	Translate Varchar to Smallint	CUST.dat	Customer_Type_Id	The unique identifier assigned to the customer type, for example, commercial, retail	SMALLINT	Yes		

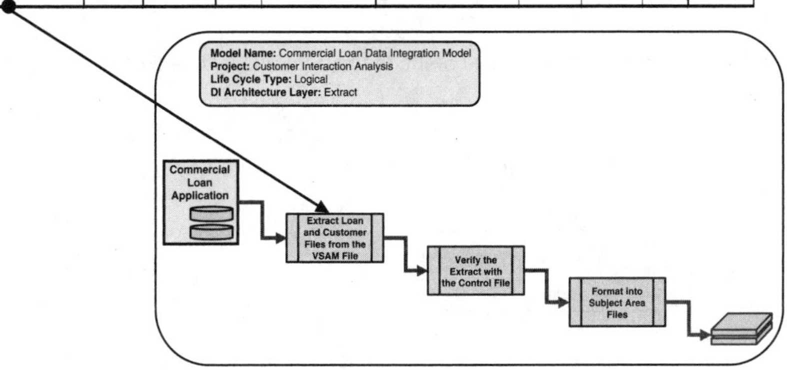

Model Name: Commercial Loan Data Integration Model
Project: Customer Interaction Analysis
Life Cycle Type: Logical
DI Architecture Layer: Extract

Commercial Loan Application

Extract Loan and Customer Files from the VSAM File

Verify the Extract with the Control File

Format into Subject Area Files

Figure 7.12 Mapping subject areas to the logical data integration extract model

Define the Logical Data Quality Data Integration Model

The logical data quality data integration model task takes the business and technical data quality criteria for the scoped data integration process and designs checkpoints to ensure that criteria is met during data integration processing.

The logical data quality integration model incorporates the processing logic or checkpoints from the data quality criteria (e.g., the critical data elements, the domain values, and the business rule ranges) for the intended target and defines them as either absolute or optional data quality rules. These business and technical checkpoints then leverage the data quality checkpoint processing architecture to instantiate the checkpoints into processing logic, as shown in Figure 7.13.

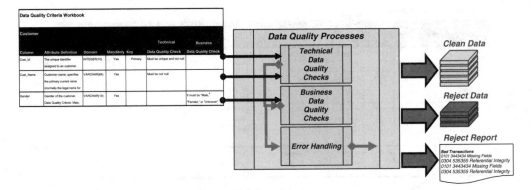

Figure 7.13   Mapping data quality criteria to the data quality checkpoint architecture

The following data quality criteria are incorporated into the logical data quality data integration model, as portrayed from Case Study 1 in Figure 7.14.

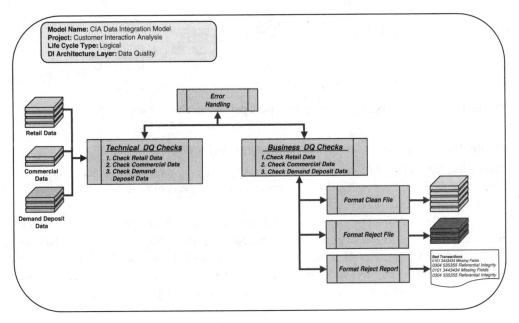

Figure 7.14   Completed logical data quality data integration model

Defining a logical data quality data integration model requires the following steps:

1. Identify critical tables and data elements.

2. Identify technical and business data quality criteria.

3. Determine which identified data quality criteria is absolute or optional.

Define the Logical Transform Data Integration Model

The logical transform data integration model task takes the business rules from the source-to-target data mapping document and determines what transformations to the source data are needed for the target data store, as illustrated in Figure 7.15.

Source File/ Table	Source Field	Source Domain	Mapping Rule	Subject Area File	Column Name	Column Definition	Target Domain
HEADER	Cust_Id	INTEGER(10)	Translate Integer to Varchar	CUST.dat	Source_Sys_Unique _Key_Text	The unique identifier of the customer in the source system.	VARCHAR(32)
HEADER	Name	VARCHAR(10)	Pad to 64	CUST.dat	Cust_Name	Customer name: specifies the primary current name (normally the legal name for the customer) as used by the Financial	VARCHAR(64)
DETAIL	City_Name	VARCHAR()	Straight move	CUST.dat	City_Code	The city of the customer	VARCHAR(20)
DETAIL	State_Code	VARCHAR()	Straight move	CUST.dat	State	The two-digit state code, e.g. "NY"	VARCHAR(2)
DETAIL	Postal_Barcode	VARCHAR()	1. Translate Varchar to Integer 2. Populate the first 5 into "Zip_Code", the final 4 into "Zip_Ext"	CUST.dat	Zip_Code	Zip_Code	INTEGER(5)
					Zip_Ext	The Zip extension	INTEGER(4)
Calculated Customer Table Attributes							
			Must be assigned "001"	CUST.dat	Source_Sys_Code	The unique identifier of the source system.	VARCHAR(20)
			Must be assigned "CUSTOMER HUB"	CUST.dat	Source_Sys_Unique _Key_Text	The unique identifier of the customer in the source system.	VARCHAR(32)
			Must be assigned "SYSTEM DATE"	CUST.dat	Last_Update_Run_Id		INTEGER(10)
			Must be assigned "SYSTEM DATE"	CUST.dat	Created_Run_Id		INTEGER(10)
			Must be system-generated by customer number	CUST.dat	Address_No	The unique identifier assigned an address	INTEGER(10)
			May or may not be populated	CUST.dat	Address_Line_2	The second address line	VARCHAR(20)

Figure 7.15 Gleaning data mapping rules for transformations

Based on the requirements of each of the business rules, a transformation type needs to be determined, and that transformation is documented in a transformation data integration model similar to the one in Figure 7.16.

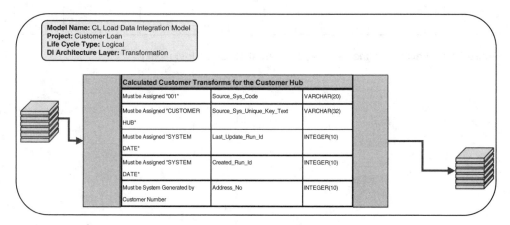

Figure 7.16 Completed logical transformation data integration model

For each business rule, an appropriate transformation type needs to be determined. A review of the types of transformations available appears in Chapter 2, including conforming, splits, processing, and enrichment, as well as aggregations and calculations.

For each business rule in the source-to-target data mapping, determine the following:

- Conforming transformation types

- Calculation and split transformation types

- Processing and enrichment transformation types

- Any additional business transformation types

Define the Logical Load Data Integration Model

The logical load data integration modeling task designs at a logical level what data needs to be loaded into the target data store from the transformed and cleansed data.

The source-to-target data mapping document provides the target data attributes by subject area, as shown in Figures 7.17 and 7.18.

Source File/ Table	Source Field	Source Domain	Mapping Rule	Subject Area File	Column Name	Column Definition	Target Domain
HEADER	Cust_Id	INTEGER(10)	Translate Integer to Varchar	CUST.dat	Source_Sys_Unique_Key_Text	The unique identifier of the customer in the source system	VARCHAR(32)
HEADER	Gender	VARCHAR(10)	Straight move	CUST.dat	Gender	Gender of the customer. Data Qualiy Criteria: Male, Female, Unknown	VARCHAR(10)
HEADER	Name	VARCHAR(10)	Pad to 64	CUST.dat	Cust_Name	Customer name: specifies the primary current name (normally the legal name for the Customer) as used by the Financial	VARCHAR(64)
HEADER	Ind_Soc_Security_Number	VARCHAR(10)	Translate Varchar to Integer, truncate last digit	CUST.dat	Social_Security_No	The government-issued identification.	INTEGER(9)
DETAIL	City_Name	VARCHAR()	Straight move	CUST.dat	City_Code	The city of the customer	VARCHAR(20)
DETAIL	State_Code	VARCHAR()	Straight move	CUST.dat	State	The two-digit state code, e.g.	VARCHAR(2)
DETAIL	Address_Line_1	VARCHAR()	Straight move	CUST.dat	Address_Line_1	The first address line	VARCHAR(20)
DETAIL	Postal_Barcode	VARCHAR()	1. Translate Varchar to Integer 2. Populate the first 5 into "Zip_Code," the final 4 into "Zip_Ext"	CUST.dat	Zip_Code	The Zip code	INTEGER(5)
					Zip_Ext	The Zip extension	INTEGER(4)

Figure 7.17   Leveraging the data mapping target attributes for loading

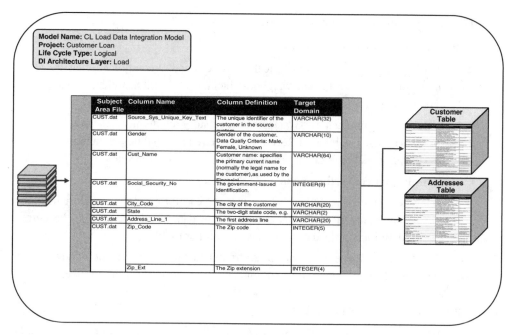

Figure 7.18   Completed logical load data integration model

Defining a logical load data integration model requires the following steps:

1. Map staged data fields to end table/columns or record/fields.

2. Determine an overwrite versus append/augment strategy.

3. Define load routines.

Defining One-Time Data Conversion Load Logical Design

One of the most difficult tasks in a data integration project is the conversion of existing history. Why? First is that transactional history is often fraught with inconsistencies in the data structure, definitions, and content. These inconsistencies are due to the fact that many systems have had two or more system conversions from organizational mergers or source systems; hence, it has a significant number of data anomalies, which makes conversions complicated and difficult. The second is that changing existing history or "conforming" it to a new target data structure can change the meaning of that data, creating definition challenges as well as potential Sarbanes-Oxley regulatory issues.

Often it makes more sense to begin building history in the new data warehouse going forward.

There are reasons for and against converting history, including the following:

- **Reasons for history conversion**
  - Historical data required for historical projections and forecasting—Often, the reporting requirements for the data warehouse include sufficient historical data to perform certain types of statistical analysis.
  - Regulatory requirements—Examples of regulatory requirements include seven years for tax records. The Internal Revenue Service requires public organizations to maintain history on all their tax information for a period of seven years.

- **Reasons for not converting history**
  - Relevance—Increasingly bad data year over year, for example, the aforementioned changes in transactional systems renders the data so different from the current, needed definition of the data that it is not useful or usable.
  - Cost—The cost/benefit in terms of effort and business involvement on how to interpret older data in context of the current definition is often cost-prohibitive.

Designing a History Conversion

There are two approaches to history conversion design. The first is a true transformation, where existing data is conformed to the new target data structures and definitions, as illustrated in Figure 7.19.

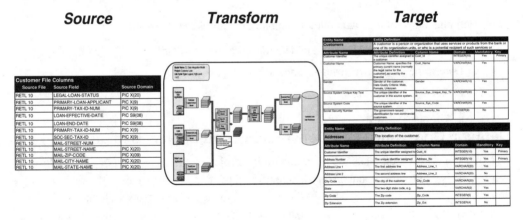

Figure 7.19   Traditional history conversion process

Rather than writing a separate set of extract, transform, and load processes for history conversion, a better approach is to leverage the target-based data integration technique and simply consider history as an additional source system extract and leverage existing transform and load processes, for example:

- History source 1 to subject area loads
- History source X to subject area loads

This significantly reduces the overall effort, and leverages existing data quality checks, transforms, and load processes.

The second approach is to simply "move" both the data and original structures into the target database environment. In terms of database design, the history tables have an additional attribute added as a key structure that provides the connection from the existing history table to the new database structure, as demonstrated in Figure 7.20.

Original Source Table

Source File/ Table	Source Field	Source Domain
	New_Cust_Id	INTEGER(10)
HEADER	Cust_Id	INTEGER(10)
HEADER	ID_Type_Code	VARCHAR(10)
HEADER	ID_Status_Type_Code	VARCHAR(10)
HEADER	Issue_Location	VARCHAR(10)
HEADER	Issuer_Id_Number	VARCHAR(10)
HEADER	Gender	VARCHAR(10)
HEADER	Name	VARCHAR(10)
HEADER	Customer_Type	VARCHAR(10)
HEADER	Fin_Viability_Type	Date
HEADER	Fin_Viability_Date	VARCHAR(10)
HEADER	Legal_Status	Date
HEADER	Legal_Status_Date	VARCHAR(10)
HEADER	Bus_Life_Cycle_Status	VARCHAR(10)
HEADER	Employee_ID	Date
HEADER	Effective_Date	Date
HEADER	End_Date	VARCHAR(10)

New Data Warehouse Tables

Entity Name	Entity Definition				
Customers	A customer is a person or organization that uses services or products from the bank or one of its organization units, or who is a potential recipient of such services or				
Attribute Name	Attribute Definition	Column Name	Domain	Mandatory	Key
Customer Identifier	The unique identifier assigned to a customer.	Cust_Id	INTEGER(10)	Yes	Primary
Customer Name	Customer Name: specifies the primary current name (normally the legal name for the customer),as used by the financial	Cust_Name	VARCHAR(64)	Yes	
Gender	Gender of the customer. Data Quality Criteria: Male, Female, Unknown	Gender	VARCHAR(10)	Yes	
Source System Unique Key Text	The unique identifier of the customer in the source system.	Source_Sys_Unique_Key_Text	VARCHAR(32)	Yes	
Source System Code	The unique identifier of the source system.	Source_Sys_Code	VARCHAR(20)	Yes	
Social Security Number	The government-issued identification for non-commercial customers.	Social_Security_No	INTEGER(9)	No	

Entity Name	Entity Definition				
Addresses	The location of the Customer.				
Attribute Name	Attribute Definition	Column Name	Domain	Mandatory	Key
Customer Identifier	The unique identifier assigned to	Cust_Id	INTEGER(10)	Yes	Primary
Address Number	The unique identifier assigned	Address_No	INTEGER(10)	Yes	Primary
Address Line 1	The first address line	Address_Line_1	VARCHAR(20)	Yes	
Address Line 2	The second address line	Address_Line_2	VARCHAR(20)	No	
City Code	The City of the Customer	City_Code	VARCHAR(20)	Yes	
State	The two-digit state code, e.g.	State	VARCHAR(2)	Yes	
Zip Code	The Zip code	Zip_Code	INTEGER(5)	Yes	
Zip Extension	The Zip extension	Zip_Ext	INTEGER(4)	No	

Figure 7.20   History movement database architecture approach

This approach has many advantages, the most important being that it

- **Keeps original data structure and definitions**—This reduces mapping time and risks.

- **Allows existing reports and queries to continue**—This provides time to migrate these end-user applications over time and reduces the overall scope and risk of the data warehouse (not just the history conversion) project.

This approach makes the history migration a movement rather than a conversion, as documented in Figure 7.21.

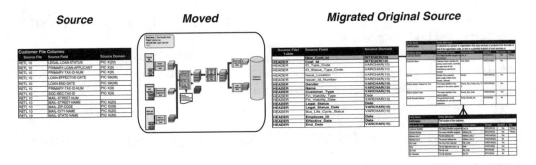

Figure 7.21   Traditional history conversion process

One-Time History Data Conversion Task Steps

Depending on the approach selected, there are two activities consisting of the following steps:

- **Steps for History Conversion**
  1. Map each source by time frame to the subject area.
  2. Design/develop extract data integration models.
  3. Design conforming transformation data integration models.
- **Steps for History Movement**
  1. Lightly conform (create key structures from old history data structure to new structures) existing data structures to the target data structures.
  2. Map sources from sources to new targets.
  3. Design extract data integration models.
  4. Design/develop conforming transformation data integration models.

Summary

This chapter covered the tasks, steps, and techniques necessary to complete a logical design for a data integration solution. It reviewed the analysis needed to size the intended data integration environment for both CPU and disk space.

The chapter spent a significant amount of time reviewing the approach for defining the target data warehouse model data quality criteria and how to integrate those criteria as checkpoints in the logical data quality model.

The chapter reviewed in detail the deliverables from the requirements phase that are used to produce logical data integration models.

The chapter also spent time detailing the differences between enterprise data integration assets and purpose-built data integration models for uses such as data mart population.

Finally, the chapter covered the complexities of two types of history conversion: traditional history conversion and history movement.

Chapter 8 utilizes the logical design techniques presented in this chapter in the Wheeler case study, using the analysis deliverables from Chapter 6, "Data Integration Analysis Case Study."

End-of-Chapter Questions

Question 1.
What are the two primary reasons to determine volumetrics?

Question 2.
What are the reasons for having an active data integration environment as early as possible in the Systems Development Life Cycle?

Question 3.
Why should the data quality criteria be defined for the target rather than the source?

Question 4.
The source-to-target data mapping document portrayed in the following image is used as input to build what logical data integration models?

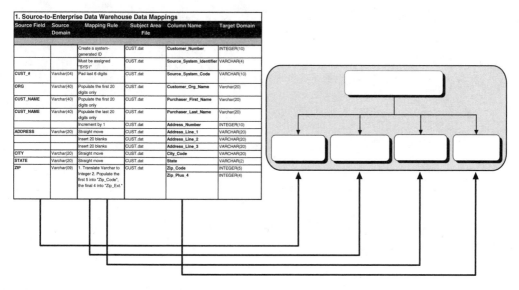

Source Field	Source Domain	Mapping Rule	Subject Area File	Column Name	Target Domain
		Create a system-generated ID	CUST.dat	Customer_Number	INTEGER(10)
		Must be assigned "SYS1"	CUST.dat	Source_System_Identifier	VARCHAR(4)
CUST_#	Varchar(04)	Pad last 6 digits	CUST.dat	Source_System_Code	VARCHAR(10)
ORG	Varchar(40)	Populate the first 20 digits only	CUST.dat	Customer_Org_Name	Varchar(20)
CUST_NAME	Varchar(40)	Populate the first 20 digits only	CUST.dat	Purchaser_First_Name	Varchar(20)
CUST_NAME	Varchar(40)	Populate the last 20 digits only	CUST.dat	Purchaser_Last_Name	Varchar(20)
		Increment by 1	CUST.dat	Address_Number	INTEGER(10)
ADDRESS	Varchar(20)	Straight move	CUST.dat	Address_Line_1	VARCHAR(20)
		Insert 20 blanks	CUST.dat	Address_Line_2	VARCHAR(20)
		Insert 20 blanks	CUST.dat	Address_Line_3	VARCHAR(20)
CITY	Varchar(20)	Straight move	CUST.dat	City_Code	VARCHAR(20)
STATE	Varchar(20)	Straight move	CUST.dat	State	VARCHAR(2)
ZIP	Varchar(09)	1. Translate Varchar to Integer 2. Populate the first 5 into "Zip_Code", the final 4 into "Zip_Ext."	CUST.dat	Zip_Code	INTEGER(5)
				Zip_Plus_4	INTEGER(4)

1. Source-to-Enterprise Data Warehouse Data Mappings

Question 5.
Identify and explain the reasons for converting or not converting history.

CHAPTER **8**

Data Integration Logical Design Case Study

This chapter continues the Wheeler Automotive Company analysis deliverables developed in Chapter 6, "Data Integration Analysis Case Study," which will be used to build out Wheeler logical designs.

Step 1: Determine High-Level Data Volumetrics

Reviewing the Wheeler Automotive case study, the following extract and high-level subject area files have been identified and are needed for the data integration project, as portrayed in Figure 8.1. These volumetrics need to be determined for environmental sizing in the data integration architecture task.

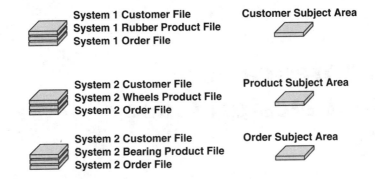

System 1 Customer File   Customer Subject Area
System 1 Rubber Product File
System 1 Order File

System 2 Customer File   Product Subject Area
System 2 Wheels Product File
System 2 Order File

System 2 Customer File   Order Subject Area
System 2 Bearing Product File
System 2 Order File

Figure 8.1   Wheeler source and target files

Steps in this activity include the following:

1. **Determine source system extract data volumetrics**—The purpose of this task is to size the source system extract files in the Wheeler source systems. The first two steps for this task are as follows:

    a.   Identify the systems and number of files—There are three source systems, which include the Domestic, Asian, and European Order Management Systems.

    b.   Determine the number of bytes per file—The total bytes per record has been calculated, as demonstrated in Figure 8.2.

System 1 Customer File

Field Name	Domain	Length
CUST_#	Varchar	4
ORG	Varchar	40
CUST_NAME	Varchar	40
ADDRESS	Varchar	20
CITY	Varchar	20
STATE	Varchar	20
ZIP		9
Record Size		153

System 2 Customer File

Field Name	Domain	Length
ID	Decimal	10
O_NAME	Char	15
F_NAME	Char	15
L_NAME	Char	15
ADDRSS 1	Char	20
ADDRSS 2	Char	20
CITY	Char	15
STATE	Char	2
ZIP	Decimal	9
Record Size		121

System 3 Customer File

Field Name	Domain	Length
CUST_ID	Decimal	10
ORGANIZATION	Varchar	20
FRST	Varchar	20
LAST	Varchar	20
ADDR 1	Char	20
ADDR 2	Char	20
ADDR 3	Char	20
CITY	Char	15
STATE	Varchar	2
ZIP	Integer	5
EXT	Integer	4
Record Size		156

System 1 Rubber Product File

Field Name	Domain	Length
Item Number	Varchar	4
Description	Char	30
Cost	Decimal	12
Price	Decimal	12
Inventory	Decimal	12
Record Size		70

System 2 Wheels Product File

Field Name	Domain	Length
Item ID	Integer	6
Inventory Name	Char	30
Cost	Decimal	12
Price	Decimal	12
Inventory	Decimal	12
Record Size		72

System 3 Bearing Product File

Field Name	Domain	Length
ID Number	Integer	6
Name	Char	30
Cost	Decimal	12
Price	Decimal	12
Inventory	Decimal	12
Record Size		72

System 1 Order File

Field Name	Domain	Length
ORDER_NO	Decimal	5
STATUS	Char	11
DATE	Integer	8
CUST_#	Varchar	4
TERMS_CD	Char	5
ITEM_NO	Varchar	4
PROD_PRICE	Decimal	5
AMNT_ORDR	Decimal	8
Record Size		50

System 2 Order File

Field Name	Domain	Length
ORD _NUM	Decimal	5
STATUS	Char	8
DATE	Integer	8
CUST_#	Varchar	4
LINE_1	Decimal	2
TERMS_CD	Char	5
ITEM_ID	Integer	6
PROD_PRICE	Decimal	5
AMNT_ORDR	Decimal	8
LINE_2	Decimal	2
TERMS_CD	Char	5
ITEM_ID	Integer	6
PROD_PRICE	Decimal	5
AMNT_ORDR	Decimal	8
Record Size		77

System 3 Order File

Field Name	Domain	Length
ORD _#	Decimal	5
STS	Char	7
DTE	Integer	8
CUST_#	Varchar	4
LN_1	Decimal	2
ID_NUMBER	Integer	6
PROD_PRICE	Decimal	5
AMNT_ORDR	Decimal	8
LN_2	Decimal	2
ID_NUMBER	Integer	6
PROD_PRICE	Decimal	5
AMNT_ORDR	Decimal	8
LN_3	Decimal	2
ID_NUMBER	Integer	6
PROD_PRICE	Decimal	5
AMNT_ORDR	Decimal	8
Record Size		87

Figure 8.2 Wheeler source file sizes

Once the individual record sizes are determined, the following information is calculated and recorded in a Source System Extract Volumetrics Report, as shown in Figure 8.3:

a. Determine the number of records per file (average on a per-run basis).

b. Multiply the number of bytes by the number of records to determine the size of each file.

c. Determine the frequency and number of generations to be kept (e.g., reruns and disaster recovery).

Wheeler Source System Extract Volumetrics Report								
System	Platform	Name	Files	Number of Bytes	Number of Records	Extract File Size	Frequency	CDC Y/N
Domestic Order	UNIX	Customer	Customer File	153	1,000	153,000		
Management		Product	Rubber Product File	70	200	14,000	Daily	Y
System		Order	Order File	50	5000	250,000		
Asian Order	UNIX	Customer	Customer File	121	1,500	181,500		
Management		Product	Wheels Product File	72	300	21,600	Daily	Y
System		Order	Order File	77	2300	177,100		
European Order	UNIX	Customer	Customer File	156	2,500	390,000		
Management		Product	Bearing Product File	72	400	28,800	Daily	Y
System		Order	Order File	87	4000	348,000		
						1,564,000	Total Number of Bytes	

Figure 8.3   Wheeler Source System Extract Volumetrics Report

For the source system extracts, there will be three days of files retained; therefore, the total disk space sizing for the extracts should be estimated (rounding up) at: 3,000MB x 3 = 9,000MB.

A good data integration guiding principle is to add an additional 30% to the estimate to account for system overhead; so for the Wheeler extract, estimate an additional 2,700MB for a total of 11,700MB for the initial staging environment.

2. **Determine subject area load data volumetrics**—Determine the number and size of the three Wheeler subject area files, as illustrated in Figure 8.4. Steps in this activity include the following:

   a. Identify the target tables (files) and ensure that they are in subject area files. For Customer, it is Customer and Address; for Product, it is simply Product; for Order, it is Order and Order Lines.

   b. Determine the number of bytes per file.

   c. Determine the number of records per file (average on a per-run basis).

   d. Multiply the number of bytes by the number of records to determine the size of each file.

   e. Determine the frequency and number of generations to be kept (e.g., reruns and disaster recovery).

Another data integration guiding principle is that subject area loads should be the same size as the sum total of the sources, as follows:

Customer Subject Area File: CUST.dat

Column Name	Domain	Size
Customer_Number	Integer	10
Source_System_Identifier	Varchar	4
Source_System_Code	Varchar	10
Customer_Org_Name	Varchar	20
Purchaser_First_Name	Varchar	20
Purchaser_Last_Name	Varchar	20
Address_Number	Integer	10
Address_Line_1	Varchar	20
Address_Line_2	Varchar	20
Address_Line_3	Varchar	20
City_Code	Varchar	20
State	Varchar	2
Zip_Code	Integer	5
Zip_Plus_4	Integer	4
Record Size		185

Order Subject Area File: ORDR.dat

Column Name	Domain	Size
Order_Number	Integer	7
Source_System_Identifier	Varchar	4
Source_System_Code	Varchar	10
Status_Code	Varchar	10
Order_Date	Date	8
Effective_Date	Date	8
Cust_Id	Integer	10
Terms	Varchar	30
Order_Number	Integer	7
Order_Line_Number	Integer	4
Product_Id	Integer	10
Product_Price	Decimal	9
Quantity_Ordered	Integer	7
Line_Amount	Decimal	11
Record Size		135

Product Subject Area File: PROD.dat

Column Name	Domain	Size
Product_Id	Integer	10
Source_System_Identifier	Varchar	4
Source_System_Code	Varchar	10
Product_Name	Char	40
Product_Type	Char	40
Product_Code	Varchar	20
Product_Cost	Decimal	9
Product_Price	Decimal	9
Inventory	Decimal	9
Record Size		151

Figure 8.4   Wheeler subject area file sizes

Wheeler Subject Area Load Volumetrics Report

Subject Area	Table Name	Number of Bytes	Number of Records	Subject Area Load File Size	Frequency	CDC Y/N
CUST.dat	Customer Addresses	185	5,000	925,000	Weekly	Y
PROD.dat	Product	151	900	135,900	Daily	N
ORDR.dat	Order Order Lines	135	11,300	1,525,500	Daily	Y
				2,586,400	Total Number of Bytes	

Figure 8.5   Wheeler Subject Area Load Volumetrics Report

Even if there is the removal of duplicate records (also known as de-duping), the number of target customer records should be equal (or very closely equal) to the source records.

File	Number of Records	Probable Size of the Target Customer Table
Customer File 1	1,000	
Customer File 2	200	
Customer File 3	<u>300</u>	
	1,500	

For the subject area loads, there will be three days of files retained; therefore, the total disk space sizing for the extracts should be estimated (rounding up) at: 3,000MB x 3 = 9,000MB.

In terms of system overhead for the subject area load estimate, estimate an additional 2,700MB (9,000 x 30%) for a total of 11,700MB for the initial staging environment.

Step 2: Establish the Data Integration Architecture

Now that the source and target/subject area volumetrics have been calculated (determined), the remaining aspects of the Wheeler data integration environment can be completed. For the sake of brevity, this exercise only considers activities through to the logical layer because most physical implementations are contingent on the brand of hardware selected.

1. **Portray the logical data integration architectural framework**—Because Wheeler is new to data warehousing and data integration, keeping the data integration architecture as close as possible to a standard blueprint is strongly recommended.

   The fact is that implementing the data integration reference architecture does not require that all the processes' staging areas are used for each data integration process, although, if needed, it is designed to be included at a later time. So for the Wheeler data integration environment, the standard blueprint will be followed.

   • Determine the number of staging areas (e.g., initial, clean staging, load-ready)—For the Wheeler environment, the size of the staging areas will leverage the work of the volumetrics task for disk space sizing.

   • Establish the data integration process (data quality and transform) architecture design—Determining the hardware requirements for processing is both an art and a science based on the concept of parallelization, as shown in Figure 8.6. The major data integration software packages provide the capability to run multiple processes in parallel, thereby reducing overall runtime. This feature is not automatic but needs to be analyzed, designed, implemented, and tuned in the data integration environment.

   The "art" is to use parallelization concepts to determine how many processes can be run at any one time based on physical constraints and other workload.

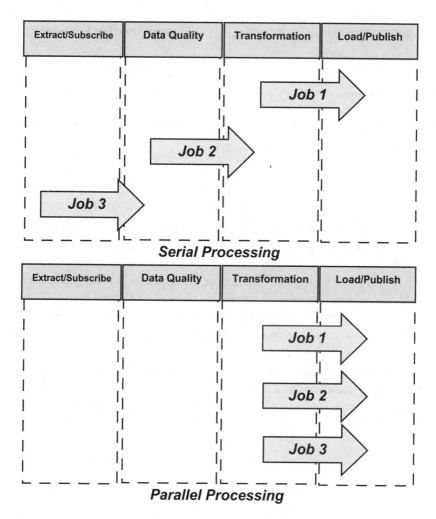

Figure 8.6 Sequential versus parallel processing

The "science" is in the estimation of CPU sizing based on the amount of memory needed per expected data integration process.

For example, if the three end-to-end data integration processes completed in 12 hours and the current estimated elapsed time per process is as follows:

23 hours is well in excess of a 12-hour batch window. The solution is to dedicate a processor per data integration process, ensuring that the three processes can run in parallel.

Data Integration Process	Elapsed Time Per Processor
Domestic Mgt. System-to-EDW	5 hours per processor
European Mgt. System-to-EDW	8 hours per processor
Asian Order Mgt. System-to-EDW	10 hours per processor
Total	23 hours

So the recommendation for a data integration server would be a four-CPU hardware platform (with an additional CPU for future growth and additional systems).

- Determine/develop the Reusable Components Library approach—As the logical architecture for the Wheeler data integration environment is completed, a configuration management approach needs to be developed for managing the data integration processes that baselines, versions, and, most important, leverages the existing processes in an ongoing basis. Chapter 12, "Data Integration Development Cycle Case Study," covers configuration management in context of data integration in more detail.

2. **Define the logical data integration architecture diagram**—The purpose of this activity is to take the sizing information and produce a blueprint for the system engineer to install, configure, and test the data integration environment for Wheeler, as shown in Figure 8.7.

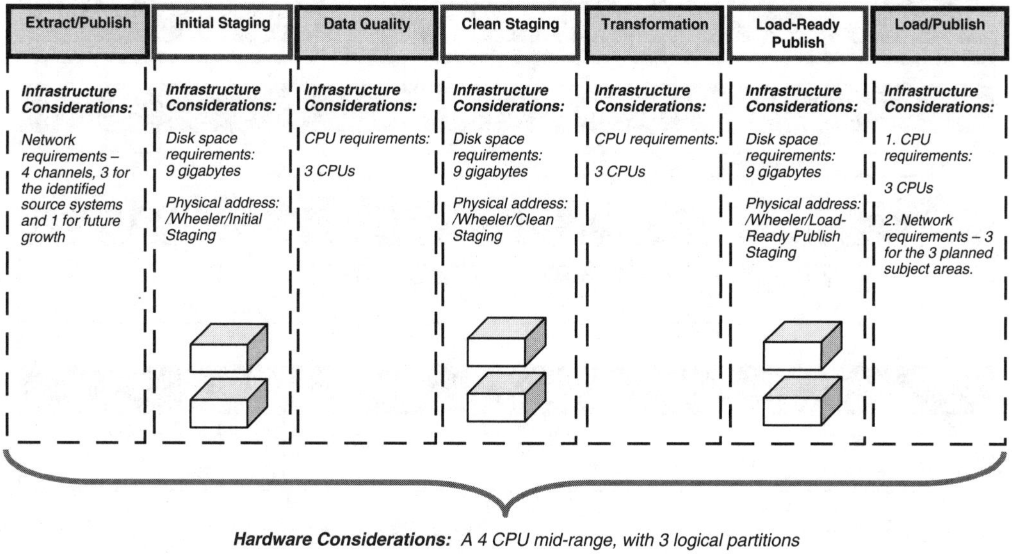

Extract/Publish	Initial Staging	Data Quality	Clean Staging	Transformation	Load-Ready Publish	Load/Publish
Infrastructure Considerations: Network requirements – 4 channels, 3 for the identified source systems and 1 for future growth	**Infrastructure Considerations:** Disk space requirements: 9 gigabytes Physical address: /Wheeler/Initial Staging	**Infrastructure Considerations:** CPU requirements: 3 CPUs	**Infrastructure Considerations:** Disk space requirements: 9 gigabytes Physical address: /Wheeler/Clean Staging	**Infrastructure Considerations:** CPU requirements: 3 CPUs	**Infrastructure Considerations:** Disk space requirements: 9 gigabytes Physical address: /Wheeler/Load-Ready Publish Staging	**Infrastructure Considerations:** 1. CPU requirements: 3 CPUs 2. Network requirements – 3 for the 3 planned subject areas.

Hardware Considerations: A 4 CPU mid-range, with 3 logical partitions

Figure 8.7 Wheeler logical data integration architecture diagram

Step 3: Identify Data Quality Criteria

While the data integration architecture is being defined and implemented, the data quality criteria can be determined and documented for the target Wheeler enterprise logical data warehouse data model.

Steps for identifying the data criteria include the following:

1. **Identify critical entities and attributes for data quality requirements**—Reviewing the Wheeler logical data model for the critical data attributes by table reveal the potential critical attributes such as primary and foreign keys, as shown in Figure 8.8.

Customer						
Attribute Name	Attribute Definition	Column Name	Domain	Mandatory	Key	Data Quality Check
Customer Identifier	The unique identifier assigned to a customer.	Cust_Id	INTEGER(10)	Yes	Primary	

Addresses						
Attribute Name	Attribute Definition	Column Name	Domain	Mandatory	Key	Data Quality Check
Customer Identifier	The unique identifier assigned to a customer.	Cust_Id	INTEGER(10)	Yes	Primary	
Address Number	The unique identifier assigned an address	Address_No	INTEGER(10)	Yes	Primary	

Loans	Entity Definition					
Attribute Name	Attribute Definition	Column Name	Domain	Mandatory	Key	Data Quality Check
Loan Number	The unique identifier of a loan between two or more	Loan_No	INTEGER(10)	Yes	Primary	
Customer Name	Customer name: specifies the primary current name (normally the legal name for the customer) as used by the financial	Cust_Name	VARCHAR(64)	Yes	Foreign	

Products						
Attribute Name	Attribute Definition	Column Name	Domain	Mandatory	Key	Data Quality Check
Product Identifier	The unique identifier of a product.	Product_Id	INTEGER(10)	Yes	Primary	
Source System Code	The unique identifier of the application or system from which the information last used to update the entity instance was populated.	Source_System_Code	VARCHAR(20)	Yes		

Figure 8.8   First-cut, identified Wheeler Data Quality Criteria Workbook

After the key attributes have been documented, then any remaining critical data attributes should be captured. These typically are those nonkey attributes that are mandatory and those with business data quality criteria.

2. **Identify the data quality criteria for each data attribute**—Once all the critical data elements have been identified from the Wheeler enterprise data model, define the technical and business data quality rules that are required for each data element. Then develop the checkpoints and document the Data Quality Criteria Workbook. This is shown completed in Figure 8.9.

Table Customer					Technical	Business
Column Name	Column Definition	Domain	Mandatory	Key	Data Quality Check	Data Quality Check
Cust_Id	The unique identifier assigned to a customer.	INTEGER(10)	Yes	Primary	1 Not Null, 2. Unique	
Cust_Name	Customer Name: specifies the	VARCHAR(64)	Yes		Not Null	
Gender	Gender of the customer. Data Quality Criteria: Male, Female, Unknown	VARCHAR(10)	Yes			It must be "Male," "Female," or "Unknown"
Source_Sys_Unique_Key_Text	The unique identifier of the Customer	VARCHAR(32)	Yes		Not Null	
Source_Sys_Code	The unique identifier of the Source	VARCHAR(20)	Yes		Not Null	
Customer_Type_Id	The unique identifier assigned to the customer type. For example,	SMALLINT	Yes		Not Null	
Cust_Effective_Date	The date on which the customer first became relevant to the financial	DATE	Yes		1 Not Null 2. Must be a date field	
Cust_End_Date	The date on which the customer ceased to be relevant to the financial	DATE	Yes		1 Not Null 2. Must be a date field	
Last_Update_Run_Id		INTEGER(10)	Yes		Not Null	
Created_Run_Id		INTEGER(10)	Yes		Not Null	
Cust_Legal_Status_Type_Id	The unique identifier of the	INTEGER(10)	Yes		Not Null	

Table Addresses					Technical	Business
Column Name	Column Definition	Domain	Mandatory	Key	Data Quality Check	Data Quality Check
Cust_Id	The unique identifier assigned to a customer.	INTEGER(10)	Yes	Primary	1 Not Null, 2. Unique	
Address_No	The unique identifier assigned an address	INTEGER(10)	Yes	Primary	1 Not Null, 2. Unique	
Address_Line_1	The first address line	VARCHAR(20)	Yes		Not Null	
City_Code	The city of the customer	VARCHAR(20)	Yes		Not Null	
State	The two-digit state code, e.g. "NY"	VARCHAR(2)	Yes		Not Null	
Zip_Code	The Zip code	INTEGER(5)	Yes		Not Null	

Table Products					Technical	Business
Column Name	Column Definition	Domain	Mandatory	Key	Data Quality Check	Data Quality Check
Product_Id	The unique identifier of a Wheeler product.	INTEGER(10)	Yes	Primary	1 Not Null, 2. Unique	
Source System Identifier	The identifier of the source system that the data was sourced.	VARCHAR(4)	Yes	Primary		In must be the unique identifier of the application or system from which the information last used to update the entity instance was populated.
Source System Code	The unique identifier of the application or system from which the information last used to update the	VARCHAR(10)	Yes	Primary	1 Not Null, 2. Unique	
Product Name	The primary name assigned to the Product. This name is used in	CHAR(40)	Yes	Yes	Not Null	
Product Type	The type of product being offered by Wheeler. Domain ranges include	CHAR(40)	Yes	Yes	Not Null	
Product Code	One or more numbers or codes by which a product can be identified; for example, code '1101' represents a	VARCHAR(20)	Yes	Yes	Not Null	
Product Cost	The per unit cost of the product item	Decimal 7,2	Yes	Yes	Not Null	
Product Price	The per unit price that Wheeler	Decimal 7,2	Yes	Yes	Not Null	
Inventory	The per unit price that Wheeler	Decimal 7,2	Yes		Not Null	

Figure 8.9   Completed Wheeler Data Quality Criteria Workbook

Table						
Order					**Technical**	**Business**
Column Name	**Column Definition**	**Domain**	**Mandatory**	**Key**	**Data Quality Check**	**Data Quality Check**
Order_Number	This number represents a single occurrence of an order.	INTEGER(07)	Yes	Primary	1 Not Null, 2. Unique	
Source_System_Identifier	The identifier of the source system that the data was sourced.	VARCHAR(4)	Yes	Primary	1 Not Null, 2. Unique	
Source_System_Code	The unique identifier of the application or system from which the information last used to update the	VARCHAR(10)	Yes	Primary	1 Not Null, 2. Unique	
Status_Code	The unique identifier for one occurrence of a status code on a	VARCHAR(10)	Yes	No	Not Null	
Order_Date	The date that the order was placed.	Date	Yes	No	Not Null	
Effective_Date	The date that the order will take effec	Date	Yes	No	Not Null	
Cust_Id	The unique identifier assigned to a customer.	INTEGER(10)	Yes	Foreign	1. Not Null 2. Must match the primary key in customer	
Terms	The terms of payment for the order.	VARCHAR(30)	Yes	No	Not Null	

Table						
Order Lines					**Technical**	**Business**
Column Name	**Column Definition**	**Domain**	**Mandatory**	**Key**	**Data Quality Check**	**Data Quality Check**
Order_Number	This number represents a single occurrence of a order.	INTEGER(07)	Yes	Primary	1. Not Null 2. Must match the primary key in order	
Order_Line_Number	The unique identifier for one occurrence of a status code on a	INTEGER(04)	Yes	Primary	1 Not Null, 2. Unique	
Product_Id	The unique identifier of a Wheeler product.	INTEGER(10)	Yes	Foreign	1. Not Null 2. Must match the primary key in product	
Product_Price	The per unit price that Wheeler	Decimal 7,2	Yes	No	Not Null	
Quantity_Ordered	The per unit quantity of the product	INTEGER(07)	Yes	No	Not Null	
Line_Amount	The product price * quantity ordered	Decimal 9,2	Yes	No	Not Null	

Figure 8.9   Completed Wheeler Data Quality Criteria Workbook

These data quality criteria will be used to design and build the data quality checkpoints in the data quality data integration model. Please note the grayed-in attributes; these data quality criteria have been identified as potential common data quality checkpoints.

Step 4: Create Logical Data Integration Models

The next task is to incorporate all the requirements for the Wheeler data integration processes in a design blueprint, the logical data integration model.

It is a good practice to ensure that all the primary inputs for the logical data integration model are ready and signed off by the appropriate stakeholders, as is depicted in Figure 8.10.

This includes some level of sign-off on the data mappings and the Data Quality Criteria Workbook to ensure that all the requirements are agreed upon and accounted for in the logical design.

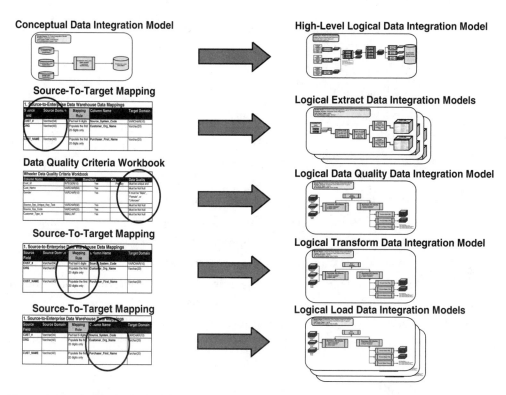

Figure 8.10   Inputs for logical data integration modeling

Define the High-Level Logical Data Integration Model

The first step in developing the logical data integration model is to provide the big-picture view of what is to be built. Because most data integration projects require a team of designers and developers to develop the data integration processes, the high-level logical data integration model provides the "context" diagram view of the entire design of the intended application. The model is also useful in explaining what is to be built to other project stakeholders, such as the business stakeholders, data modelers, and database administrators.

To build the Wheeler data warehouse high-level logical data integration model, we will use the Wheeler conceptual data integration model and refine the following questions:

- **What is in the logical extraction data integration model?**

  The Domestic Order Management System, with the following files:

  - System 1 Customer File

  - System 1 Rubber Product File

  - System 1 Order File

The Asian Order Management System, with the following files:

- System 2 Customer File
- System 2 Wheels Product File
- System 2 Order File

The European Order Management System, with the following files:

- System 3 Customer File
- System 3 Bearing Product File
- System 3 Order File

- **What is in the logical data quality data integration model?**
  - Data Quality Criteria Workbook—Technical: 25 checkpoints
  - Data Quality Criteria Workbook—Business: 2 checkpoints
- **What is in the logical transform data integration model?**
  - Source-to-EDW target mapping document—100 conforming transforms (format changes, trimming, and padding), 20 calculations
- **What is in the logical load data integration model (if known)?**

  The data warehouse subject areas are as follows:

  - Customer (CUST.dat)
  - Product (PROD.dat)
  - Order (ORDR.dat)

With the big-picture diagram complete, as illustrated in Figure 8.11, the remaining work can be subdivided into separate pieces of work that can be accomplished in parallel.

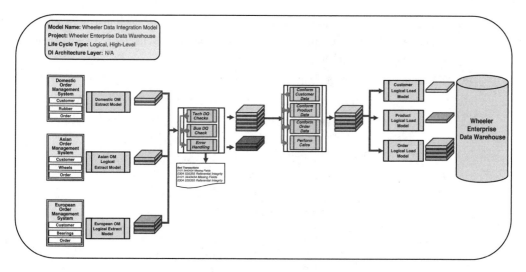

Figure 8.11   The Wheeler high-level logical data integration model

Define the Logical Extraction Data Integration Model

The first consideration in developing the Wheeler logical extraction data integration model is whether one extraction diagram or many extraction diagrams are needed.

What determines one or many? The simple answer is readability. If all sources can fit into one logical diagram, it makes sense to keep it together. Keep in mind that for physical data integration models and actual source code, the diagram and code will be split into one and only one function per data integration process.

Because the number of icons on the diagram would exceed the ability for anyone to read the diagrams and because there will most likely be three separate data integration jobs when complete, there will be three separate logical extract data integration models by source system.

1. **Confirm the subject area focus from the data mapping document**—In reviewing the Wheeler source-to-target data mapping document, the three subject areas that are cross-referenced in the Wheeler conceptual data integration model are as follows:

   • Customer (CUST.dat)

   • Product (PROD.dat)

   • Order (ORDR.dat)

2. **Review whether the existing data integration environment can fulfill the requirements**—Because the Wheeler environment is new, there are no existing physical data integration models or code to leverage. It is always important to confirm first that there are not components to leverage on the very next data integration project.

3. **Determine the business extraction rules**—In determining what needs to occur to extract or capture the data from the source system, all three Wheeler order management systems will be batch captures with the following times:

- Domestic Order Management System

    - From what extract directory? The three Domestic Order Management Systems will land three files into the /Wheeler/Initial Staging directory.
    - When? 7:00 p.m.
    - What files?
        - SYS_1_CUST
        - SYS_1_PROD
        - SYS_1_ORDR
    - What control files?
        - SYS_1_CUST_CNTL
        - SYS_1_PROD_CNTL
        - SYS_1_ORDR_CNTL

- Asian Order Management System

    - From what extract directory? The three Asian Order Management Systems will land three files into the /Wheeler/Initial Staging directory.
    - When? 6:00 p.m.
    - What files?
        - SYS_2_CST
        - SYS_2_PRD
        - SYS_2_ORD
    - What control files?
        - SYS_2_CST_CNTL
        - SYS_2_PRD_CNTL
        - SYS_2_ORD_CNTL

- European Order Management System

    - From what extract directory? The three European Order Management Systems will land three files into the /Wheeler/Initial Staging directory.
    - When? 6:00 p.m.

- What files?
  - SYS_3_CUSTOMR
  - SYS_3_PRODCT
  - SYS_3_ORDER
- What control files?
  - SYS_3_CUSTOMR_CNTL
  - SYS_3_PRODCT_CNTL
  - SYS_3_ORDER_CNTL

4. **Map source file formats to the attribute level**—This step segments the source attributes of the Wheeler source-to-EDW target mapping document into those subject area–focused components needed for the extract models.

Figure 8.12 portrays how to use the data mapping document to segment out and provide the subject area mappings for the Wheeler logical extract data integration models shown in Figures 8.13, 8.14, and 8.15 that have been created for Wheeler.

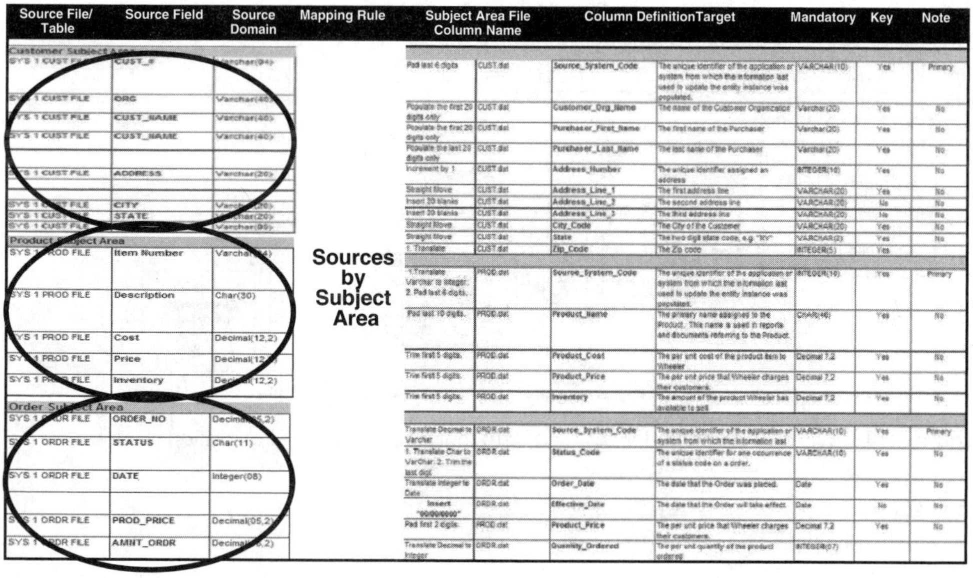

Figure 8.12 Leveraging the Wheeler source-to-EDW target mapping for the extract data integration models

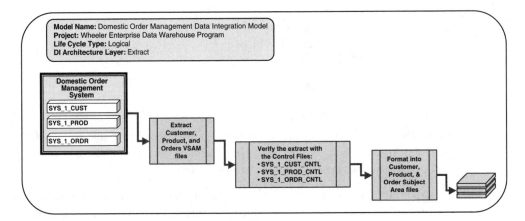

Figure 8.13   Wheeler Domestic Order Management logical extract data integration model

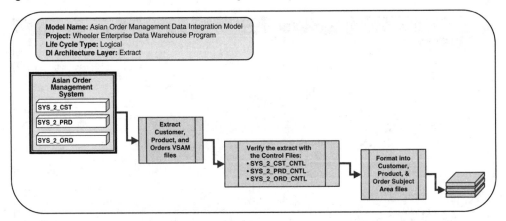

Figure 8.14   Wheeler Asian Order Management logical extract data integration model

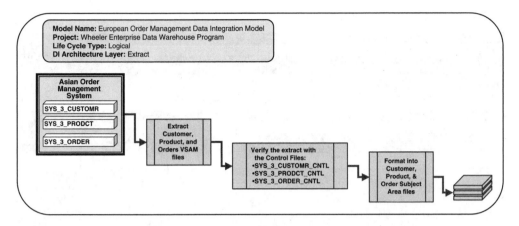

Figure 8.15   Wheeler European Order Management logical extract data integration model

Define the Logical Data Quality Data Integration Model

To define the Wheeler logical data quality model, you need to review the Data Quality Criteria Workbook and then include the technical data quality checkpoints into a technical data quality component and the business data quality checkpoints into a business data quality component.

1. **Identify critical tables and data elements columns**—This step is in the approach for those projects that have not developed a Data Quality Criteria Workbook. Because one exists, this step is not necessary.

2. **Identify technical and business data quality criteria from the Data Quality Criteria Workbook**—This step performs that "filtering" of the technical and business data quality checkpoints into two buckets or subcomponents. In the completed Wheeler Data Quality Criteria Workbook, shown in Figure 8.16, we will glean only the few business (highlight rows) data quality checkpoints, assuming that the remainder is technical data quality checkpoints.

    Figure 8.16 also shows the business data quality criteria that need to be designed into the logical data quality data integration model.

Wheeler Business Data Quality Criteria Workbook

Table

Customer

Column Name	Column Definition	Domain	Mandatory	Key	Technical Data Quality Check	Business Data Quality Check
Gender	Gender of the customer. Data Quality Criteria: Male, Female, Unknown	VARCHAR(10)	Yes			It must be "Male," "Female," or "Unknown"

Table

Products

Column Name	Column Definition	Domain	Mandatory	Key	Technical Data Quality Check	Business Data Quality Check
Product_Id	The unique identifier of a Wheeler product.	INTEGER(10)	Yes	Primary	1 Not Null, 2. Unique	
Source System Identifier	The identifier of the source system that the data was sourced.	VARCHAR(4)	Yes	Primary		In must be the unique identifier of the application or system from which the information last used to update the entity instance was populated.

Figure 8.16   Wheeler business data quality criteria

As mentioned in Chapter 4, "Case Study: Customer Loan Data Warehouse Project," it is not unusual to have significantly more technical data quality checkpoints than business data quality checkpoints.

3. **Determine which identified data quality criteria is absolute or optional**—This step reviews each of the data quality checkpoints to evaluate if they are significant enough to terminate processing of the file or simply "flag and pass." For this case study, all Wheeler data quality checkpoints will be simply flag-and-pass checks, as it is in most data integration projects.

4. **Assemble the logical data quality data integration model**—The final step is to assemble all the input in to the logical Wheeler data quality data integration model, as shown in Figure 8.17.

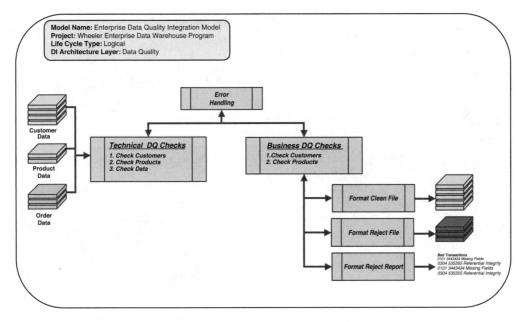

Figure 8.17   Wheeler logical data quality data integration model

Figure 8.18 illustrates the organization of the technical data quality checkpoint in the data integration model, and Figure 8.19 shows the Business Data Quality view.

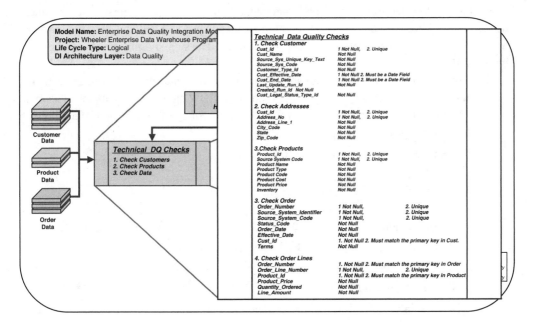

Figure 8.18   Wheeler logical data quality data integration model—Technical Data Quality view

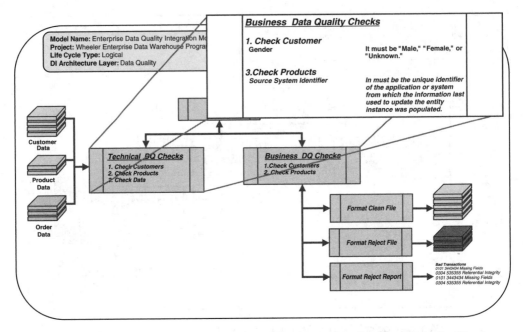

Figure 8.19   Wheeler logical data quality data integration model—Business Data Quality view

Define Logical Transform Data Integration Model

Developing the Wheeler logical transform data integration model requires gleaning the business rules from the Wheeler source-to-EDW target data mapping document and determining what transformations to the source data are needed for the target data store by subject area, as shown in Figure 8.20.

1. **For each business rule in the source-to-target data mapping, determine a transform type**—Reviewing the Wheeler source-to-EDW target data mapping document (found in the online appendix, Appendix D, "Case Study Models") finds the following transform types:

   • Generating system keys for the following:

      • Customer

      • Product

      • Order

   • Conforming/translating over 40 elements with trims, pads, or format conversions

   • Performing two domain checks, testing for "Must be either 'Rubber,' 'Wheels,' or 'Bearings'"

   • Performing seven foreign key lookups

   As discussed in Chapter 4, most transformations from multiple source systems to a data warehouse are primarily translating and conforming transform types.

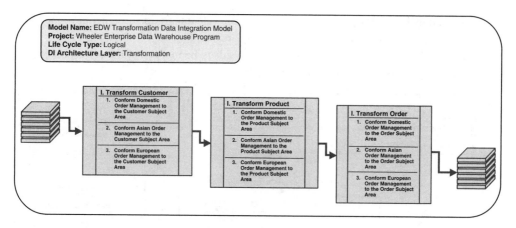

Figure 8.20   Wheeler logical transform data integration model

Define Logical Load Data Integration Model

The Wheeler logical load data integration model requires the EDW target mappings from the source-to-EDW target data mapping document, as shown in Figure 8.21.

Source File/ Table	Source Field	Source Domain	Mapping Rule	Subject Area File Column Name		Column Definition	Target Domain	Mandatory	Key	Note
Customer Subject Area										
SYS 1 CUST FILE	CUST_#	Varchar(94)	Pad last 6 digits	CUST.dat		Source_System_Co	The unique identifier of the application or system from which the information last used to update the entity instance was populated.	VARCHAR(10)			Primary
SYS 1 CUST FILE	ORG	Varchar(40)	Populate the first 20 digits only	CUST.dat		Customer_Org_Name	The name of the Customer Organization	Varchar(20)	Yes		
SYS 1 CUST FILE	CUST_NAME	Varchar(40)	Populate the first 20 digits only	CUST.dat		Purchaser_First_Name	The first name of the Purchaser	Varchar(20)	Yes		No
SYS 1 CUST FILE	CUST_NAME	Varchar(40)	Populate the last 20 digits only	CUST.dat		Purchaser_Last_Name	The last name of the Purchaser	Varchar(20)	Yes		
			Increment by 1	CUST.dat		Address_Number	The unique identifier assigned an address	INTEGER(10)	Yes		No
						Address_Line_1	The first address line	VARCHAR(20)	Yes		No
SYS 1 CUST FILE	ADDRESS	Varchar(20)	Straight Move	CUST.dat		Address_Line_2	The second address line	VARCHAR(20)	No		No
			Insert 20 blanks	CUST.dat		Address_Line_3	The third address line	VARCHAR(20)	No		No
			Insert 20 blanks	CUST.dat		City_Code	The City	VARCHAR(20)	Yes		No
SYS 1 CUST FILE	CITY	Varchar(20)	Straight Move	CUST.dat		State	The two digit state code, e.g. "NY"	VARCHAR(2)	Yes		No
SYS 1 CUST FILE	STATE	Varchar(20)	Straight Move	CUST.dat		Zip_Code	The Zip code	INTEGER(5)			
SYS 1 CUST FILE	ZIP	Varchar(09)	1. Translate	CUST.dat						
Product Subject Area										
SYS 1 PROD FILE	Item Number	Varchar(04)	1.Translate Varchar to integer. 2. Pad last 6 digits.	PROD.dat		Source_System_Code	The unique identifier of the application or system from which the information last used to update the entity instance was populated.	INTEGER(10)	Yes		Primary
SYS 1 PROD FILE	Description	Char(30)	Pad last 10 digits.	PROD.dat		Product_Name	The primary name assigned to the Product. This name is used in reports and documents referring to the Product.	Char(40)	Yes		
SYS 1 PROD FILE	Cost	Decimal(12,2)	Trim first 5 digits.	PROD.dat		Product_Cost	The per unit cost of the product item to Wheeler	Decimal 7,2	Yes		No
SYS 1 PROD FILE	Price	Decimal(12,2)	Trim first 5 digits.	PROD.dat		Product_Price	The per unit price that Wheeler charges their customers.	Decimal 7,2	Yes		No
SYS 1 PROD FILE	Inventory	Decimal(12,2)	Trim first 5 digits.	PROD.dat		Inventory	The amount of the product Wheeler has available	Decimal	Yes		No
Order Subject Area										
SYS 1 ORDR FILE	ORDER_NO	Decimal(05,2)	Translate Decimal to Varchar	ORDR.dat		Source_System_Code	The unique identifier of the application or system from which the information last used to update the entity instance was populated.	VARCHAR(10)	Yes		Primary
SYS 1 ORDR FILE	STATUS	Char(11)	1. Translate Char to VarChar. 2. Trim the last digit	ORDR.dat		Status_Code	The unique identifier for one occurrence of a status code on a order.	VARCHAR(10)	Yes		No
SYS 1 ORDR FILE	DATE	Integer(08)	Translate Integer to Date	ORDR.dat		Order_Date	The date that the Order was placed.	Date	Yes		
			Insert "00/00/0000"	ORDR.dat		Effective_Date	The date that the Order will take effect.	Date	No		
SYS 1 ORDR FILE	PROD_PRICE	Decimal(05,2)	Pad first 2 digits.	PROD.dat		Product_Price	The per unit price that Wheeler charges their customers.	Decimal 7,2	Yes		No
SYS 1 ORDR FILE	AMNT_ORDR	Decimal(08,2)	Translate Decimal to integer	ORDR.dat		Quantity_Ordered	The per unit quantity of the product ordered	INTEGER(07)			

Sources by Subject Area

Figure 8.21   Leveraging the Wheeler source-to-EDW target mapping for the logical load data integration model

Segmenting the loads by subject area provides the data integration designer the opportunity to create one logical load model or many, by subject area.

Each set of subject area load target elements needs to be mapped to the corresponding target database table column, as shown in Figure 8.22.

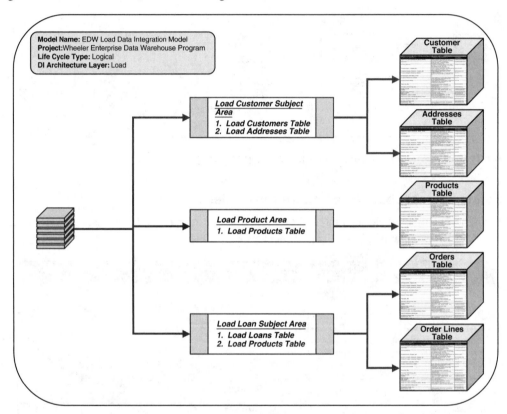

Figure 8.22   Wheeler logical load data integration model

As reviewed in the extract data integration models, as the project moves to physical design, this model will most likely be segmented into three physical data integration models, usually by source systems.

Define Logical Data Mart Data Integration Model

The one process yet to be defined is the extract, transform, and load from the Wheeler enterprise data warehouse to the product line profitability data mart displayed in Figure 8.23.

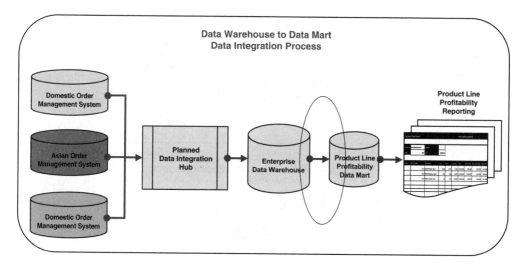

Figure 8.23 Wheeler data warehouse to data mart data integration process

For this data integration process, the extraction from the data warehouse, transformation, and load will all occur in one data integration process model.

Why is this approach different?

For most of this text, we have advocated the concept of separating functionality into components for both ease of maintenance and reuse. Yet for this data integration process, we are promoting everything in one model/job.

The reason is enterprise versus local use. The concept of reuse is applicable for those enterprise-level assets that can take advantage of reuse, such as extract, loads, and common components.

It is best practice (as discussed in earlier chapters) to have only one extract per source or one process to load a set of related tables. However, when there is a specifically purposed data integration process, such as loading a data mart from a data warehouse, it makes sense to have only one data integration job that will extract the data needed for the data mart, perform the transforms (calculations and aggregations), and then load it into the data mart tables.

One question to consider: Where do you extract the data from? There are two potential sources, as shown in Figure 8.24.

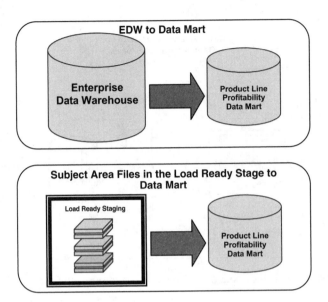

Figure 8.24   Data mart sourcing options

The first option is to use the data warehouse for sourcing data into the data mart (the traditional approach).

Advantages:

- The data warehouse is the source for all downstream analytic data stores such as data marts leveraging common, consistent data.

Disadvantages:

- You must wait for the data warehouse to be loaded before the extract for the data mart can begin.
- The data warehouse tables that are required for the data mart will be unavailable while the extract occurs.

The second option is to use the data integration environment's load-ready staging data for sourcing data into the data mart.

Advantages:

- There is no availability impact on the data warehouse tables from an extract perspective.
- The data for the data mart can be loaded in parallel to the data warehouse, cutting down the overall source-to-DW data mart load time.

Disadvantages:

- If there is history calculation requirements in the data warehouse required for the data mart transforms, the load-ready approach might not be practical.

For the Wheeler EDW-to-data mart data integration process, the data warehouse will be used as the source, as shown in Figure 8.25.

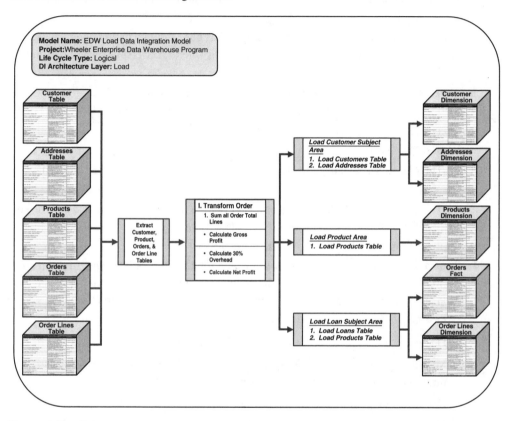

Figure 8.25 Wheeler enterprise data warehouse to product line profitability data mart data integration model

Develop the History Conversion Design

The first step is to confirm what history if any is needed for the Wheeler enterprise data warehouse and, second, if the three source systems are "clean" enough and capable of providing the data for the history conversion.

Once analyzed, the following steps must be performed:

1. **Determine Wheeler enterprise data warehouse history requirements**—The one known end-user requirement for the data warehouse is the product line profitability data mart. Through analysis, it is discovered that three years of history are needed to forecast profitability by product line.

2. **Review the source systems**—Upon review of the history of the three source systems, the following is discovered:

- The Domestic Order Management System contains 90% of the needed order history.
- The Asian Order Management System went online one month ago and does not have any history.
- The European Order Management System has gone through three major conversions in the past two years. The data is problematic due to conversion-related data anomalies but is needed.

3. **Determine the history conversion approach for each source system**—Based on the status and "shape" of the history, the following approach is recommended:

   - The Domestic Order Management System—The history will be converted for the past three years.
   - The Asian Order Management System—This history will not be used due to the lack of data.
   - The European Order Management System—Due to the need of the data and the cost benefit of attempting to rationalize the data to the new data warehouse data model, the data will simply be moved (History Approach Two).

4. **Determine the history conversion approach for the Domestic Order Management System**—For the Domestic Order Management System, the traditional history conversion approach will be used (shown in Figure 8.26) and will require the following steps:

   a. Profile each of the three years' prior history for anomalies.

   b. Document any needed source-based data quality checkpoints.

   c. Map the Domestic Order Management System to subject area files for each of the three years (to account for any year-over-year format changes).

   d. Design/develop the year-over-tear extract data integration model.

   e. Design the subject area–conforming transformation data integration model.

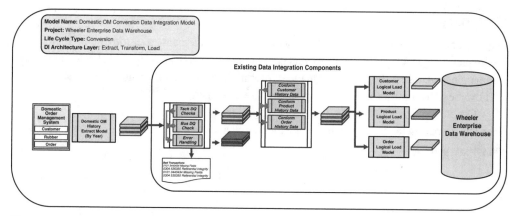

Figure 8.26 Domestic Order Management System history conversion logical data integration model

5. **Determine the history movement for the European Order Management System—** This approach, illustrated in Figure 8.27, is to simply find a common key and port the existing database structures and data to the new database environment. This approach entails the following:

a. "Lightly conform" the European (create key structures from old history data structure to new structures) existing data structures to the target data structures.

b. Map the existing European database structure into the new Wheeler EDW with the extended European data structures.

c. Design the European extract data integration model.

d. Design/develop the transformation data integration model for the additional key structure.

e. Design the extended Wheeler EDW load model.

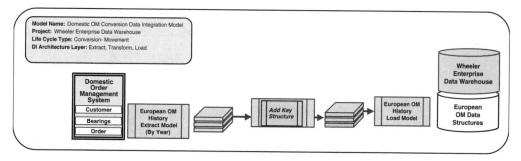

Figure 8.27 Wheeler history conversion data integration model

Summary

In this chapter, we further extended the Wheeler order management case study in the logical design phase by developing a set of logical data integration models using the Wheeler source target mappings and the Wheeler Data Quality Criteria Workbook from the analysis phase, showing how the deliverables for earlier work efforts are leveraged.

Chapter 9, "Data Integration Physical Design," focuses on taking the logical design deliverables and preparing them for physical implementation and initial performance tuning in the physical design phase.

Data Integration Physical Design

The physical data integration phase transforms the logical business designs into physical design specifications that will be optimally tuned in the targeted data integration technology. Upon completion, there will be a set of physical data integration models and operational requirements that will be ready for final build activities.

This chapter also covers how to best convert the models into component-based designs in the selected data integration software package that will be optimized for performance, maintainability, and reusability.

In this phase, there is a focus on ensuring that the designs have accounted for the intended volumes and frequencies (collected in the data volumetrics task in logical design) and has "tuned" the designs to ensure maximum throughput of data.

It also covers how the physical data integration models can be leveraged in architectural patterns such as service-oriented architecture (SOA) components.

Finally, it reviews the requirements that are necessary to prepare the data integration processes (e.g., jobs scheduling and production support) to run in a production environment.

The tasks for the data integration physical design phase include the following:

1. Create component-based physical designs.
2. Prepare the data integration development environment.

3. Create physical data integration models.

    3.1.   Develop physical common components models.

    3.2.   Design physical source system data integration models.

    3.3.   Design physical subject area load data integration models.

4. Design parallelism into the data integration models.

5. Design Change Data Capture.

6. Finalize the history conversion design.

7. Define data integration operational requirements.

8. Design data integration components for SOA.

Creating Component-Based Physical Designs

The first data integration physical design task reviews the logical data integration models and uses the data integration reference architecture as a framework to further apply component techniques against them, as first discussed in Chapter 3, "A Design Technique: Data Integration Modeling."

Reviewing the Rationale for a Component-Based Design

One of the primary objectives of the data integration reference architecture is that logical units of work should be separated into extract, data quality, transform, and load physical processes or components because of reasons such as the following:

- If an extract is successful, the file should not need to be re-extracted because of errors in downstream processing.
- Fatal transformation errors should not create a need for cleanup in downstream loads.
- Downstream loads can be postponed until all dependent loads are successful. The net effect is that any fatal errors in a transformation component can be fixed and rerun without regard to the effects from upstream or downstream processing.

In other words, splitting up processes into components provides flexibility in processing data with different timings and levels of data quality without creating unneeded constraints.

Modularity Design Principles

To drive that next level of componentization or modularity in the data integration models, each model needs to be looked at in terms of coupling versus cohesion. Coupling is the degree to which components of a design depend on each other. Cohesion is determined by how tightly related or focused a single component is. Coupling and cohesion are traditional design principles for component-based design.

Tight coupling implies that a component interacts with many other components. A good design should limit the coupling of components.

Loosely coupled systems are easier to maintain, to test, and to recover. It also facilitates implementing core performance capabilities such as parallelization, which reduces overall runtimes and demand on resources.

The best-practice design techniques for coupling and cohesion are to

- Limit coupling by decomposing where possible the design into smaller, logical parts.
- Ensure that the smaller parts work well together (e.g., are highly cohesive).

Key Component-Based Physical Designs Creation Task Steps

The three steps in ensuring that the data integration processes have been made as modular for componentization as possible are as follows:

1. **Review across the data integration reference architecture for further componentization opportunities**—The purpose of this step is to determine additional decomposition of logical model designs into physical components, such as any specific extract or load logic that could be leveraged at an enterprise or application level.

2. **Review data integration models for further componentization**—The purpose of this step is to determine if there is any opportunity to split components within a model or layer. The classic example is separating technical and business data quality into separate components, embedding the technical data quality with the source system extract data integration models that will need that subject area focus and moving the business data quality functionality into its own enterprise-level common component data integration model.

3. **Design parameterization into the data integration models for maximum reuse**—Once all the data integration models have been componentized as much as possible, review the entire job flow of data integration model designs for the opportunity to maximize the use of parameterization (depending on the data integration technology used), providing the potential for as much future reuse as possible.

   It is important to note that this task is iterative in nature and can be performed before or after the data integration models are instantiated in the selected technology.

Preparing the DI Development Environment

This task ensures that adequate facilities are provided to allow the data integration development and testing activities to be carried out effectively. It covers the provisioning of physical facilities such as work areas and workstations as well as system facilities such as the data integration software, test databases, component libraries, and tools for the generation and preparation of data integration application.

NOTE

This task is unnecessary if the environment was configured in the data integration logical design phase.

The design and development environment needs to ensure that the designer/developer will be able to convert the logical data integration models into physical data integration model/jobs in the intended data integration software for each of the various layers of the data integration reference architecture, as shown in Figure 9.1.

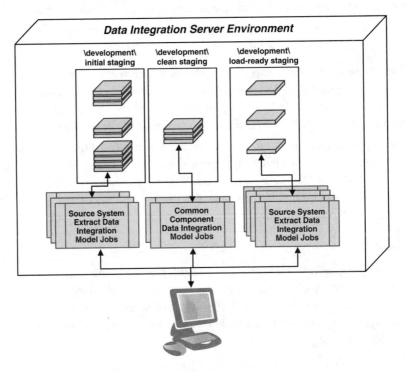

Figure 9.1   Data integration server development environment

Key Data Integration Development Environment Preparation Task Steps

Preparing the data integration development environment includes the following steps:

1. **Load and configure the data integration software**—In this step, the selected data integration software should be loaded and configured with the following activities:

    a. Load the data integration architecture software.

    b. Configure the software to the staging directories.

    c. Configure the software to the required source system directories, databases, and file systems.

    d. Test the software through the network and middleware.

    e. Configure the software to the planned target databases, development, test, and production.

2. **Establish transformation environment constraints**—This task establishes the security and system constraints in the development environment. It should be noted that there will be different levels of security based on the environment (development, test, production).

3. **Create DDL for tables to be loaded and alter/create tables in the development environment**—Create and configure the development target database.

4. **Check out of source control, any existing scripts, jobs, or components that will be used/modified**—This step is for existing data integration environments that have pre-built data integration components established in a source configuration management repository.

5. **Obtain and validate initial sample data**—Obtain test data from the source systems that represents a sufficient sample size of data that will used to test the source extract logic, test the technical and business data quality checkpoints, exercise the transformations, and provide the ability to test referential integrity in the subject area load jobs.

Creating Physical Data Integration Models

The purpose of this task is to convert the logical data integration models into the selected data integration technology, while at the same time apply the target-based, component-based design technique discussed in Chapter 3.

There have been a number of discussions about the need for componentization and modularity threaded throughout the book. Why the emphasis? The nature of the design and development approaches used in data integration development to date have relied on traditional development techniques, and to truly take advantage of both the data integration architecture and modeling technique, the final aspects of design and development cannot use those traditional methods.

Point-to-Point Application Development—The Evolution of Data Integration Development

First, what are those traditional design and development techniques for data integration?

Data integration development techniques have evolved out of traditional application development disciplines. As the discipline of data warehousing developed in the late 1980s and early 1990s, data sources were few, the data volumes small, and load frequencies were monthly or quarterly. With these low expectations, the need for a well-thought-out, scalable architecture for integrating data into a data warehouse is not required based on the low volumes and frequencies.

Original development techniques used were the point-to-point application development processes based on either traditional 3GLs such as COBOL or Java™ or simple procedural SQL scripts written by database administrators. These traditional development approaches led to the design and development of very linear or serial data integration processes that do not promote highly scalable, reusable components, as displayed in Figure 9.2.

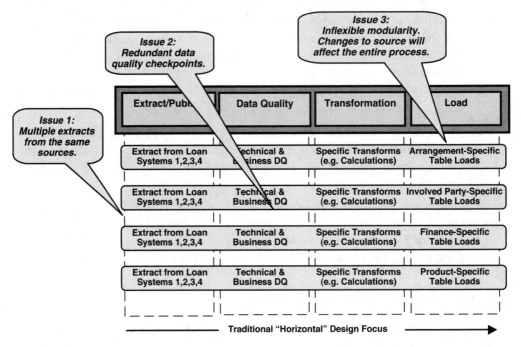

Figure 9.2   Issues with point-to-point data integration development

One of the major reasons for data integration modeling is to encourage modular designs based on the data integration reference architecture and away from point-to-point design.

In physical data integration design, there is the temptation to abandon the component approach taken in logical data integration modeling and design the processes in the technology using the old point-to-point approach. It is at this stage in design that taking logical designs and incorporating them into the selected technology, with that extra vigilance of following the rules of modularity, will ensure highly maintainable and reusable components, as shown in Figure 9.3.

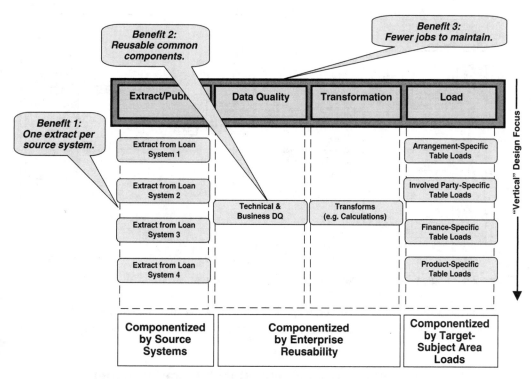

Figure 9.3   Target state of componentized data integration processes

The High-Level Logical Data Integration Model in Physical Design

In logical design, the high-level logical data integration model provided the context for the models/components needed for the final data integration application. However, there is no real need to extend or change this data integration model to instantiate the logical data integration models into the data integration development software package, as shown in Figure 9.4.

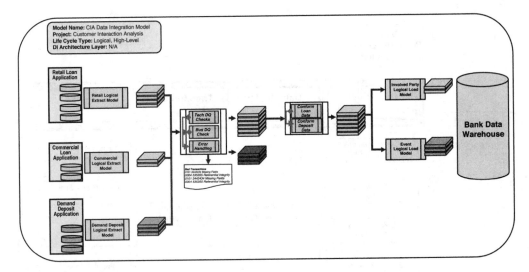

Figure 9.4   Logical high-level data integration model review

It is interesting to note that in certain projects, the high-level data integration model has still been built in the physical design model process for no other reason than to show the overall job flow and aid in the componentization process.

Design Physical Common Components Data Integration Models

The first step in developing physical data integration models is determining what data quality and transformations will be common and what should be moved to either source system extracts or subject area loads.

As discussed in Chapter 3, that certain data quality or transformation logic will only apply to a source system or subject area load and should be moved to that area of functionality, as displayed again in Figure 9.5.

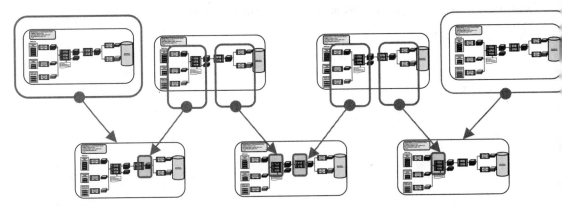

Figure 9.5   Logical to physical common componentization

There is no importance on whether to start with transformations or data quality in modularizing or componentizing the functionality for physical design.

The two steps for creating physical common components include the following:

1. **Partition the logical data quality data integration model**—Use the following steps to partition the logical data quality model shown in Figure 9.6:

   a. Sort and segment the logical data quality checkpoints, first by source, second by subject area.

   b. Consolidate and review nonsource system data quality into either common technical or business data quality components.

   c. Prepare to incorporate those source system data quality components into the appropriate physical source system extract models.

   d. Create or modify/extend the enterprise-level technical data quality components in the appropriate data integration development package.

   e. Create or modify/extend the enterprise-level business data quality components in the appropriate data integration development package.

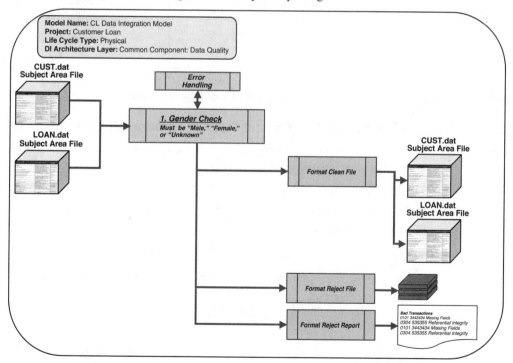

Figure 9.6 Physical data quality common component data integration model sample

2. **Partition the logical transformation data integration model**—Use similar steps to partition the logical transformation model (Figure 9.7):

a. Sort and segment the logical transformations by source subject area load.

b. Prepare to incorporate those subject area transformation components into the appropriate physical subject area load models.

c. Create or modify/extend the enterprise-level transformation components in data integration development software package.

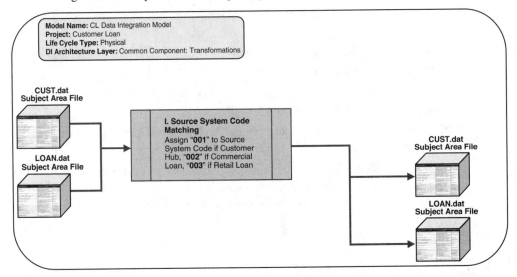

Figure 9.7   Physical transforms common component data integration model sample

Design Physical Source System Extract Data Integration Models

The physical source system extraction data integration model task starts with the logical extract model and instantiates that logic into the selected data integration technology package. The logic is typically componentized into three logical units of work:

• The extract, file/capture logic

• The subject area file conforming logic

• The source system data quality logic (from the logical data quality data integration model)

The method for creating these components will differ slightly from each of the commercial data integration software packages.

The steps for creating a physical source system extract data integration model (illustrated in Figure 9.8) include

1. Instantiate the base physical source system data integration model into the data integration development software package.

2. Instantiate the extract, file/capture logic into the physical source system data integration model.

3. Instantiate the subject area file conforming logic into the physical source system data integration model.

4. Include the source system data quality logic from the logical data quality data integration model.

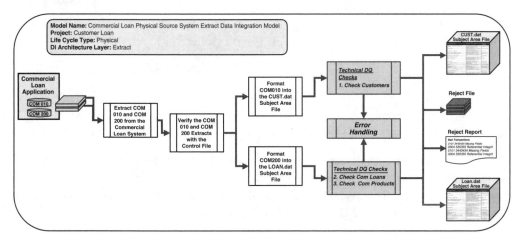

Figure 9.8   Physical source system extract data integration model sample

Design Physical Subject Area Load Data Integration Models

The physical subject area load data integration modeling task converts the logical load data integration model into the selected data integration technology package componentized by subject area. During this activity, the specific transformations for that subject area are applied within that subject area load data integration model, as shown in Figure 9.9.

The three substeps for creating the physical source system extract data integration model include the following:

*   Create the base physical subject area load data integration model into the data integration development software package.

*   Include the subject area transformation logic from the logical transformation data integration model.

*   Instantiate the subject area load logic into the physical source system data integration model from the logical extract data integration model by subject area.

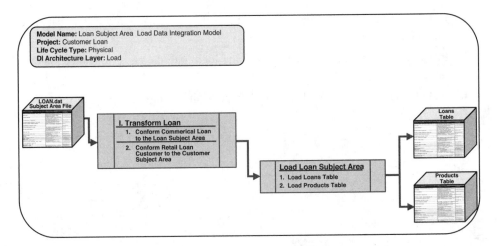

Figure 9.9   Physical subject area load data integration model sample

It is important to consider the run order of the table loads in terms of referential integrity of the target database as the tables in the subject area are loaded. For example, it is important to first load the lookup tables, then base tables, and, finally, detail tables. This topic is discussed further in this chapter in the "Defining Data Integration Operational Requirements" section.

Designing Parallelism into the Data Integration Models

This task focuses on how to best optimize the execution of data integration jobs through parallel processing.

The concept of parallel processing was first discussed in Chapter 7, "Data Integration Logical Design," while discussing the partitioning of staged data. Parallel processing is the ability to break large data integration processes and/or data into smaller pieces that are run in parallel, thereby reducing overall runtime, as demonstrated in Figure 9.10.

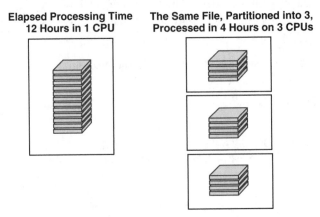

Figure 9.10   File-based parallel processing example

Types of Data Integration Parallel Processing

Although each of the data integration development software packages provides a different view on how to best implement parallel processing, there are two common approaches to parallelizing a data integration application: between data integration processes and within a data integration process, which are discussed in the following sections.

Between Data Integration Processes

The first approach is demonstrated in the following scenario, where there are three source systems that need to be extracted for downstream processing:

- A customer file system—4 hours
- A commercial loan system—5 hours
- A retail loan system—3 hours

If these data integration processes are executed serially, the elapsed runtime would take 12 hours; however, if these processes are run in parallel, the elapsed time is only 5 hours, as displayed in Figure 9.11.

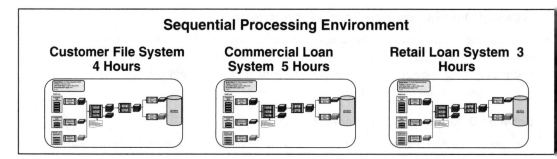

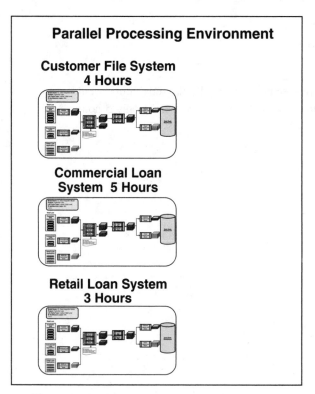

Figure 9.11   Sequential versus parallel process processing

Within a Data Integration Process

The second approach is to parallelize where possible within a data integration process. This normally revolves around parallel processing large data sets. Using the prior scenario, the longest running data integration process was the five-hour commercial loan system. Upon further analysis, it is found that the reason for the five-hour runtime is that the commercial loan file is 250GB. If the file can be partitioned into five segments and run in five separate partitions, the overall elapsed time for the commercial loan extract processing will be reduced to only one hour, as shown in Figure 9.12.

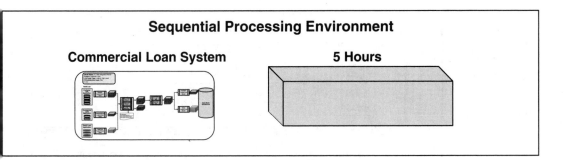

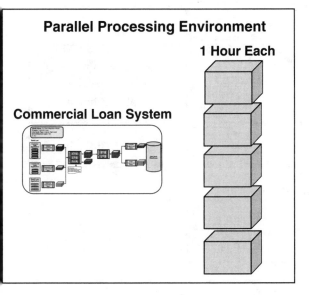

Figure 9.12   Sequential versus parallel file processing

Using these two approaches, a data integration architect should be able to review the entire data integration process flow for opportunities to optimize using parallel processing techniques. Figure 9.13 portrays the optimized extract processing along with the underlying physical environment needed for that processing.

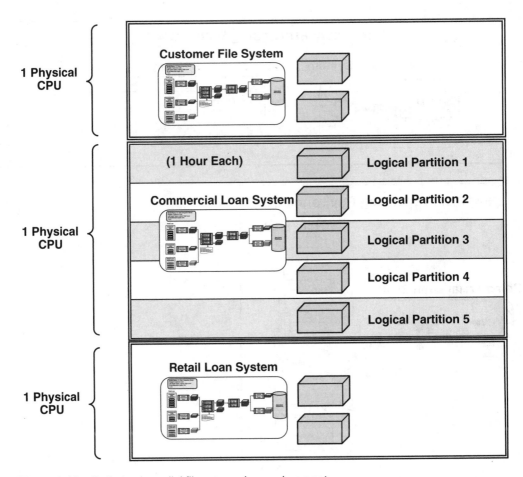

Figure 9.13   Optimized parallel file processing environment

It should be noted again that the technical implementation of each of these two approaches is highly dependent on the selected data integration technology package.

Other Parallel Processing Design Considerations

Parallelization design is also based on a combination of the following factors:

- The degree of parallelization must be a divisor or multiple of the number of available CPUs in the server.
- The number of potential logical partitions in the CPU must be accounted for in determining the logical constraint in terms of processing capability.
- The total data volumes and frequencies are another factor in the formula in terms of the size of the data compared with the size of the network pipe. Frequency refers to how often the data is being pushed through that network pipe.

Optimizing parallel performance includes the following:

• Selecting an intelligent key for partitioning of data

• Avoiding hot spot data access

Parallel processing, like other complex design techniques, is not a "one and done" task. Usually, a good first cut at a parallel design is required based on the parameters discussed previously. However, each environment with its data volumes, frequencies, and types of processing will be different and require its own set of metrics for parallel processing. This is the reason that after the initial test, there will be a number of performance tuning cycles based on test runs with test data in the development environment.

Parallel Processing Pitfalls

Setting up parallel processing must be a well-thought-through design process. Poorly designed parallel processing environments often perform less efficiently than a finely tuned sequential process.

When implementing parallel processing, the *entire* work flow must be considered to prevent creating bottlenecks along the path, as displayed in Figure 9.14.

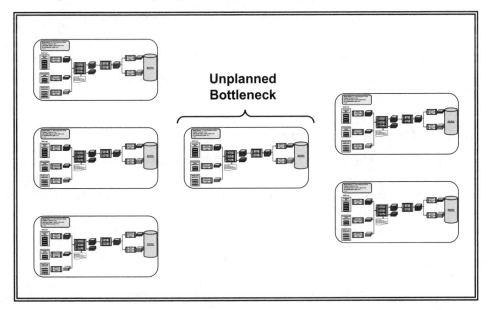

Figure 9.14   Examples of parallel processing issues

The final comment on parallel processing is that it should be apparent that in order to run data integration processes in parallel, it is critical to have the jobs as modular as possible, the common theme in the early part of this chapter.

Key Parallelism Design Task Steps

The two steps for designing parallelism into the data integration design are as follows:

1. **Designing parallelism between data integration processes**—In this step, the data integration job flow is reviewed for opportunities for running multiple jobs simultaneously and, where appropriate, configures those jobs for parallelism. Steps in this activity include the following:

   a. Review the entire job flow.

   b. Identify and configure those data integration processes for parallel processing.

   c. Test (in the development environment) parallel process, tune any potential bottlenecks.

   d. Configure job schedule and/or data integration software package parameters (package-specific).

2. **Designing parallelism within a data integration process**—This step parallelizes the processes within a data integration process. Steps in this activity include the following:

   a. Review any subprocesses or components within a data integration process.

   b. Review the input files for segmentation for parallel processing.

   c. Plan test for running parallelization within a data integration process.

   d. Configure job schedule and/or data integration software package parameters (package-specific).

Designing Change Data Capture

The focus of this task is how to best capture the transactional changes generated in the transactional databases periodically for the target analytic (e.g., data warehouse, data mart) database.

One of the most complex challenges in data integration is how to update the target data warehouse with transactional changes. Every day the transactional systems generate new transactions that create new records, edit records, and delete records, as shown in Figure 9.15.

Existing Data Warehouse

Record Number	Date	Transaction Amount	Status	Customer Name
001	06/02/2005	$15,000	New	JP Morgan
002	06/02/2005	$35,000	Open	Citicorp
003	06/02/2005	$27,000	Open	Wachovia

Changed Transactions

Record Number	Date	Transaction Amount	Status	Customer Name	
004	06/07/2005	$29,000	Edit	Wachovia	Edit Transaction
005	06/07/2005	$40,000	New	Wells Fargo	New Transaction
006	06/07/2005	$35,000	Del	Citicorp	Delete Transaction

Figure 9.15   Changed transactions

Change Data Capture is the technique to capture those transactions and apply them to the target database. There are two basic approaches for capturing and applying the edited, new, and deleted transaction records:

- **Overwrite Change Data Capture approach**—This approach, illustrated in Figure 9.16. simply replaces the existing data with a complete "refresh."

Record Number	Date	Transaction Amount	Status	Customer Name
001	06/02/2005	$15,000	New	JP Morgan
002	06/02/2005	$35,000	Open	Citicorp
003	06/02/2005	$27,000	Open	Wachovia
004	06/07/2005	$29,000	Edit	Wachovia
005	06/07/2005	$40,000	New	Wells Fargo
006	06/07/2005	$35,000	Del	Citicorp

Record Number	Date	Transaction Amount	Status	Customer Name
001	06/02/2005	$15,000	New	JP Morgan
002	06/02/2005	$35,000	Open	Citicorp
003	06/02/2005	$27,000	Open	Wachovia

Figure 9.16   Overwrite Change Data Capture approach

Although it is a simple method of updating data, it is not very practical for large transactional systems. The refresh approach is most often used for reference data Change Data Capture updating.

- **Append Change Data Capture approach**—This Change Data Capture approach shown in Figure 9.17 updates the database with the transactional changes only.

Record Number	Date	Transaction Amount	Status	Customer Name
001	06/02/2005	$15,000	New	JP Morgan
003	06/02/2005	$27,000	Open	Wachovia
004	06/07/2005	$29,000	Edit	Wachovia
005	06/07/2005	$40,000	New	Wells Fargo
006	06/07/2005	$35,000	Del	Citicorp

002	06/02/2005	$35,000	Open	Citicorp

Figure 9.17   Append Change Data Capture approach—moving only the transactional changes

Append Change Data Capture Design Complexities

The Append Change Data Capture approach is the method most used for systems with high-volume transactions. Although it is the more pragmatic method for high transactional systems, it requires more complex data integration design patterns and data structure to implement. There are several challenges, such as how to capture the new or changed transactions, how to mark and load the transactions into the target data model, and, finally, how to handle deleted transactions.

Capturing the New or Changed Transactions

The first step to Change Data Capture design is to determine how the new or changed transactions will be captured. There are several techniques and technologies to perform this task, including the following:

- **Log scrapers**—This technique takes the changed data from the transaction logs of the relational database. While appearing simple, this process cannot affect or, worse yet, impact the transactional system. Log scraping must also ensure that as it captures and moves sets of data, it does not miss transactions in a capture or capture the same transaction twice, creating a data anomaly.

- **File-to-file matching**—This technique saves a transaction file for a time period, say a day, and uses that file the next day to compare the two files and sort the changes into a Change Data Capture file. Although a relatively simple process, it is often not very practical due to the large size of some organizations' transaction files.

- **Commercial Change Data Capture applications**—Most of the commercial data integration software packages have either Change Data Capture built in to their platforms or provide add-on Change Data Capture functionality, each with different levels of functionality.

Designing the Target Data Model for Change Data Capture Transactions

For many reasons, including restart/recovery and time series analysis, the target data model will need an additional key to capture the version of the Change Data Capture update batch. The most common approach is to place a time stamp on the row of the changed data. The time stamp simply the reflects the time data was updated and is often the simplest approach to documenting the Change Data Capture and can leverage existing SQL-based database utilities such as Last Update to create the time stamp in the Change Data Capture process.

There are other patterns, which include using status indicators and version numbers. Each of these patterns can have multiple techniques associated with them in Change Data Capture processing.

Addressing Deleted Transactions

One of the complexities in the Append Change Data Capture approach is the issue of deleted transactions. The question has always been, "Do you leave the record out there in a changed state or physically remove the record from disk?" There are two basic delete transaction types based on that question:

- **Hard deletes**—Hard deletes physically remove existing records.

- **Soft deletes**—Soft deletes, shown in Figure 9.18, leave the record in a changed state.

Soft Delete

Record Number	Date	Transaction Amount	Status	Customer Name
001	06/02/2005	$15,000	New	JP Morgan
002	06/02/2005	$35,000	Open	Citicorp
003	06/02/2005	$27,000	Open	Wachovia
004	06/07/2005	$29,000	Edit	Wachovia
005	06/07/2005	$40,000	New	Wells Fargo
006	06/07/2005	$35,000	Del	Citicorp

Data Lineage

Figure 9.18   Lineage of deleted transactions

Although there are legitimate reasons for physically removing transactions, the best practice is to implement soft deletes due to the following reasons:

- **Traceability of the data lineage**—To have the ability to analyze and trace the life cycle of a transaction from new, to open, to close, the soft delete option is required.

- **Regulatory and tax reasons**—Often for tax reasons (e.g., previously mentioned seven years of history for the IRS) and Sarbanes-Oxley regulations, the soft delete approach must be used.

Do not underestimate the time it will take to thoroughly design and test the Change Data Capture process. It is highly recommended that it be prototyped with as large a set of test data as possible in this physical design phase to ensure that any data anomalies or design defects are caught now and not in the build or testing phase.

Key Change Data Capture Design Task Steps

The five steps required in developing a Change Data Capture design include the following:

1. **Determine Change Data Capture approach**—Determine whether it will be Overwrite or Append, based on table type (transactional or reference data).

2. **Determine Change Data Capture technique**—Determine what technique will be used to capture the changed or new transactions (e.g., log scraping).

3. **Design target data model for Change Data Capture batches**—Determine the design approach for the target data model (e.g., time stamp).

4. **Design tables**—Based on the target data model, design those tables (usually a subset).

5. **Prototype, evaluate, and complete the Change Data Capture design**—Model the Change Data Capture process with as wide a breadth of data as possible, tune and remediate where necessary, and prep the process for the final build phase.

NOTE

Because Change Data Capture is so specific to the environment and dependent on the technologies used, there will not be an exercise on it in the Wheeler case study.

Finalizing the History Conversion Design

This task converts the history conversion data integration model to the selected commercial data integration software and runs scenarios using prototyping techniques against the complex logic.

From Hypothesis to Fact

As stated in Chapter 7, history conversions are often the most difficult aspect of a data integration project. In physical design, the tasks are few but every bit as important as in logical design. It is important that after the designs are created in the commercial data integration package, that key transformation logic for each of the time periods of history are prototyped with sample data and results evaluated.

Isn't this just unit testing? Yes and no. Certain components (especially transformation logic) are being driven through to completion, but not the entire application, plus it provides the designer\developer the opportunity to confirm core data design assumptions before finalizing the code in the build cycle phase.

Why is this necessary? Because often despite all the time spent on profiling and mapping history to a new target, there are mistaken assumptions that can only be corrected by end users "seeing" the data. Often, the end users have not "seen" the data in the target database, and it is only when they can actually evaluate data in the target structures that they will be able to determine mistakes in the mappings of old history to the new target data model.

Finalize History Data Conversion Design Task Steps

Depending on the history conversion approach selected, there is a series of tasks, which include the following:

1. **Convert the logical design in to a physical design**—Instantiate the logical history data conversion model into the commercial data integration package, further componentized for performance where possible.

2. **Test the physical subject area load jobs with sample data**—Ensure that any load issues in regard to mapping are not a result of the history conversion but due to mapping issues in the load jobs first.

3. **Prototype the complex history load key logic**—Determine the potentially trouble-some areas for load logic, for example across subject area keys for each time period (such as month) and prototype those areas of functionality into run-ready jobs. Run these selected critical jobs through the subject area load jobs, ensuring that historical data is conformed as expected.

4. **Confirm results and prepare for final build**—Confirm the prototype results with both IT and business stakeholders to modify logic and code as needed.

Defining Data Integration Operational Requirements

This task specifies the operational requirements that are needed to run the data integration code in a production environment. This includes the numbers and types of resources needed and the impacts of the new code on the existing job schedule (if any), as well as production support and maintenance resource requirements. Do not underestimate or take lightly the time it will take to develop a job schedule and support team requirements.

Determining a Job Schedule for the Data Integration Jobs

Once in production, the data integration jobs must be scheduled to run in a particular sequence and time. There is nothing different about scheduling the execution of data integration jobs in comparison with other technologies; however, job scheduling is every bit as important in plan-ning and testing as the data integration jobs themselves.

Although the commercial data integration software packages all have their own job sched-uling software and also the ability to tie in to commercial job scheduling packages such as CA-7, Tivoli®, and CTL-M, the heavy lifting is in determining the job flow, documenting, and testing the schedule.

It is important to note that early perceptions of the success or more likely the lack of suc-cess in the new data integration application is often attributed to a poorly planned and tested job scheduling system. Job execution issues are just as often a result of a missing file or job being run out of sequence in the job schedule that results in a data quality issue as are coding or design defects. The following considerations need to be designed and tested for a complete job schedule:

- Determine the frequencies of the job runs, for example, daily, monthly, quarterly, or other. Determine if there are special runs that need to be scheduled.
- Define the high-level job process steps, for example:
  - Source-to-subject area files process
  - Subject area files-to-data warehouse process
  - Data warehouse-to-data mart process

- Determine the job sequences within each of the high-level steps. For example, in the commercial loan data warehouse case study, the source system extract jobs had a sequence that had to be run due to business logic reasons, as follows:

  1. Run Customer to have a baseline set of customer to reconcile against.

  2. Run Commercial Loans to have a baseline set of loans to reconcile against.

  3. Run Retail Loans.

  4. Confirm the run order for each of the data integration jobs within each of the job steps.

- For each job, develop a Job Run Check List that includes

  - Parameters settings (if any)

  - Source system data directory information and availability timing

  - Wrapper scripts

  - Business date logic

- For any additional application-level job, determine and develop additional processing activities, such as the following:

  - Archive and purge

  - Recovery and restart

  - Rerun procedures

  - Control file processing

    - Control file processing objective

    - Control file processing assumptions

    - Control file processing flow

  - Error reject file processing

  - Error reject file processing overview

  - Notification process

  - Error/reject file contents

Determining a Production Support Team

With a production schedule developed, the next operational requirement to determine is who will execute and monitor the data integration job runs. There are a number of initial considerations to determine when sizing a production support team:

- **Production support coverage hours**—The frequency of the data integration job runs (e.g., intraday) and when the input files are available (often late at night after daily transactional runs) will determine what type of coverage is required. Examples of coverage hours include

- 7 x 24 onsite
- 5 x 8 business hours
- 5 x 8 business hours with after-hours pager support and some weekend support
- **Data integration application size**—The number and complexity of the data integration jobs that make the data integration application factors in the number and type of support staff needed.
  - Number of applications/jobs/programs/databases/tables/etc.
  - Number of monthly job executions
  - Data volume: size of files/tables
  - Number of sources
  - Number of users/reports/output files/etc.
- **Stability**—Despite the best efforts, extremely complex data integration processes are more likely to fail than simpler processes, hence the purpose for using the data integration reference architecture to reduce complexity in the design and, hence, code. There are, however, certain business requirements that will create highly complex jobs that will create a higher level of production incidents. The following are the criteria that help determine stability:
  - Number of monthly production incidents by severity level
  - System uptime
  - History of downtime (application/databases/servers/network/DASD/etc.)
  - Problem areas
  - Currency of software (i.e., current or current minus one or older)
- **Rate of change**—Is the application fairly stable, or does it have a high level of complexity in terms of processes and data? Determine the rate of change by asking the following:
  - Number of changes being deployed or expected to be deployed into production
  - Quality of the changes being deployed
  - Number of development projects
  - Number of enhancements in pipeline

Following are some other support team size structure considerations:

- Enhancement activities—Will enhancement activities be in or out of scope for the support team? For example, will there be a pool of enhancement hours for changes/small enhancements requiring 40 hours or less, or as time permits, or absolutely no enhancements?
- Hardware and software upgrades and activities

- Maintenance windows
- Backup and recovery processes
- Capacity planning
- Disaster recovery exercises and participation

It is important also to consider whether this is a new department or organization or simply another data integration application being added to an existing portfolio of applications.

Key Data Integration Operational Requirements Task Steps

The following four steps in developing the data integration application operational requirements include the following:

1. **Develop a data integration job schedule**—Develop the schedule of what jobs and when those data integration jobs need to run. This includes the following steps:

    a. Document the frequency of the data integration job runs—The purpose of this step is to develop a first-cut data integration job schedule and plan on how to best sequence the workflow, such as daily, monthly, quarterly, or special runs.

    b. Determine the high-level jobs steps—For example, source-to-subject area files processing and/or subject area files to data warehouse.

    c. Determine the job sequences within each of the steps—For example, customer loads before transactions.

    d. For each job, develop a job run checklist—For example, what are the tasks to be run by a checklist?

    e. Determine application-level job processing activities—For example, archive and purge or control file processing.

2. **Review impact on contingency plans**—The purpose of this step is to determine how the new data integration application "fits" into the existing contingency plans.

3. **Review impact on capacity plans**—The purpose of this step is to confirm that the sizing determined in logical design is vetted and built in to the final production support processes.

4. **Determine operations resource requirements**—The purpose of this step is to determine the resources needed to execute and, if needed, correct execution issues in the data integration jobs.

Designing Data Integration Components for SOA

This task reviews the physical data integration models for potential reuse in an SOA-enabled framework and then reviews what tasks are necessary to ensure the SOA enablement.

Leveraging Traditional Data Integration Processes as SOA Services

As discussed in Chapter 2, "An Architecture for Data Integration," service-oriented architecture (SOA) is a standard framework for components to interact over a network and is a recognized data integration pattern. As batch, real-time, and other data integration patterns converge due to technology advancements and business needs, the ability to leverage the data integration processes as SOA components will continue to move from "interesting technology abilities" to required capability.

Fitting Traditional Data Integration Processes into an SOA Architecture

The development of SOA components in the Information Technology press conjures discussions of modern custom application development languages such as Java and C#. However, one of the major premises of SOA is reusability of existing application logic.

One of the major premises of SOA is that components may be custom-built in-house components, in-house ERP application components, and outside-the-firewall applications such as Salesforce.com.

Based on this premise, components such as traditional data integration processes are ideal for being leveraged in an SOA environment, as displayed in Figure 9.19, where the data integration environment is connected to an SOA framework via an enterprise service bus providing access to traditional data integration processes.

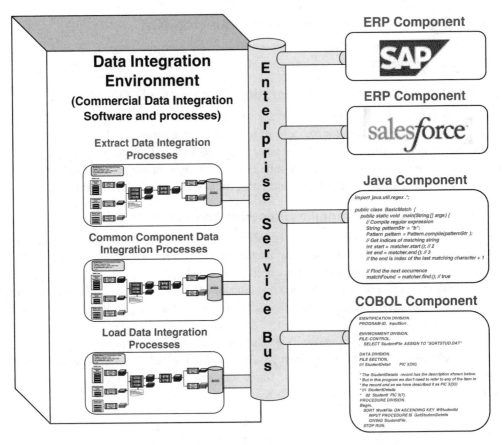

Figure 9.19   Traditional data integration processes in an SOA framework

Connecting Data Integration Processes into an SOA Framework

All of the major data integration software vendors (Informatica, Ab Initio, and IBM Data Stage) have built the SOA framework protocols into their core data integration process engines. Protocols such as Enterprise JavaBeans, Web Service Definition Language (WSDL), and Simple Object Access Protocol (SOAP) provide other SOA components connected to the enterprise service bus the ability to invoke or execute the SOA-enabled data integration processes on the data integration server.

What Data Integration Processes to Use in an SOA Framework?

By designing highly modular data integration processes using the data integration framework and the design techniques discussed for both logical and physical data integration design, the resulting data integration job code can be easily leveraged as both coarse-grained (general) and fine-grained (specific) SOA components. Examples of both types include the following:

- **Coarse-grained SOA object**—A source system extract job. One that performs the three tasks of every source system job: extracts the data, conforms the data, and checks the technical data quality.

- **Fine-grained SOA object**—The gender data quality common component job, which performs one and only one task.

Appropriate Data Integration Job Types

Based on the data integration reference architecture and business requirements, there are ample types of data integration jobs that would be appropriate candidates for being leveraged in an SOA framework; however, there are three design patterns that would have specific applicability:

- **Source system extract data integration jobs**—Following the best practice of "Read once, write many," for nondata warehouse applications that may need to use source system data, having the ability to execute these types of data integration processes would provide value.

- **Common component data integration jobs**—These data integration jobs, based on their component-based design, are particularly well fitted for being leveraged in an SOA environment.

- **Data access processes**—By leveraging the subject area load data mappings, data access data integration jobs can be easily built to extract data from the target database through data integration jobs instantiated through an SOA framework.

At the time of this writing, leveraging data integration code on an SOA enterprise service bus as a service is not widely used in many organizations but is expected to become more prevalent in the future.

Key Data Integration Design for SOA Task Steps

The three steps for using the data integration jobs in an SOA framework are as follows:

1. **Review the designed data integration application for appropriate leverage in an SOA framework**—The purpose of this step is to evaluate the entire data integration application for fit of use in an SOA environment.

2. **Determine which physical data integration model designs would be appropriate as course-grained SOA components in an SOA framework**—The purpose of this step is to determine if there is business need for such a general data integration component.

3. **Determine physical components for SOA**—The purpose of this step is to determine which physical data integration model designs would be appropriate as fine-grained SOA components in an SOA framework based on business need for such a specific-purpose data integration component.

Any changes necessary for these data integration processes to be leveraged in an SOA framework should be based on any impact for the original business and technical purpose of the process.

Summary

This chapter covered the physical design tasks, steps, and techniques necessary to complete the design for a data integration solution and prepare it for final build tasks. It also covered the need to analyze from multiple dimensions the need to modularize the design into compact components and then how to apply those techniques in the conversion from logical data integration models to physical data integration models instantiated in the intended commercial data integration software.

It discussed how to use those design components to determine parallel processing techniques, used to optimize performance.

The chapter covered the complexities of Change Data Capture and reviewed the technical approaches to capture new transactional history.

It reviewed the need to verify the expected results of the history conversion in the physical design phase to ensure that the conversion results have been cleaned and verified prior to the final build and test tasks.

The chapter covered the individual specifications for job scheduling and production support staffing for ongoing operational requirements.

Finally, the chapter covered the potential for leveraging the data integration model designs as SOA components within an SOA framework. It reviewed how certain data integration jobs could fulfill the requirements of both course-grained and fine-grained SOA components.

Chapter 10, "Data Integration Physical Design Case Study," applies the physical design tasks and techniques discussed in this chapter to refine the Wheeler logical design deliverables into physical design artifacts and prepare the Wheeler operations team for running these data integration jobs.

End-of-Chapter Questions

Question 1.
Define coupling and cohesion.
Question 2.
Define the two types of parallel processing discussed in the chapter.
Question 3.
What are the factors for which parallelization design is based?
Question 4.
For Change Data Capture, what are three of the methods discussed on capturing the changed transactions?
Question 5.
What would be appropriate candidates for leveraging data integration jobs in an SOA environment?

CHAPTER 10

Data Integration Physical Design Case Study

The physical design case study in this chapter refines the Wheeler order management logical data integration models into physical data integration model components and instantiates them into the selected data integration technology.

Step 1: Create Physical Data Integration Models

The first task is to incorporate all the requirements for the Wheeler data integration processes in a design blueprint, the physical data integration model.

Instantiating the Logical Data Integration Models into a Data Integration Package

Every "what" (e.g., transform type) has a "how" in the commercial data integration software package. Expertise in these technologies is a function of both training and experience. Having designers with the experience and training in the package is critical to the success of developing physical data integration models.

The Wheeler physical data integration models will be created for these examples in a generic data integration technology to emulate a commercial data integration package, as shown in Figure 10.1.

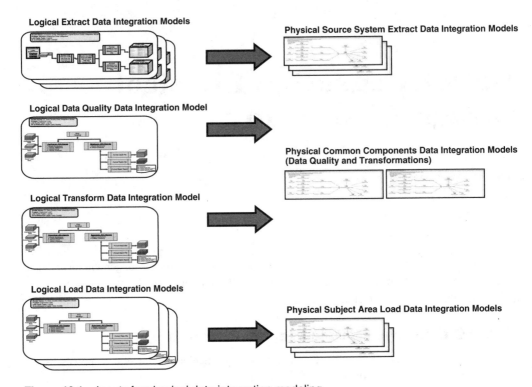

Figure 10.1   Inputs for physical data integration modeling

As in logical design, the end of physical design needs some level of sign-off on the physical data integration models and operational requirements.

Design Physical Common Components Data Integration Models

The first step in developing the Wheeler physical data integration models is applying the component techniques against the logical data quality and then transformation models to determine what is common and what is source-specific or subject area-specific.

Determine the local versus common data quality components by taking the logical data quality data integration model through the following steps:

1. Sort and segment the logical data quality checkpoints, first by source, second by subject area, which results in the following:

    *   Technical Data Quality Checkpoints
        *   Domestic Order Management Extract
            a.   Customer
            b.   Product
            c.   Order
        *   Asian Order Management Extract

          a.   Customer

          b.   Product

          c.   Order

- European Order Management Extract

          a.   Customer

          b.   Product

          c.   Order

- Business Data Quality Checkpoints
  - Check Customer Gender
  - Check Products Source System Id

2. Consolidate and review nonsource system data quality into either common technical or business data quality components.

3. Prepare to incorporate the Wheeler source system data quality components into the appropriate physical source system extract models (see the next section).

4. Create or modify/extend the Wheeler enterprise-level business data quality components in the appropriate data integration development package illustrated in Figure 10.2.

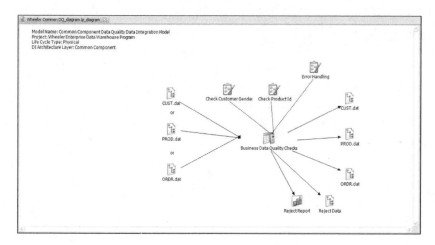

Figure 10.2   The Wheeler data quality common component data integration model sample

Next partition the Wheeler logical transformation data integration model through similar steps:

1. Sort and segment the logical Wheeler transformations, by source subject area load, which results in:

- Customer Subject Area
  - Conform Domestic Order Management
  - Conform Asian Order Management
  - Conform European Order Management
- Product Subject Area
  - Conform Domestic Order Management
  - Conform Asian Order Management
  - Conform European Order Management
- Order Subject Area
  - Conform Domestic Order Management
  - Conform Asian Order Management
  - Conform European Order Management

2. Prepare to incorporate those subject area transformation components into the appropriate physical subject area load models.

For the Wheeler source-to-EDW data integration processes, there is only one enterprise level, common transformation component, which is illustrated in Figure 10.3.

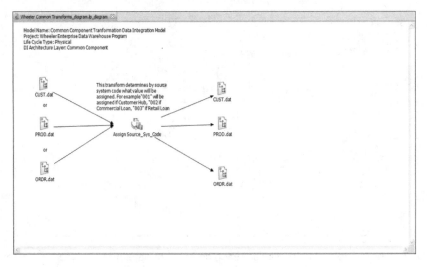

Figure 10.3   The Wheeler transform common component data integration model sample

Design Physical Source System Extraction Data Integration Models

The second step is to create the Wheeler physical source system extract model by instantiating the extract and conforming logic for each of the three sources into three jobs of the selected data integration software package with the following steps:

1. Create the base physical source system data integration model into the data integration development software package, which includes the following:
   - Domestic Order Management Source System Extract job
   - Asian Order Management Source System Extract job
   - European Order Management Source System Extract job
2. Instantiate the extract, file/capture logic into each of the three Wheeler data integration jobs.
3. Instantiate the subject area file conforming logic into each of the three Wheeler data integration jobs.
4. Include the source system data quality logic from the logical data quality data integration model for each of the three Wheeler data integration jobs, as illustrated in Figures 10.4, 10.5, and 10.6.

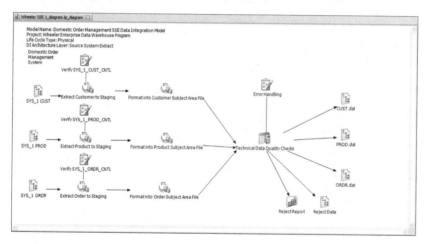

Figure 10.4   Wheeler Domestic Order Management System physical source system extract data integration model

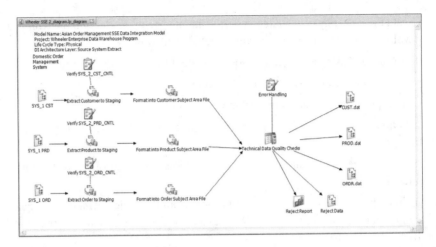

Figure 10.5   Wheeler Asian Order Management System physical source system extract data integration model

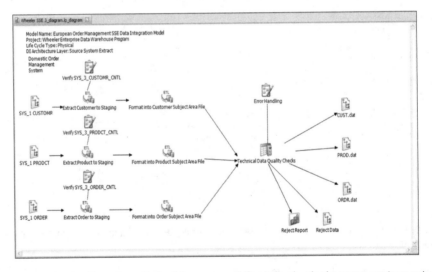

Figure 10.6   Wheeler European Order Management System physical source system extract data integration model

Design the Physical Subject Area Load Data Integration Model

The third step converts the Wheeler logical load data integration models into the selected data integration technology package componentized by subject area and then adds the three subject area specific transformations that are illustrated in the three subject area load physical data integration models in Figures 10.7, 10.8, and 10.9.

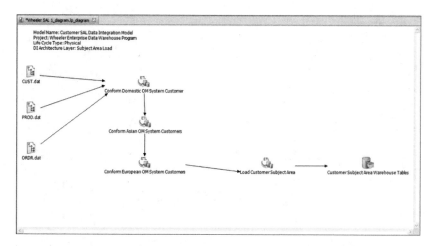

Figure 10.7   Physical customer subject area load data integration model

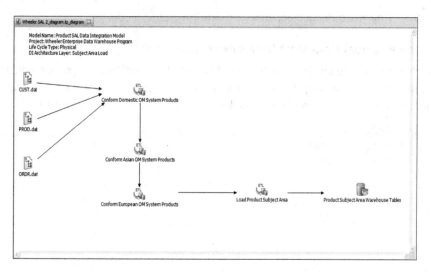

Figure 10.8   Physical product subject area load data integration model

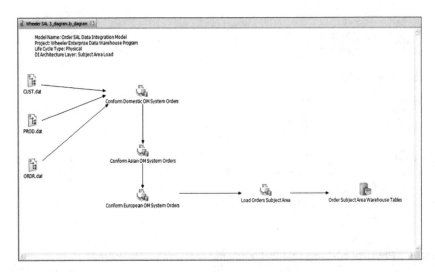

Figure 10.9   Physical order subject area load data integration model

Design the Physical Data Mart Data Integration Model

The fourth and final step involves the Wheeler EDW-to-data mart data integration model, which was designed as a stand-alone process, and for physical design simply needs to be converted into the commercial data integration software package as a job, as shown in Figure 10.10.

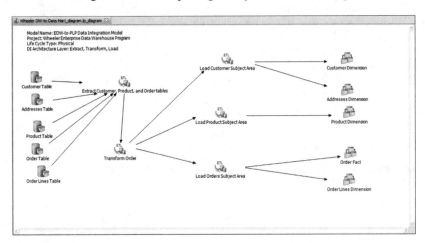

Figure 10.10   Wheeler enterprise data warehouse to product line profitability data mart data integration model

Once implemented in the commercial data integration software, the Wheeler EDW-to-data mart data integration model is ready for any final build tasks and testing.

Step 2: Find Opportunities to Tune through Parallel Processing

Step 2 reviews the entire job flow of the Wheeler data integration process and looks for opportunities to improve performance with parallel processing. In logical design, the volumetrics sizing determined that the Domestic Order file would be 600GB per run, taking at least three hours, as shown in Figure 10.11.

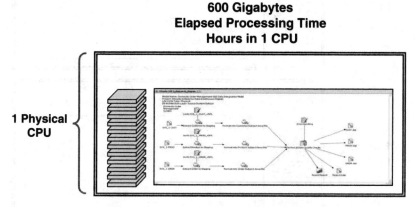

Figure 10.11   Domestic OM source system extract before parallelism

By splitting the file and running it in parallel on separate CPUs, the estimated Domestic Order Management extract time would be reduced to one hour, as shown in Figure 10.12.

**The same file, partitioned into 3,
processed in 4 hours on 3 CPUs.**

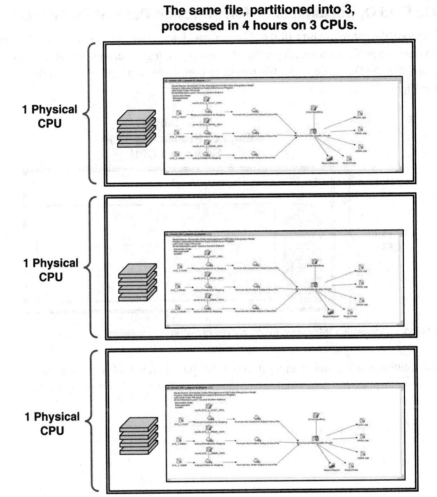

**1 Physical
CPU**

**1 Physical
CPU**

**1 Physical
CPU**

Figure 10.12   Domestic OM source system extract after parallelism

Step 3: Complete Wheeler History Conversion Design

Step 3 converts the Wheeler history conversion data integration model to the selected commercial data integration software; afterwards, a series of test scenarios will be run with known control totals to verify each month's run along with reviews of critical fields. Step 3's activities include the following:

1. **Convert the logical design into a physical design**—We are able to leverage the Domestic Order Management physical source system extract model as a base for the conversion of the history model due to using similar source data.

The sources in the diagram simply need to be repointed to the history tables, as illustrated in Figure 10.13.

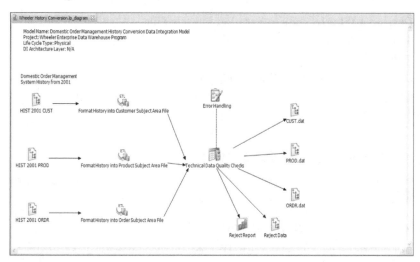

Figure 10.13 Wheeler history conversion data integration model

| Domestic Order History 2001 Month 1 | | | | | |
Order_Number	Order_Line_Number	Product_Id	Product_Price	Quantity_Ordered	Line_Amount
1101	1		$135	1,000	$135,000
1102	1	Extra field	$89	450	$40,050
1103	1	1112	$147	670	$98,490
1104	1	1112	$147	874	$128,478
1105	1	1112	$147	343	$50,421
1106	1	1111	$135	1,222	$164,970
ax08*	1107	1	1112	$147	350
1108	1	1113	$89	560	$49,840
1109	1	1111	$135	760	$102,600
1110	1	1113	$89	1,343	$119,527

Figure 10.14 Wheeler history conversion prototype test results

2. **Test the physical subject area load jobs with sample data**—To ensure that any load issues in regard to mapping the Wheeler Domestic Order Management history is not a result of the history conversion but due to mapping issues in the load jobs first, we will test key logic and critical fields.

Figure 10.14 demonstrates as expected that despite the best efforts of the data mappers and business analyst, data anomalies will be found. It is best to correct these anomalies in the source system before executing the history load.

Step 4: Define Data Integration Operational Requirements

Step 4 defines the operation requirements for the Wheeler data integration process. First, a job schedule will be produced for the monthly run of the Wheeler data integration application and then a proposed production support organizational model will be developed, which will address the following tasks:

1. **Develop a Wheeler data integration job schedule**—What are the jobs, and when are they executed? A sample job schedule for the Wheeler data integration jobs is included in the following section.

2. **Determine operations resource requirements**—The purpose of this step is to determine the resources needed to execute and, if needed, correct execution issues in the data integration jobs.

Developing a Job Schedule for Wheeler

The Wheeler data integration jobs must be scheduled to run in a particular sequence and time. The following sections include instructions for loading the Wheeler data warehouse.

The Wheeler Monthly Job Schedule

The Wheeler enterprise data warehouse (**EDW**) monthly load process gathers extract files from the three order management source systems (Domestic, Asian, and European), conforms them into three subject area (**SA**) files (Customer, Product, and Order), and then loads those files into the EDW via subject area load jobs. After completion of the load of the EDW, a final process extracts data from the EDW and loads it into the product line profitability data mart customer profitability dimensional data mart.

This schedule will be documented by the sequential steps of this monthly process. At a high level, these include the following:

Process Step 1: Perform job execution preparation.

Process Step 2: Execute source system to subject area file jobs.

Process Step 3: Execute subject area files to EDW load jobs.

Process Step 4: Execute EDW to product line profitability data mart jobs.

The Wheeler Monthly Job Flow

Figure 10.15 illustrates the monthly Wheeler job schedule.

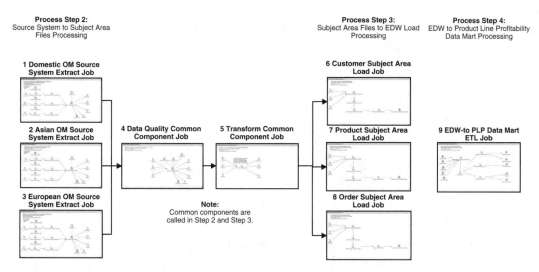

Figure 10.15   Wheeler monthly job diagram

Process Step 1: Preparation for the EDW Load Processing

These are the tasks that need to be performed prior to the execution of the daily run:

Task 1: Set the date and run parameters
1.   Set the batch date and run number
2.   Verify the batch date and run number

Task 2: Verify the extract files
1.   The Domestic Order Management System, with the following files:

•   System 1 Customer File

•   System 1 Rubber Product File

•   System 1 Order File

2.   The Asian Order Management System, with the following files:

•   System 2 Customer File

•   System 2 Wheels Product File

•   System 2 Order File

3.   The European Order Management System, with the following files:

•   System 3 Customer File

•   System 3 Bearing Product File

•   System 3 Order File

Process Step 2: Source System to Subject Area File Processing

These are the jobs that take the extract files from the Wheeler source systems and conform them to the EDW subject area files.

Run Source to Subject Area Jobs Checklist

These are the source-to-SA jobs in order of execution:

     ___ **Wheeler_SSE1.job**

     ___ **Wheeler_SSE2.job**

     ___ **Wheeler_SSE3.job**

     ___ **Wheeler_Common_DQ.job**

Detailed Source-to-Subject Area Jobs Checklist

Wheeler Domestic Order Management Source System Extract Job   Job   Name: Wheeler_SSE1.job

    Job Description: This job uses files from the Domestic Order Management System to create the corresponding subject area (SA) files.

    Input Files:

- SYS_1_CUST
- SYS_1_PROD
- SYS_1_ORDR

    The input files will be read by the Wheeler_SSE1.job from the \production\initial staging\ directory.

    External Calls:

- Wheeler_Common_DQ.job

    Control Files:

- SYS_1_CUST_CNTL
- SYS_1_PROD_CNTL
- SYS_1_ORDR_CNTL

    Output Files:

- CUST.dat
- PROD.dat
- ORD.dat

    The output file will be stored in the \production\clean staging\ directory.

    Additional Resources:

    The batch job requires no additional resources.

Expected Execution Time:

Based on expected volume and the parallelization steps, this batch job should execute for approximately 1 hour.

Wheeler Asian Order Management Source System Extract Job Overview   Job Name: Wheeler_SSE2.job

Job Description: This job uses files from the Asian Order Management System to create the corresponding subject area (SA) files.

Input Files:

- SYS_2_CST
- SYS_2_PRD
- SYS_2_ORD

The input files will be read by the Wheeler_SSE2.job from the \production\initial staging\ directory.

External Calls:

- Wheeler_Common_DQ.job

Control Files:

- SYS_2_CST_CNTL
- SYS_2_PRD_CNTL
- SYS_2_ORD_CNTL

Output Files:

- CUST.dat
- PROD.dat
- ORD.dat

The output file will be stored in the \production\clean staging\ directory.

Additional Resources:

The batch job requires no additional resources.

Expected Execution Time:

Based on expected volume and the parallelization steps, this batch job should execute for approximately 20 minutes.

Wheeler European Order Management Source System Extract Job Overview   Job Name: Wheeler_SSE3.job

Job Description: This job uses files from the European Order Management System to create the corresponding subject area (SA) files.

Input Files:

- SYS_3_CUSTOMR

- SYS_3_PRODCT
- SYS_3_ORDER

The input files will be read by the Wheeler_SSE3.job from the \production\initial staging\ directory.

External Calls:

- Wheeler_Common_DQ.job

Control Files:

- SYS_3_CUSTOMR_CNTL
- SYS_3_PRODCT_CNTL
- SYS_3_ORDER_CNTL

Output Files:

- CUST.dat
- PROD.dat
- ORD.dat

The output file will be stored in the \production\clean staging\ directory.

Additional Resources:

The batch job requires no additional resources.

Expected Execution Time:

Based on expected volume and the parallelization steps, this batch job should execute for approximately 30 minutes.

Wheeler Data Quality Common Component Job Overview
Job Name: Wheeler_Common_DQ.job

Job Description: This on-demand job checks, flags, and passes nonsource-specific data quality in the extracted data.

Input Files:

- CUST.dat
- PROD.dat
- ORD.dat

The input files will be read by the Wheeler_SSE3.job from the \production\initial staging\ directory.

External Calls:

- None

Control Files:

- SYS_3_CUSTOMR_CNTL
- SYS_3_PRODCT_CNTL
- SYS_3_ORDER_CNTL

Output Files:

- CUST.dat
- PROD.dat
- ORD.dat

The output file will be stored in the \production\clean staging\ directory.

Additional Resources:

The batch job requires no additional resources.

Expected Execution Time:

Based on expected volume and the parallelization steps, this batch job should execute for 15 to 20 minutes.

Process Step 3: Subject Area Files to EDW Load Processing

These are the jobs that take the EDW subject area files, apply subject-area specific transformations, and then load them to the EDW database tables.

Run Subject Area-to-EDW Jobs Checklist

These are the SA-to-EDW jobs in order of execution:

___ **Wheeler_SAL1.job**

___ **Wheeler_SAL2.job**

___ **Wheeler_SAL3.job**

___ **Wheeler_Common_Transforms.job**

Detailed Subject Area-to-EDW Jobs Checklist

Wheeler Customer Subject Area Load Job Overview   Job Name: Wheeler_SAL1.job

Job Description: This job uses the Common Transformation job to allocate source system IDs, then applies subject area specific transformation, and then loads the data into the Customer Subject Area tables.

Input Files:

- CUST.dat

The input files will be read by the Wheeler_SAL1.job from the \production\clean staging\ directory, landed temporarily if needed in the \production\load-ready staging directory.

External Calls:

- Wheeler_Common_Transforms.job

Output Files:

- \EDW database\Customer tables

The output file will be stored in the \production\load-ready staging\ directory.

Additional Resources:

The batch job requires no additional resources.

Expected Execution Time:

Based on expected volume, this batch job should execute for approximately 2 hours.

Wheeler Product Subject Area Load Job Overview   Job Name: Wheeler_SAL2.job

Job Description: This job uses the Common Transformation job to allocate source system IDs, then applies subject area specific transformation, and then loads the data into the Product Subject Area tables.

Input Files:

- PROD.dat

The input files will be read by the Wheeler_SAL2.job from the \production\clean staging\ directory, landed temporarily if needed in the \production\load-ready staging directory.

External Calls:

- Wheeler_Common_Transforms.job

Output Files:

- \EDW database\Product tables

The output file will be stored in the \production\load-ready staging\ directory.

Additional Resources:

The batch job requires no additional resources.

Expected Execution Time:

Based on expected volume, this batch job should execute for approximately 1 hour.

Wheeler Order Subject Area Load Job Overview   Job Name: Wheeler_SAL3.job

Job Description: This job uses the Common Transformation job to allocate source system IDs, then applies subject area specific transformation, and then loads the data into the Order Subject Area tables.

Input Files:

- ORDR.dat

The input files will be read by the Wheeler_SAL3.job from the \production\clean staging\ directory, landed temporarily if needed in the \production\load-ready staging directory.

External Calls:

- Wheeler_Common_Transforms.job

Output Files:

- \EDW database\Order tables

Additional Resources:

The batch job requires no additional resources.

Expected Execution Time:

Based on expected volume, this batch job should execute for approximately 3 hours.

Wheeler Transform Common Component Job Overview Job Name: Wheeler_Common_Transforms.job

Job Description: This on-demand job assigns "001" if Customer Hub, "002" if Commercial Loan, "003" if Retail Loan to the Source_Sys_Code field.

Input Files:

- CUST.dat
- PROD.dat
- ORD.dat

The input files will be read by the Wheeler_Common_Transforms.job from the \production\initial staging\ directory.

External Calls:

- None

Output Files:

- CUST.dat
- PROD.dat
- ORD.dat

The output file will be stored in the \production\transform staging\ directory.

Additional Resources:

The batch job requires no additional resources.

Expected Execution Time:

Based on expected volume, this batch job should execute between 20 and 30 minutes.

Process Step 4: EDW-to-Product Line Profitability Data Mart Load Processing

These are the jobs that extract EDW data and perform calculations and aggregations for downstream data marts.

Run EDW-to-PLP Data Mart Job Checklist

The only job is the Wheeler DW-to-Data Mart.job that is executed upon completion of the EDW loads.

Detailed EDW-to-Data Mart Jobs Checklist

Job Name: Wheeler DW-to-Data Mart.job

    Job Description: This job extracts EDW data, performs order line calculations and aggregations for customer product line profitability, and then loads the raw and calculated data into the product line profitability data mart.

    Input Files:

- \EDW database\Customer tables
- \EDW database\Product tables
- \EDW database\Order tables

    The input files will be read by the Wheeler DW-to-Data Mart.job from the \production\clean staging\ directory, landed temporarily if needed in the \production\load-ready staging directory.

    External Calls:

- Wheeler_Common_Transforms.job

    Output Files:

- \PLP Data Mart database\Customer dimension tables
- \PLP Data Mart database\Product dimension tables
- \PLP Data Mart database\Order fact table

    Additional Resources:

    The batch job requires no additional resources.

    Expected Execution Time:

    Based on expected volume, this batch job should execute for approximately 3 to 4 hours.

Production Support Staffing

Based on the daily and monthly frequency of the Wheeler data integration job runs, it is proposed that a three-person support team will be needed between the hours of 8:00 a.m. and 8:00 p.m. Monday through Friday with expectations of having to work one weekend a month.

Summary

The Wheeler physical design case study in this chapter used the Wheeler enterprise data warehouse logical data integration models created in Chapter 8, "Data Integration Logical Design Case Study," and created physical source system extract data integration models, physical common component data integration models, and, finally, subject area load data integration models. We also built a job schedule based on those intended Wheeler enterprise data warehouse data integration jobs.

Chapter 11, "Data Integration Development Cycle," focuses on taking the physical design deliverables and completing the build cycle Tasks. These tasks include any final development standards and best practices that need to be applied. The next chapter also reviews how to leverage prototyping techniques for final build and test activities.

Data Integration Development Cycle

One of the common themes in this book is that data integration is not traditional application development, where in the development phase there is still a considerable amount of work in terms of coding.

In data integration, the bulk of the work is completed prior to what is considered traditional development. The "diamond" nature of the data integration development life cycle places the bulk of the effort in the design phases, as illustrated in Figure 11.1.

Data Integration Development   Application Development

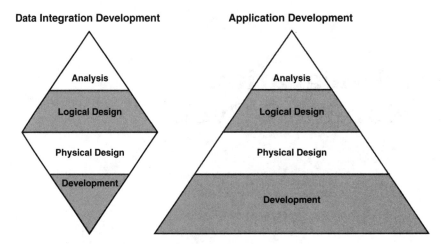

Figure 11.1   Application versus data integration development cycle

For the data integration Systems Development Life Cycle, the development phase completes any remaining final construction tasks for the data integration application and prepares the application's data integration jobs and runs scripts for the testing and configuration management tasks, which prepares the application for deployment.

These final development tasks include preparing the code for production and leveraging prototyping techniques to confirm the finalized code in development and test cycles. Prototyping (also called Agile development) is an excellent technique to confirm the entire application and pay particular attention to complex transformation logic and field mapping to ensure that they are correct not only to specifications, but to actual need, as shown in Figure 11.2.

Figure 11.2   Prototyping in the development phase

NOTE

Many of the final development tasks and activities are dependent on the commercial data integration software package selected for the project. This book discusses what those activities are without referring to any specific package. Refer to the user manuals of those packages for clarification on the implementation of those tasks and activities.

The tasks for the development cycle phase include the following:

1. Perform general data integration development activities.

2. Prototype a set of data integration functionality.

3. Complete/extend data integration job code.

   3.1   Complete/extend common components jobs.
   3.2   Complete/extend source system jobs.
   3.3   Complete/extend subject area load jobs.

4. Perform data integration testing.

   4.1   Perform data warehouse unit tests.
   4.2   Execute data warehouse integration tests.
   4.3   Perform data warehouse system and performance tests.
   4.4   Execute data warehouse user acceptance tests.

Performing General Data Integration Development Activities

The first task in the development phase focuses on ensuring that the data integration jobs are developed and/or completed using correct coding standards such as naming standards and error-handling procedures.

Data Integration Development Standards

The use of proper data integration development standards ensures that the production data integration job code is reliable and consistent, making the data integration jobs easier to understand, maintain, enhance, and adapt for reuse.

Many organizations have developed data integration Centers of Excellence to help architect and design data integration applications as well as help to enforce data integration development standards.

Adherence to coding standards also makes it easier to transition existing data integration jobs to other teams for deployment and transition. It reduces the time (and, hence, the cost) that data integration designers and developers must spend coming "up to speed" on existing data integration jobs. Good job coding standards include the following:

- **Job code structure**—The code within a data integration job should have a discernable structure. The use of the component-based design technique propagated from the analysis phase through the design phase using the data integration reference architecture should have influenced the creation of highly componentized jobs, functions, scripts, and other objects, which should be easily documented. Any code with these components should be composed of clearly defined, modular sections.

It is important in the development phase that any additional objects (e.g., scripts or data integration jobs) that need to be created are not "thrown together" but adhere to the component design patterns.

- **Job logs**—All data integration jobs should write operational information into a job log file. Information such as the status of the job, the sequence of steps and their completion, any errors, and all relevant information pertaining to the job should all be included in the job log as well as a job log purge strategy.

> **NOTE**
>
> Whenever possible, avoid cluttering the log file with repetitive information or information that would be of little use.

- **Variables and functions**—The names of global variables and functions in a data integration job should aid in understanding the job and its underlying code. Do not use terse, cryptic names for variables and functions; use names that indicate the meaning or use of that variable or function. Use comments to explain the purpose, meaning, and use of variables and functions. Use global variables only when truly required. Otherwise, use local variables where their meaning in context will be clearer and side effects minimized.

  If abbreviations are used, they should be defined in the comments and used consistently throughout the data integration job. Avoid obscure abbreviations, such as "TTE." Stick to lowercase and use underscores to separate words or use camel case such as "CustomerTable" to distinguish between words. Avoid all uppercase variable and function names! (Exception: UNIX® environment variables are, by convention, UPPER_CASE. Follow the convention in this case.)

- **Data integration job commenting**—Data integration job code should be commented *during* the design and development phases, not at the end of the development phase. Inserting comments into data integration jobs as they are developed is far easier than having to complete it later. Keep the comments clear and concise. Describe why a technique is used in the code as well as the "what" and "how."

  Subsequent data integration developers should not have to guess at the purpose of a section of a job, variable, or component.

  If errors are discovered during testing and require changes to the job, document the problem and resolution in the comment section. Others will learn from these efforts.

- **Documenting nonstandard code**—If critical requirements lead to the creation of nonstandard code, those requirements must be clearly documented in the data integration job and in the data integration design documentation. The impact and potential problems (if any) caused should be identified and documented. Nonstandard code should be isolated in a separate program, function, or module so that it can be replaced later.

Error-Handling Requirements

All data integration jobs that call components or functions must check a job return code for error conditions and provide guidance (e.g., documentation) for how to address that particular error code. Include the error source text in every error message for ease of use.

Error-Handling Design Approach

Most errors that occur in a data integration application can be categorized as either:

- Expected (e.g., invalid input record)
- Unexpected (e.g., database crashes or file system fills up)

Good development methods will insulate a data integration job from both types of errors and facilitate a smooth recovery.

Error-Handling Requirement Steps

The creation of error handling in data integration jobs should include the following best practices:

- Design precise, detailed, and meaningful error reports to simplify maintenance and support.
- Create system notifications/alerts/job run reports when errors occur.
- Design error-handling capabilities for *both* expected and unexpected errors for ill-behaving or corrupt records.
- Design error logging and restartability using a job scheduler. For example, do not use a restart file if it can be broken into two separate jobs and handled with dependencies in the job scheduler.
- Diligently check return codes for all function calls and external interfaces in the data integration jobs (e.g., APIs).
- Centralize the error handling and logging design within an application where appropriate.
- Create anomaly and variance reporting in the data integration layer to track data types and counts from systems of record, then compare with expected results, and measure the variance.

Naming Standards

Naming standards in data integration is every bit as important as in traditional application development languages such as Java or C#.

The following data integration component labeling convention has the following structure using the data integration reference architecture:

<Component Layer> – **<Component Name>** [(additional information)]
where:

- **<Component Layer>**—The data integration component layer that the job represents, for example, source system extract, DQ, transform, subject area load.

- **<Component Name>**—The data integration component name comes first followed by a hyphen (-) and any additional component information. The additional information is optional and must adhere to the following rules:

  - The hyphen has a space on either side.

  - The label will contain only alphanumeric characters and some special characters (",", "(", ")", ".").

  - If the labels are not unique, use a number sequence prefixed with a hyphen to make the label unique (Example: Sort – Account by AcctNumber(m)– 1, Sort – Account by AcctNumber(m) – 2).

  - Blank keys are represented with the word "no-key" in the label.

  - If the label includes keys and if there are multiple fields in the key, one field will be chosen to be a part of the label appended with an "(m)" to indicate that the key contains many fields.

Following is a naming standard example:
Transform.Sort – Account by AcctNumber(m)

Key General Development Task Steps

The three general development steps include the following:

1. **Implement\confirm data integration standards**—This step reviews the data integration jobs to ensure that the general development standards have been implemented during development. These include the following:

   - Reviewing the final data integration for modular structure with the data integration job code

   - Building and/or implementing job log functionality

   - Reviewing for code comments in both standard and nonstandard data integration job code

2. **Build in error-handling capability**—The purpose of this step is to ensure that all data integration jobs contain error-handling capability.

3. **Ensure naming standards**—This step ensures that standard naming conventions have been applied to data integration job code, scripts, and other objects.

Prototyping a Set of Data Integration Functionality

In this task, core transformation, mapping, and data quality processing logic is prototyped for accuracy and correctness. This task is optional but highly recommended prior to any final development tasks, especially for large, complex, data integration applications.

In the development phase, much of the work is not traditional application development coding, but confirming the data output in the data integration jobs. Prototyping provides a good approach to verifying not only unit test cases with business and\or IT users, but to confirm critical cross-functional database key logic that spans multiple data integration processes.

Prototyping provides a very flexible approach to the final development tasks of the data integration application.

The Rationale for Prototyping

Prototyping is a technique, also known as Agile, that is as applicable to data integration development as any other Information Technology approaches. In fact, prototyping is more conducive to better understood data requirements in comparison with traditional waterfall Systems Development Life Cycles.

Software development for large, sophisticated information systems has been traditionally an extremely structured process using a traditional Systems Development Life Cycle, with many days spent on requirements analysis documentation, design reviews, and so on. The strategy for these types of projects is to invest as much time early, when mistakes are cheaper to fix.

However, this approach is not optimal in the business intelligence space, where the nature of data warehousing projects is that requirements have to be "discovered" rather than "defined."

Benefits of Prototyping

There are many benefits for using prototyping techniques for both traditional application development and data integration, the most important of which include the following:

- **Adjusting for fluid requirements**—Just when you are about to deliver, expect the rules to change—then change again. In other words, the entire nature of the project development cycle is fluid.

  This is especially true in data integration where assumptions on mapping rules are often made and need to be vetted.

- **Developing buy-in**—Prototyping provides the ability to gain support among potential users. A working prototype can be used to display the end result of the data integration in a report or user view of the data in order to get buy-in from interested parties and increase the probability of a project's success.

- **Confirming scope and value**—Prototyping also demonstrates to the users that a project is on track and that the output was useful. The following case study demonstrates that by using prototyping techniques, critical data design and transformation logic was visually discovered.

Prototyping Example

Overview: A development team for a financial services organization had been attempting for six months to determine the data requirements for moving financial billing information into a commercial off-the-shelf general ledger package. Their issue revolved around their inability to determine the requirements for a complex data structure, a nine-level deep product hierarchy, that needed to be designed and data aggregated to fill each of nine levels of the hierarchy in the new general ledger.

Needing to change the way the team worked with their business users, the project manager brought in an external team of data integration experts to address the requirements and at that time, they had only seven months to analyze, design, and develop the application.

The Problem Statement: The business users had never seen what the product hierarchy should contain.

The Opportunity: To prototype the product hierarchy to visualize and confirm the data structure and, more important, the business transformation rules for the aggregations.

The Prototype Approach: The data integration experts proposed a three-step approach to iteratively present the data and aggregations in increasing size and complexity to the business users to confirm assumptions within the requirements.

Step 1 – Present the Data: The first step was to take the requirements developed to date, take a subset of production data, and model the data in Microsoft Excel. Business role aggregations were simply Excel calculations, as shown in Figure 11.3.

Project Hierarchy											
FISCAL_YEA	ACCOUNTIN	OPERATING	DEPTID	PRODUCT_I	CHANNEL_I	OBJ_ID	PROJECT_I	FUND_CODE	GEOGRAPH	CHARTFIELD	CHARTFIELD	CHARTFIELD
2004	3	11001	OR00038	PR00084	CH0001	OB0001	PI0001	FU0001	GE0001	V2000	<Null>	CF0001
2004	3	11001	OR00038	PR00084	CH0001	OB0001	PI0001	FU0001	GE0001	V2002	<Null>	CF0001
2004	3	11001	OR00038	PR00084	CH0001	OB0001	PI0001	FU0001	GE0001	V2003	<Null>	CF0001
2004	3	11001	OR00038	PR00084	CH0001	OB0001	PI0001	FU0001	GE0001	V2003	<Null>	CF0001
2004	3	11001	OR00038	PR00084	CH0001	OB0001	PI0001	FU0001	GE0001	V2003	<Null>	CF0001
2004	3	11001	OR00038	PR00084	CH0001	OB0001	PI0001	FU0001	GE0001	V2003	<Null>	CF0001
2004	3	11001	OR00038	PR00084	CH0001	OB0001	PI0001	FU0001	GE0001	V2003	<Null>	CF0001
2004	3	11001	OR00038	PR00084	CH0001	OB0001	PI0001	FU0001	GE0001	V2003	<Null>	CF0001
2004	3	11001	OR00038	PR00084	CH0001	OB0001	PI0001	FU0001	GE0001	V2003	<Null>	CF0001
2004	3	11001	OR00038	PR00084	CH0001	OB0001	PI0001	FU0001	GE0001	V2003	<Null>	CF0001
2004	3	11001	OR00038	PR00147	CH0001	OB0001	PI0001	FU0001	GE0001	V2003	<Null>	CF0001
2004	3	11001	OR00038	PR00147	CH0001	OB0001	PI0001	FU0001	GE0001	V2003	<Null>	CF0001
2004	3	11001	OR00038	PR00147	CH0001	OB0001	PI0001	FU0001	GE0001	VN0022	<Null>	CF0001
2004	3	11001	OR00038	PR00147	CH0001	OB0001	PI0001	FU0001	GE0001	VN0022	<Null>	CF0001
2004	3	11001	OR00038	PR00K84	CH0001	OB0001	PI0001	FU0001	GE0001	V2003	<Null>	CF0001
2004	3	11001	OR00038	PR00K84	CH0001	OB0001	PI0001	FU0001	GE0001	V2003	<Null>	CF0001
2004	3	85000	OR00038	P9TOH	CH0001	OB0001	PI0001	FU0001	GE0001	V2002	<Null>	CF0001
2004	3	85000	OR00038	P9TOH	CH0001	OB0001	PI0001	FU0001	GE0001	V2003	<Null>	CF0001
2004	3	85000	OR00038	P9TOH	CH0001	OB0001	PI0001	FU0001	GE0001	V2003	<Null>	CF0001
2004	3	85000	OR00038	P9TOH	CH0001	OB0001	PI0001	FU0001	GE0001	V2003	<Null>	CF0001
2004	3	85000	OR00038	P9TOH	CH0001	OB0001	PI0001	FU0001	GE0001	V2003	<Null>	CF0001
2004	3	85000	OR00038	P9TOH	CH0001	OB0001	PI0001	FU0001	GE0001	V2003	<Null>	CF0001
2004	3	85000	OR00038	P9TOH	CH0001	OB0001	PI0001	FU0001	GE0001	V2003	<Null>	CF0001
2004	3	85000	OR00038	PR00084	CH0001	OB0001	PI0001	FU0001	GE0001	V1998	<Null>	CF0001
2004	3	85000	OR00038	PR00084	CH0001	OB0001	PI0001	FU0001	GE0001	V2000	<Null>	CF0001
2004	3	85000	OR00038	PR00084	CH0001	OB0001	PI0001	FU0001	GE0001	V2000	<Null>	CF0001
2004	3	85000	OR00038	PR00084	CH0001	OB0001	PI0001	FU0001	GE0001	V2002	<Null>	CF0001
2004	3	85000	OR00038	PR00084	CH0001	OB0001	PI0001	FU0001	GE0001	V2002	<Null>	CF0001
2004	3	85000	OR00038	PR00084	CH0001	OB0001	PI0001	FU0001	GE0001	V2003	<Null>	CF0001
2004	3	85000	OR00038	PR00084	CH0001	OB0001	PI0001	FU0001	GE0001	V2003	<Null>	CF0001

Figure 11.3   Product hierarchy prototype data

Step 1 Result: This first step provided the users the first opportunity to see how the data would actually look within the product hierarchy and view the issues in the data in terms of sparsity. This allowed both the business and the data integration experts the opportunity to refine what data would be needed and the business rules used to aggregate the data.

Step 2 – Refine the Business Rules: The second step was to refine the business transformation rules, build them into a commercial data integration package, and then test the augmented logic against a larger test data set, as illustrated in Figure 11.4.

Project Hierarchy												
FISCAL_YEA	ACCOUNTIN	OPERATING	DEPTID	PRODUCT_I	CHANNEL_I	OBJ_ID	PROJECT_I	FUND_CODE	GEOGRAPH	CHARTFIELD	CHARTFIELD	CHARTFIELD
2004	3	11001	OR00038	PR00084	CH0001	OB0001	PI0001	FU0001	GE0001	V2000	\<Null\>	CF0001
2004	3	11001	OR00038	PR00084	CH0001	OB0001	PI0001	FU0001	GE0001	V2002	\<Null\>	CF0001
2004	3	11001	OR00038	PR00084	CH0001	OB0001	PI0001	FU0001	GE0001	V2003	\<Null\>	CF0001
2004	3	11001	OR00038	PR00084	CH0001	OB0001	PI0001	FU0001	GE0001	V2003	\<Null\>	CF0001
2004	3	11001	OR00038	PR00084	CH0001	OB0001	PI0001	FU0001	GE0001	V2003	\<Null\>	CF0001
2004	3	11001	OR00038	PR00084	CH0001	OB0001	PI0001	FU0001	GE0001	V2003	\<Null\>	CF0001
2004	3	11001	OR00038	PR00084	CH0001	OB0001	PI0001	FU0001	GE0001	V2003	\<Null\>	CF0001
2004	3	11001	OR00038	PR00084	CH0001	OB0001	PI0001	FU0001	GE0001	V2003	\<Null\>	CF0001
2004	3	11001	OR00038	PR00084	CH0001	OB0001	PI0001	FU0001	GE0001	V2003	\<Null\>	CF0001
2004	3	11001	OR00038	PR00084	CH0001	OB0001	PI0001	FU0001	GE0001	V2003	\<Null\>	CF0001
2004	3	11001	OR00038	PR00147	CH0001	OB0001	PI0001	FU0001	GE0001	V2003	\<Null\>	CF0001
2004	3	11001	OR00038	PR00147	CH0001	OB0001	PI0001	FU0001	GE0001	V2003	\<Null\>	CF0001
2004	3	11001	OR00038	PR00147	CH0001	OB0001	PI0001	FU0001	GE0001	VN0022	\<Null\>	CF0001
2004	3	11001	OR00038	PR00147	CH0001	OB0001	PI0001	FU0001	GE0001	VN0022	\<Null\>	CF0001
2004	3	11001	OR00038	PR00K84	CH0001	OB0001	PI0001	FU0001	GE0001	V2003	\<Null\>	CF0001
2004	3	11001	OR00038	PR00K84	CH0001	OB0001	PI0001	FU0001	GE0001	V2003	\<Null\>	CF0001
2004	3	85000	OR00038	P9TOH	CH0001	OB0001	PI0001	FU0001	GE0001	V2002	\<Null\>	CF0001
2004	3	85000	OR00038	P9TOH	CH0001	OB0001	PI0001	FU0001	GE0001	V2003	\<Null\>	CF0001
2004	3	85000	OR00038	P9TOH	CH0001	OB0001	PI0001	FU0001	GE0001	V2003	\<Null\>	CF0001
2004	3	85000	OR00038	P9TOH	CH0001	OB0001	PI0001	FU0001	GE0001	V2003	\<Null\>	CF0001
2004	3	85000	OR00038	P9TOH	CH0001	OB0001	PI0001	FU0001	GE0001	V2003	\<Null\>	CF0001
2004	3	85000	OR00038	P9TOH	CH0001	OB0001	PI0001	FU0001	GE0001	V2003	\<Null\>	CF0001
2004	3	85000	OR00038	PR00084	CH0001	OB0001	PI0001	FU0001	GE0001	V1998	\<Null\>	CF0001
2004	3	85000	OR00038	PR00084	CH0001	OB0001	PI0001	FU0001	GE0001	V2000	\<Null\>	CF0001
2004	3	85000	OR00038	PR00084	CH0001	OB0001	PI0001	FU0001	GE0001	V2000	\<Null\>	CF0001
2004	3	85000	OR00038	PR00084	CH0001	OB0001	PI0001	FU0001	GE0001	V2002	\<Null\>	CF0001
2004	3	85000	OR00038	PR00084	CH0001	OB0001	PI0001	FU0001	GE0001	V2002	\<Null\>	CF0001
2004	3	85000	OR00038	PR00084	CH0001	OB0001	PI0001	FU0001	GE0001	V2003	\<Null\>	CF0001
2004	3	85000	OR00038	PR00084	CH0001	OB0001	PI0001	FU0001	GE0001	V2003	\<Null\>	CF0001

Figure 11.4 Second product hierarchy prototype data set

Step 2 Result: The second, larger set of test data generated this time through a data integration tool allowed the data integration experts and business users to "see" how the rules would react within the tool and against a larger data set, getting closer to not only the actual business requirements, but also the final application. In addition, running against a larger data set provided the data integration experts and business users the opportunity to ferret out additional data anomalies and create methods to cleanse the anomalies.

Step 3 – Refine for Production: With the product hierarchy data structure complete and the transformation logic confirmed, the final step was to incorporate the additional cleansing rules, tune the process for production, and perform one final test on an entire production data set, as shown in Figure 11.5.

Project Hierarchy												
FISCAL_YEA	ACCOUNTIN	OPERATING	DEPTID	PRODUCT_I	CHANNEL_I	OBJ_ID	PROJECT_I	FUND_CODE	GEOGRAPHY	CHARTFIELD	CHARTFIELD	CHARTFIELD
2004	3	11001	OR00038	PR00084	CH0001	OB0001	PI0001	FU0001	GE0001	V2000	<Null>	CF0001
2004	3	11001	OR00038	PR00084	CH0001	OB0001	PI0001	FU0001	GE0001	V2002	<Null>	CF0001
2004	3	11001	OR00038	PR00084	CH0001	OB0001	PI0001	FU0001	GE0001	V2003	<Null>	CF0001
2004	3	11001	OR00038	PR00084	CH0001	OB0001	PI0001	FU0001	GE0001	V2003	<Null>	CF0001
2004	3	11001	OR00038	PR00084	CH0001	OB0001	PI0001	FU0001	GE0001	V2003	<Null>	CF0001
2004	3	11001	OR00038	PR00084	CH0001	OB0001	PI0001	FU0001	GE0001	V2003	<Null>	CF0001
2004	3	11001	OR00038	PR00084	CH0001	OB0001	PI0001	FU0001	GE0001	V2003	<Null>	CF0001
2004	3	11001	OR00038	PR00084	CH0001	OB0001	PI0001	FU0001	GE0001	V2003	<Null>	CF0001
2004	3	11001	OR00038	PR00084	CH0001	OB0001	PI0001	FU0001	GE0001	V2003	<Null>	CF0001
2004	3	11001	OR00038	PR00147	CH0001	OB0001	PI0001	FU0001	GE0001	V2003	<Null>	CF0001
2004	3	11001	OR00038	PR00147	CH0001	OB0001	PI0001	FU0001	GE0001	V2003	<Null>	CF0001
2004	3	11001	OR00038	PR00147	CH0001	OB0001	PI0001	FU0001	GE0001	VN0022	<Null>	CF0001
2004	3	11001	OR00038	PR00147	CH0001	OB0001	PI0001	FU0001	GE0001	VN0022	<Null>	CF0001
2004	3	11001	OR00038	PR00K84	CH0001	OB0001	PI0001	FU0001	GE0001	V2003	<Null>	CF0001
2004	3	11001	OR00038	PR00K84	CH0001	OB0001	PI0001	FU0001	GE0001	V2003	<Null>	CF0001
2004	3	85000	OR00038	P9TOH	CH0001	OB0001	PI0001	FU0001	GE0001	V2002	<Null>	CF0001
2004	3	85000	OR00038	P9TOH	CH0001	OB0001	PI0001	FU0001	GE0001	V2003	<Null>	CF0001
2004	3	85000	OR00038	P9TOH	CH0001	OB0001	PI0001	FU0001	GE0001	V2003	<Null>	CF0001
2004	3	85000	OR00038	P9TOH	CH0001	OB0001	PI0001	FU0001	GE0001	V2003	<Null>	CF0001
2004	3	85000	OR00038	P9TOH	CH0001	OB0001	PI0001	FU0001	GE0001	V2003	<Null>	CF0001
2004	3	85000	OR00038	P9TOH	CH0001	OB0001	PI0001	FU0001	GE0001	V2003	<Null>	CF0001
2004	3	85000	OR00038	PR00084	CH0001	OB0001	PI0001	FU0001	GE0001	V1998	<Null>	CF0001
2004	3	85000	OR00038	PR00084	CH0001	OB0001	PI0001	FU0001	GE0001	V2000	<Null>	CF0001
2004	3	85000	OR00038	PR00084	CH0001	OB0001	PI0001	FU0001	GE0001	V2000	<Null>	CF0001
2004	3	85000	OR00038	PR00084	CH0001	OB0001	PI0001	FU0001	GE0001	V2002	<Null>	CF0001
2004	3	85000	OR00038	PR00084	CH0001	OB0001	PI0001	FU0001	GE0001	V2002	<Null>	CF0001
2004	3	85000	OR00038	PR00084	CH0001	OB0001	PI0001	FU0001	GE0001	V2003	<Null>	CF0001
2004	3	85000	OR00038	PR00084	CH0001	OB0001	PI0001	FU0001	GE0001	V2003	<Null>	CF0001

Figure 11.5   Final product hierarchy prototype data set

Step 3 Result: The final test run came through complete and correct, which confirmed with a high level of assurance that the final data anomalies had been captured and addressed. It also provided the business users the opportunity to "see" how the product hierarchy would appear in production.

The result of using prototyping rather than a traditional Systems Development Life Cycle approach was that in nine weeks, the data integration experts had defined, designed, and coded what the first team could not accomplish in six months.

Observations: In addition to finally determining the requirements, user acceptance testing of the product hierarchy data integration process was a simple task of confirmation with the business users rather than a discovery process. Often, many of the issues the business users have in user acceptance testing in data warehousing applications are the result of seeing the raw, aggregated, and calculated data for the first time.

By prototyping complex data structures and the transformation logic with the business users, the discovery and actual confirmation process begins earlier in the process and prevents costly reengineering in testing.

As demonstrated, prototyping can be a very useful technique that can be used in data integration development to facilitate the discovery of the rules to qualify and transform the data in a very visual method that assists in business rule confirmation and early user adoption.

It is interesting to note that the exercise was not a pure data integration one; the product hierarchy is a classic data modeling deliverable. Often, to derive the transformation business logic, significant work needs to occur as well on the data model.

It is important to note that prototyping can be performed during any phase of the data integration development life cycle, as shown in Figure 11.6.

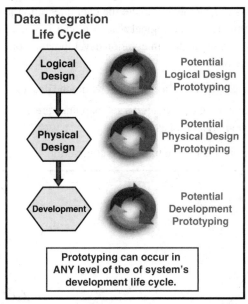

Figure 11.6   Prototyping in the data integration life cycle

Key Data Integration Prototyping Task Steps

The five key steps for data integration prototyping include the following:

1. **Define the scope of the prototype**—The purpose of this step is to determine what logic and target data structures need to be proven. Often, these are subject areas of target data model and/or cross-subject area key creation transformation logic.

2. **Set up the prototyping environment**—The purpose of this step is to ensure that the development environment, tools, and sample data are ready for the prototyping. The prototyping sessions with the business users should also be scheduled.

3. **Leverage existing physical data integration models to complete a prototype**—This step builds out the prototype using existing data integration model designs to verify requirements and design assumptions.

4. **Review the results with the business users**—Verify the results with the business users against expected and unexpected requirements and assumptions.

5. **Renovate and reperform prototyping session, if necessary**—Determine if the feedback from the business users is sufficient to complete development or if additional iterations of user review are necessary.

Completing/Extending Data Integration Job Code

The purpose of this task is to generate/complete the data integration job code required for each physical data integration model. If the logical design model is sound, and the physical design models have been instantiated in the data integration development tool, then this task is generally short in duration. There are two reasons:

- The data integration jobs have been created within the data integration development tool.

- The transformation logic and source/target mappings are already embedded through the design in the development tool as well.

Figure 11.7 illustrates the data integration job completion.

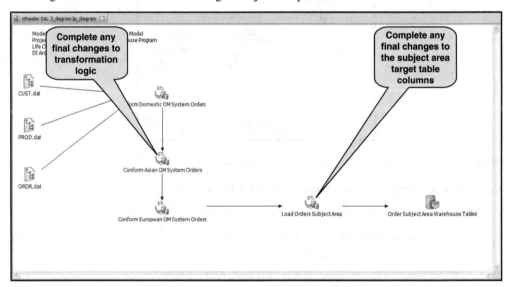

Figure 11.7   Completing development on the data integration jobs

---

NOTE

Most of the final development techniques and steps are data integration technology-specific. So for the reader, it is highly recommended to augment this task and chapter with the specific activities required of the commercial data integration tool that will be used for your effort.

Complete/Extend Common Component Data Integration Jobs

The first step in completing the development of the data integration jobs is finishing the development of the common component data integration jobs.

Although it expected that much of the functionality is complete, certain logic or functions may have been "stubbed" or commented out in the physical design phase that now needs to be developed and completed.

Wrapping up final development includes two steps.

The first step is to extend and/or complete the common data quality data integration jobs, as illustrated in Figure 11.8, as follows:

- Verify that data quality criteria and tolerances are available for the entities and elements/attributes in the target data source.

- Develop/complete any file integrity cleansing components.

- Develop/complete any record-level cleansing components.

- Develop/complete any error threshold cleansing components.

- Develop/complete any data quality error and exception handling reporting components.

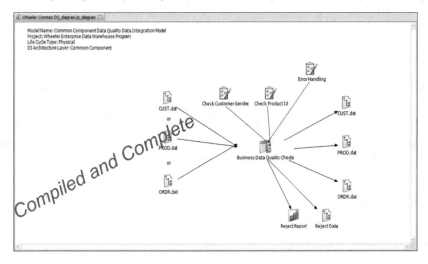

Figure 11.8   Completed data quality common component job sample

The second step is to then extend and/or complete the common transform data integration jobs shown in Figure 11.9 as follows:

- Develop/complete any calculation components.

- Develop/complete any split components.

- Develop/complete any processing components.
- Develop/complete any enrichment components.
- Develop/complete any joins components.
- Develop/complete any aggregations components.
- Develop/complete any Change Data Capture components.

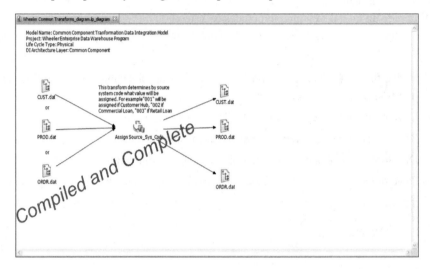

Figure 11.9   Completed transforms common component data integration job sample

Complete/Extend the Source System Extract Data Integration Jobs

The second step is completing the development of the source system extract data integration jobs shown in Figure 11.10. In this task, the data integration developer needs to complete/extend the following:

- Extract, file/capture functionality, which includes
  - Develop/complete source system extract logic.
- Subject area file conforming functionality, which includes
  - Develop/complete subject area file conforming logic.
- Source system data quality functionality, which includes
  - Verify that data quality criteria and tolerances are available for the entities and elements/attributes in the target data source.
  - Develop/complete any source-specific file integrity cleansing components.
  - Develop/complete any source-specific record-level cleansing components.

- Develop/complete any source-specific error threshold cleansing components.
- Integrate the code with the common error and exception-handing reporting components.

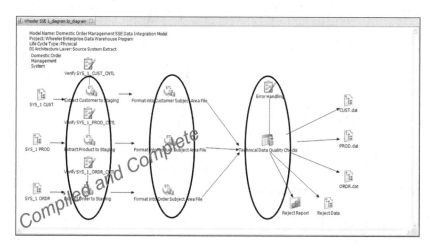

Figure 11.10   Completed source system extract data integration job sample

Complete/Extend the Subject Area Load Data Integration Jobs

The final step is completing the development of the subject area load data integration jobs, as shown in Figure 11.11. The final development activities include the following:

- The subject area transformation functionality.
  - Develop/complete any subject area-specific calculation components.
  - Develop/complete any subject area-specific split components.
  - Develop/complete any subject area-specific processing components.
  - Develop/complete any subject area-specific enrichment components.
  - Develop/complete any subject area-specific joins components.
  - Develop/complete any subject area-specific aggregations components.
  - Develop/complete any subject area-specific Change Data Capture components.
- The subject area load functionality.
  - Develop/complete any subject area load logic.
- Code load error-handling (automated and manual) components.
- Configure any database load processes.

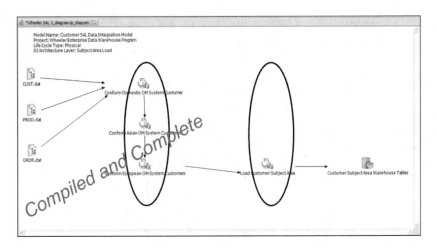

Figure 11.11   Completed subject area load data integration job sample

With all design and development activities complete, attention is directed on testing the data integration application.

Performing Data Integration Testing

The purpose of this task is to develop a test strategy for both the overall data warehouse and in particular the data integration applications that will ensure that the future data warehouse environment and enabling technology will provide the expected business benefits in terms of requirements and performance. The test strategy will include all activities required to conduct thorough and accurate tests of analytic capabilities and parameters, database performance, data integration extract, transform, and load accuracy and performance.

Figure 11.12 portrays the breadth of testing in a data warehouse. Testing in a data warehouse environment is very different from traditional transactional systems testing.

Because most data integration projects are aspects of a larger data warehouse project or program, is it important to understand the context of data integration testing within a data warehouse testing life cycle.

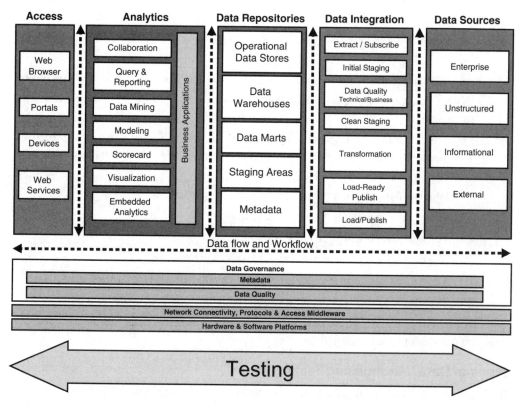

Figure 11.12   Testing a data warehousing project

The remainder of this task focuses on end-to-end data warehousing testing with a deeper emphasis on the data integration tasks and activities.

Data Warehousing Testing Overview

Determining testing requirements for a data warehousing project is very different from a traditional application development project. For example, a data warehousing project is not concerned with the issue of transactional integrity.

Traditional application development projects for transactional systems have to deal with the creation, update, and deletion of business transactions. Data warehouse projects collect those transactions and rationalize them into database structures that facilitate analysis. The type of testing required to verify the correctness and completeness of a transactional system is much more comprehensive and different from that of a data warehouse in that:

- A transactional system must test:
  - Whether a transaction has been created properly.
  - Whether the transaction was created in the right sequence, at the right time, and at the right speed (e.g., service-level agreements).

- A data warehouse must test:
  - Whether the transactions were collected at the right time, in the right format, and in the right quantity.
  - Whether the calculations were necessary to aggregate the data performed correctly.
- Data warehouse projects have analytic requirements, not business requirements, for example:
  - Creating a loan transaction is a business requirement. The rules necessary to create the loan transaction must be tested as a part of any OLTP testing approach.
  - Determining the total loan portfolio amount, number of loans by geography are traditional analytic requirements.
- Data integration testing is meant to verify that:
  - The right data is extracted at the right time.
  - The data is cleansed with the defined levels of data quality.
  - The data is transformed (e.g., aggregated, calculated) with the defined business rules.
  - The data is loaded into the right targets, with the right data, at the right time.

To perform this verification, data integration testing involves verifying row counts, file sizes, test calculations, and aggregations.

Types of Data Warehousing Testing

Testing for a data warehousing effort should ensure each of the layers of a data warehouse: The analytic components, database objects, and data integration processes work end-to-end. In a data warehouse, each of the following testing types should be performed as shown in Figure 11.13:

- **Unit testing**—This should involve testing each component of each layer of the data warehouse environment. For data integration, each component should be tested individually first such as
  - Individual source system extract data integration jobs
  - Individual common component data integration jobs
  - Individual subject area load data integration jobs
- **Integration testing**—This testing ensures that all components work together as expected end-to-end from a functionality perspective for correctness and completeness. For data integration, the following occurs:
  1. The source system extract data integration jobs are executed in sequence.
  2. The common component data integration jobs are executed in sequence.
  3. The subject area load data integration jobs are executed in sequence.

- **System and performance testing**—This testing exercises the end-to-end data ware-housing environment in the context of the entire application for the
  - Anticipated source-to-target data load demands (size and timing)
  - Anticipated query and reporting database demands
- **User acceptance testing**—This type of testing usually exercises only the analytic layer and confirms the underlying data in the database. Rarely are there direct user acceptance tests conducted on the data integration layer applications.

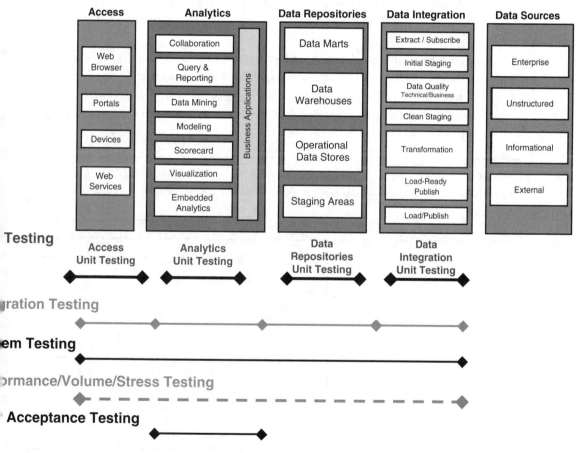

Figure 11.13 Types of testing in a data warehouse project

Perform Data Warehouse Unit Testing

Unit testing in a data warehouse environment requires the testing of the "components" (DI job, database script, Analytics Report) developed in each of the layers of the business intelligence reference architecture. The following is the approach for each of the data warehouse layers.

Perform Data Integration Layer Unit Testing

Data integration unit test cases (with an example in Figure 11.14) may be defined as the verification and validation of an individual data integration model or component. It is the most "micro" scale of testing for testing particular functions or job logic. Each data integration process between source and target sources will be checked for the following criteria:

- **Source system extraction completeness and correctness**—Was all the data extracted that was intended? For both initial extraction and Change Data Capture?

- **Data quality completeness and correctness**—Was the intended level of data quality checking (completeness and correctness) achieved? Did exception handling occur as intended?

- **Transformation completeness and correctness**—Was all the data transformed as intended? Did the data transformation algorithms work as intended?

- **Subject area load completeness and correctness**—Was the transformed data loaded into the target system correctly? Did the data load perform either data overlay or appending per the load requirements?

Sample **Unit Test Plan**

Component Name:

Description: *This component assigns instrument id to the PS_C1_FCAL_DIM_F00 work file and creates the PS_C1_FCAL_DIM_F00 load-ready file. It also creates PS_C1_IBAL_R00 load-ready file.*

Condition	Condition Description	Step	Step Description	Expected Results	Actual Results
1	The input PS_C1_FCAL_DIM_F00 work file confirms to the expected file layout.	1.1	Check to ensure that the data file layout and the expected data file DML match.	Data is read successfully from input file.	Data is read successfully from input file.
2	Instrument Id is correctly assigned.	2.1	Create records in the Synthetic Instrument Reference lookup file such that Org, LE, Product Level 9, Weekly Vintage combinations match the combinations in the input file.	Data is read successfully from input file.	Data is read successfully from input file.
		2.2	Create records in the PS_C1_FCAL_DIM_F00 work file such that Org, LE, Product Level 9, Weekly Vintage combination does not exist in the synthetic instrument reference lookup file.		
		2.3	Execute the graph.		
		2.4	Validate that instrument id values have been correctly assigned.	For dimension combinations that have matching data in synthetic instrument reference lookup file, the corresponding instrument id from the lookup file is assigned. For dimension combinations that do not find a match in the lookup file, the defined default value is assigned.	For dimension combinations that have matching data in synthetic instrument reference lookup file, the corresponding instrument id from the lookup file is assigned. For dimension combinations that do not find a match in the lookup file, the defined default value is assigned.
3	Fields in PS_C1_FCAL_DIM_F00 that are not being populated using apex data are assigned the defined default values.	3.1	Execute the graph.		

Figure 11.14   Sample data integration unit test case

Following are the data integration testing tasks:

1. Unit test cases need to be created for each individual data integration specification/component. Each test case should have a test case description to outline the purpose of the test. Each test case can then have multiple steps to execute that test. Each step should be numbered, have a description associated with it, have a column for the expected result, and have a column for actual result.

2. Once the component has run, the unit test cases need to be executed and validated. Any issues need to be resolved, and the test should be rerun. It is recommended (not required) to restart the running of the test from the beginning rather than from the point of failure.

3. For larger components, as a standard for unit testing, it is highly recommended that it be broken up by functionality into smaller testable units (for example, by having intermediary files in between). Each unit should have its own test case(s). Once each unit has been tested, the entire graph can be tested in its entirety.

4. Every component should have a reject/log file associated with it during the testing process to facilitate debugging. The reject/log files should be named as per the naming standards of data integration files. These files may be deleted prior to promoting the components into the production area.

Perform Data Warehouse Layer Unit Testing

Unit testing the data warehouse layer includes confirming the different data warehouse database structures:

- Data warehouse structures:
  - Subject area load completeness and correctness—Ensure that the transformed data loaded.
  - Volume testing—Ensure that the physical data model can handle the amounts of data to be stored, both for loading and querying.
  - Referential integrity—Ensure that the data model contains the necessary data rules to prevent data anomalies.
- Data mart or dimensional structures:
  - Aggregation testing—Ensure that the data dimensions will provide the correct rollups, subtotals, and totals.

Perform Analytics Layer Unit Testing

The reporting and ad hoc query environments should be verified with the following criteria:

- **Completeness**—Each analytic report/ad hoc environment should be confirmed that the right data elements are in the right column and row in the report.

- **Correctness**—Each analytic report/ad hoc environment should be tested to ensure that report subtotals and totals are correct in their signed-off requirements.

- **Look and feel**—The report (views) should be checked to ensure the information appears as documented in the requirements and prototypes.

- **Drill-path verification**—For interactive reports (views) with drill up/down functionality, it should be confirmed that each major drill path drills into the correct data, to the correct level of granularity.

Perform Data Warehouse Integration Testing

Integration testing is a logical extension of unit testing. In its simplest form, two components that have already been tested are combined into a larger application, and the interface between them is tested. It verifies that all the components of the data warehouse environment will work together. A component, in this sense, refers to an integrated aggregate of the entire data warehouse environment.

This will be accomplished through the end-to-end process of data integration (extract, DQ, transform, load), storage, and reporting/analytics. It will focus on testing the information flow between the data integration environment, the data warehouse database environment, and the analytics environment. It is recommended that a common test data set will be used to verify the data integration, databases, and reporting components from both a completeness and correctness perspective.

Integration testing identifies problems that occur when components are combined. By using a test plan that requires the testing of each component to ensure the viability of that component before combining components, any errors discovered when combining components are a likely result of the interface between those components and not the components themselves. This method reduces the number of possibilities to a far simpler level of analysis. Requirements of integration testing include the following:

- Integration test cases/scenarios need to be created. These test cases are for testing end-to-end functionality of the system.

- Various components/tools must be compatible with one another.

- Test cases must be executed and validated.

Data Warehouse Database Integration Testing Approach

The methodology for assembling a data warehouse integration test is to "string" together the unit test cases from the data warehouse layer components and execute them in proper sequence. The focus of this approach is to ensure that the

- Data integration unit test cases load the data properly.

- Database unit test cases display the correct amount and types of data in the data warehouse structures.

- Data mart data integration properly moves and manipulates the data into the data mart.

- The analytic environment/reporting environment reads and displays the correct data and reporting format, and the correct reports are displayed to the correct user community.

Data Warehouse Security Testing Approach

One of the facets of integration testing is confirming the security requirements (e.g., user types) of the data warehouse environment. Examples of these tests include the following:

- **Source extract data integration jobs**—Security testing will verify that the data integration job can connect to only the correct database structure.

- **Data mart load data integration jobs**—Security testing will verify that only the approved user ID can connect and browse the approved data warehouse structures and update the customer profitability data mart.

- **Data warehouse and data mart database structures**—Security testing will verify that only the approved database user ID can connect and read the approved tables.

- **Analytic reports and ad hoc query environments**—Security testing will verify that only the approved user types are defined and can only access those reports that are specified.

Perform Data Warehouse System and Performance Testing

Data warehouse system testing examines how the new or extended data warehouse application works within the overall application environment.

A data warehouse performance test is conducted to evaluate the compliance of a data warehouse application or its components with specified performance requirements. It is a process of observing the operations of the overall data warehouse application and making adjustments to its different components based on those observations for optimal performance. Determining performance testing success metrics involves many technical and managerial aspects.

The ultimate requirement for performance testing is to produce the most efficient data warehouse environment. The definition of "efficient" needs to be defined for each project to be based on performance requirements such as data volumes, complexity of transformations, frequency, and expected timing to determine performance expectations. It is best practice to build these performance metrics using the service-level agreements (SLAs) with the business that were established in the analysis phase. These SLAs should include the following:

- Defined performance metrics (and other metrics)

- Definitions around what is acceptable performance if users increase and/or the data load increases

Note that the percentage of time these SLAs need to be met may vary from application to application.

For data integration, the performance testing again leverages the same unit test cases but runs them in sequence using higher volume test data to exercise each layer of the data integration application. For example, test the volumes and timing of the data integration jobs, which includes the following:

- Testing if the jobs execute in the expected time frame with the sample data volumes

- Testing whether the data integration jobs execution cause issues (e.g., slowdown) with other applications in the environment

When preparing for data warehouse system testing, it is important that a test environment is configured as closely as possible to the intended production server in the number of CPUs, LPARs, and SAN configuration.

The data volumes for the test should go beyond the highest expected level of source data to know at what point the data integration process fails and how they fail.

Perform Data Warehouse User Acceptance Testing

User acceptance testing in a data warehouse is the verification that the data and reporting environment (whether standard or ad hoc) meet the business requirements and analytic use cases. This testing is usually performed by the users executing a set of analytic use cases for the reporting /ad hoc query environment exercising the access and analytic unit test cases and then approving or declaring defects as they execute each of the testing use cases.

Despite all the profiling, mapping, and prototyping, there are expected to be some level of defects in the final application. There are several types of defects to be aware of, including the following:

- **First-time view of the data**—Often, when a business user executes a test and views the result, it is the first time that they have actually "seen" the data. Despite the documentation developed and signed off on these, defects can be quite contentious with the common comment that "It is what I asked for but not what I need." Many of these defect types are reduced or eliminated in environments that use prototyping to provide the visualization needed to manage the expectations to the actual data.

- **Scope creep**—Often in user acceptance testing, users will find "missing" data (both raw and calculated) that they expected to find in the data. It is important to manage the user expectations that the user acceptance testing is supposed to only verify the data warehouse application to the signed-off requirements.

- **Analytic/reporting defect**—Analytic defects are either issues that are found in the reporting tool metadata or issues in the database (or further downstream). Analytic/reporting defects can be classified as:

- **Formatting defects**—In situations where the data model is not in sync with the actual database tables, formatting defects are often found.

- **Completeness defects**—Errors where the correct data elements are in the wrong column or row in the report.

- **Correctness defects**—Where report subtotals and totals are incorrect to the signed-off requirements.

- **Look-and-feel formatting defects**—Where the report formatting does not match the view presenting the requirements and prototypes.

- **Drill-path errors**—Where either the organizational hierarchies or aggregations are incorrect in the correct levels of granularity.

- **Database defect**—Usually, these defects are actually symptoms of either reporting defects or more likely bad data from the data integration processes. Here are defect types that are directly attributed to the database:

  - **Formatting defects**—In situations where the data model is not in sync with the actual database tables, formatting defects are often found.

  - **Aggregation defects**—These are defects that are found in data warehouse environments that leverage view technology, and the aggregation or join calculations (either business or technical) are incorrect.

- **Data integration defect**—There are several types of data integration errors, which include:

  - **Formatting defects**—These are the most common, where a trim or pad of a field from source to target is incorrect, causing keys to not connect or incorrect calculations.

  - **Source-to-subject area mapping defects**—These are typically where complex key mappings (despite prototyping!) are incorrect due to incorrect understanding of the key fields in the source systems.

  - **Subject area-to-load mapping defects**—Rarer than source-to-subject area, these defects are usually due to miscommunication from the data integration mapping analyst and the data modeler.

  - **Incorrect common or subject area calculation defects**—These defects are either a result of misunderstanding of the business requirements for the calculation or incorrect physical implementation of that requirement.

The Role of Configuration Management in Data Integration

With testing complete, it is important to catalog and deploy the data integration application into production. The purpose of this section is to discuss the procedures and standards for the data integration software promotion life cycle and version control.

What Is Configuration Management?

Configuration management is a software management process that manages the creation and management of software assets such as data integration jobs as configuration items. It is a series of standards and techniques that coordinates the process of data integration application component development, quality assurance, testing, and data integration job promotion.

The goal for the data integration architecture is to provide a long-term framework and foundation that can be maintained and grown as the business requirements change and expand. Configuration management manages the changes to the components within that framework such as data integration jobs, code, scripts, and other environmental objects. Configuration management in the context of data integration primarily addresses the following key areas:

- **Data integration job migration**—Throughout the development process, the developer must be consciously aware of migration and promotion issues. Because the same data integration jobs must be executable in multiple environments, including those used for development, testing, and production, the goal is to develop code in such a manner that it can be easily promoted and then executed without modification from one environment to another, potentially even on a different platform.

  To make this possible, the code must be highly configurable. One primary method of achieving this is through the use of parameters contained apart from the data integration jobs. These parameters are used to configure or define each environment and include values for database schemas, middleware connection strings, directory paths, and run identifiers. These types of configuration parameters should never be hard-coded within the data integration jobs.

- **Data integration job recovery**—Even with the best development practices and effort, data integration jobs will sometimes fail in production. Independent of job logic, data integration jobs can fail because of environmental conditions, other application failures, other system failures, and data errors.

  When failure occurs, the process "falls back" to a recoverable point—the last known good point in the data flow. One way of accomplishing the recovery point in the data integration jobs is by landing files at critical points in the data integration environment.

  To take advantage of landed files, critical dependencies must be identified so processing does not progress until all jobs are complete for that stage. The job stream must also be designed to allow a restart at any checkpoint. Ideally, the job stream will always start at the beginning and track its own completion status, minimizing the dependency on an operator to follow complicated restart instructions.

To manage data integration job migration and recovery, the following configuration management processes are required.

Data Integration Version Control

One of the major processes of configuration management is configuration control. Configuration control are the processes that identify and control configuration items. Configuration items are the components that make up an application, and for data integration, they are the data integration jobs, scripts, and associated objects. Version control is the configuration control process that identifies and manages the data integration configuration items such as source code, user test plans, and sample data.

This includes evaluating, approving or disapproving, coordinating, and tracking changes to those data integration configuration items.

It is important that a version control naming convention is implemented with the data integration application as well as having the data integration configuration items managed within the version control capabilities of the commercial data integration package, and/or a configuration management package.

Data Integration Software Promotion Life Cycle

Maintenance and enhancement to existing data integration jobs as well as adding new jobs require that these changes are thoroughly tested as an application version. Once tested, the version of tested jobs scripts and other objects need to be moved from the developer testing environment to production. The Software Promotion Life Cycle (SPLC) includes the quality assurance/control stages, which data integration jobs pass through to production.

A Software Promotion Life Cycle for data integration should consist of the procedures and technology for moving data integration jobs and components from development to test and on to production, as shown in Figure 11.15.

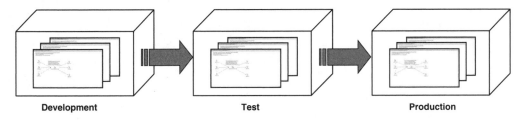

| Development | Test | Production |

Figure 11.15 Data integration Software Promotion Life Cycle

Most commercial data integration packages have built-in promotion functionality or the ability to "hook" into commercial configuration management packages with release management capability.

Summary

This chapter covered the development phase of a data integration project. It discussed development phase coding standards in detail and reviewed the concepts of prototyping with users in terms of the benefits and approaches to building prototypes to ensure that the requirements are correct as well as ferret out issues earlier than formal user acceptance testing.

It covered testing not only for data integration but also for the entire discipline of data warehousing in terms of unit, integration, system, and user acceptance testing for each of the layers of a data warehouse. The chapter focused on the key data integration testing concept of counts and amounts, using control totals.

Finally, the chapter reviewed data integration job assets in terms of configuration management, specifically version control and release management.

Chapter 12, "Data Integration Development Cycle Case Study," completes the application of the Build tasks reviewed in this chapter against the physical Wheeler data integration models.

End-of-Chapter Questions

Question 1.
What are two of the benefits of prototyping?
Question 2.
Why is the testing required to verify the correctness and completeness of a transactional system much more comprehensive and different than that of a data warehouse?
Question 3.
What are the four types of data integration unit testing?
Question 4.
What are the common types of data integration defects found in testing?
Question 5.
Configuration management in the context of data integration primarily addresses what two key areas?

Data Integration Development Cycle Case Study

The last section of the Wheeler order management data integration project case study is the development phase, which will consist of two key development tasks:

1. Prototyping cross-functional key logic, the common customer key

2. Building a unit test case for one of the source system extract jobs

Step 1: Prototype the Common Customer Key

Because many organizations have multiple customer information files and databases, one of the most complex tasks in data warehousing is determining how to link all the customer files together in a common customer key.

In fact, common customer data is such a critical requirement to organizations that the discipline of Master Data Management emerged.

Unfortunately, the Wheeler Automotive Company does not have a Master Data Management customer integration process in place, so it will fall upon the data integration team to rationalize the customer data sources from the three order management systems into a common structure with a common key.

Because this is one of the most critical aspects of the Wheeler Automotive Company project, we will use the customer source-to-target mapping in Figure 12.1 to prototype out with sample Wheeler customer data to ensure that either the data or logic is flawed.

1. Source-to-Enterprise Data Warehouse Data Mappings							
Source File/ Table	Source Field	Source Domain	Mapping Rule	Subject Area File	Column Name	Column Definition	Target Domain
			Create a system-generated ID	CUST.dat	Customer_Number	The unique identifier assigned to a customer.	INTEGER(10)
			Must be assigned "SYS1"	CUST.dat	Source_System_Identifier	The identifier of the source system that the data was sourced.	VARCHAR(4)
SYS 1 CUST FILE	CUST_#	Varchar(04)	Pad last 6 digits	CUST.dat	Source_System_Code	The unique identifier of the application or system from which the information last used to update the entity instance was populated.	VARCHAR(10)
			Create a system-generated ID	CUST.dat	Customer_Number	The unique identifier assigned to a customer.	INTEGER(10)
			Must be assigned "SYS2"	CUST.dat	Source_System_Identifier	The identifier of the source system that the data was sourced.	VARCHAR(4)
SYS 2 CUST FILE	ID	Decimal(10)	Translate Decimal to Varchar	CUST.dat	Source_System_Code	The unique identifier of the application or system from which the information last used to update the entity instance was populated.	VARCHAR(10)
			Create a system-generated ID	CUST.dat	Customer_Number	The unique identifier assigned to a customer.	INTEGER(10)
			Must be assigned "SYS3"	CUST.dat	Source_System_Identifier	The identifier of the source system that the data was sourced.	VARCHAR(4)
SYS 3 CUST FILE	CUST_ID	Decimal(10)	Translate Decimal to Varchar	CUST.dat	Source_System_Code	The unique identifier of the application or system from which the information last used to update the entity instance was populated.	VARCHAR(10)

Figure 12.1   Wheeler common customer key prototype target

For developing the Wheeler common customer key prototype, the following steps will be performed:

1. **Define the scope of the prototype**—The scope of the prototype is to rationalize the key logic for combining customer records from the three different customer files from the Wheeler order management systems.

2. **Set up the prototyping environment**—The data needed for the prototype consists of a narrow scope of sample records from the Wheeler order management customer files; for this task, it will be five records from each customer source, using the Customer Id field, as shown in Figure 12.2.

3. **Leverage the existing physical data integration models to complete a prototype**— For the prototype, leverage the customer key consolidation logic found in the physical subject area load data integration job, as shown in Figure 12.3.

System 1 Customer File

CUST_#	ORG	CUST_NAME	ADDRESS	CITY	STATE	ZIP
410	General Motors	Mr. Jones	1230 Main Street	Warren	Michigan	48010
520	Toyota	Ms. Smith	444 Elm Street	Pontiac	Michigan	48120
660	Ford Motor	Mr. Cartwright	510 Amber St	Detroit	Michigan	48434
200	Nissan	Ms. Wheelright	626 Anderson	Lansing	Michigan	48232
300	Kia	Mr. Spokeright	923 Maiden Lane	Ann Arbor	Michigan	48932

System 2 Customer File

ID	O_NAME	F_NAME	L_NAME	ADDRSS 1	ADDRSS 2	CITY	STATE	ZIP
11100011	General Motors	Jasper	Jones	1230 Main St		Warren	Michigan	48010
11100012	Chrysler	Katie	Harvey	03 Daimler	Gate 2	Pontiac	Michigan	48120
11100013	Ford Motor	Mr. Angel	Mr. Cartwright	510 Amber St		Dearborn	Michigan	48012
11100014	Hyndai	Mr. Jose	Gonzelez	410 Main	Gate 1	Wyandotte	Michigan	48011
11100015	Nissan	Kelsie	Harvey	626 Anderson		Lansing	Michigan	48232

System 3 Customer File

CUST_ID	ORGANIZATION	FRST	LAST	ADDR 1	ADDR 2	ADDR 3	CITY	STATE	ZIP	EXT
310001	Ford Motor	Mr. Cartwright	Mr. Cartwright	510 Amber St			Dearborn	Michigan	48012	1234
310002	Chrysler	June	Jones	03 Daimler	Gate 2	Dock 1	Pontiac	Michigan	48120	4321
310003	General Motors	Jasper	Jones	1230 Main St		Warren	Michigan	Michigan	48012	1232
310004	Hyndai	Mr. Jose	Gonzelez	410 Main	Gate 1		Wyandotte	Michigan	48011	
310005	Nissan	Kelsie	Harvey	626 Anders			Lansing	Michigan	48232	2331

Figure 12.2   Sample Wheeler customer data

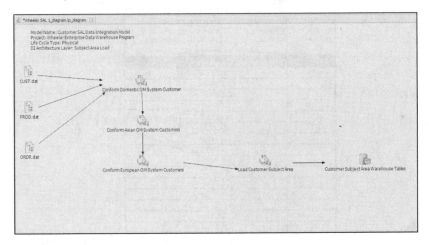

Figure 12.3   Leveraging the customer subject area load DI model for the prototype

4. **Develop the prototype and review the results with the business users**—As the Wheeler subject area load data integration job is prepared to be executed, an expected output is created to benchmark the results against, which is displayed in Figure 12.4.

Unfortunately, the first prototype results were not the expected results, with results as shown in Figure 12.5.

Customer_ Number	Source_System_ Identifier	Source_System_Code
The unique identifier assigned to a customer.	The identifier of the source system that the data was sourced.	The unique identifier of the application or system from which the information last used to update the entity instance was populated.
1	410	SYS1
2	520	SYS1
3	660	SYS1
4	200	SYS1
5	300	SYS1
6	11100011	SYS2
7	11100012	SYS2
8	11100013	SYS2
9	11100014	SYS2
10	11100015	SYS2
11	310001	SYS3
12	310002	SYS3
13	310003	SYS3
14	310004	SYS3
15	310005	SYS3

Figure 12.4   Expected prototype results

Customer_ Number	Source_System_ Identifier	Source_System_Code
The unique identifier assigned to a customer.	The identifier of the source system that the data was sourced.	The unique identifier of the application or system from which the information last used to update the entity instance was populated.
INTEGER(10)	VARCHAR(4)	VARCHAR(10)
1	410	SYS1
2	520	SYS1
3	660	SYS1
4	200	SYS1
5	300	SYS1
6	11	SYS2
7	12	SYS2
8	13	SYS2
9	14	SYS2
10	15	SYS2
11	1	SYS3
12	2	SYS3
13	3	SYS3
14	4	SYS3
15	5	SYS3

Incorrect Mappings

Figure 12.5   First set of prototype results

5. **Renovate and re-execute the prototyping session, if necessary**—It is discovered that the source system identifier for the Domestic Order Management System is correct but incorrect for the Asian and Domestic Order Management Systems. For those two order management systems, the first six characters of their source system primary keys have been truncated.

Reviewing the output with the technical users of the systems pointed out this issue. Upon further research, the Source_System_Identifier column and Source_System_Code column sizes were switched.

With the redefined column lengths in the Wheeler data warehouse data model and then database, the test is rerun, and the expected outcome is found.

In this case study, the prototyping session with users uncovered a critical mapping error early in the development process rather than completing the code, performing multiple cycles of testing, and then finding the error in user acceptance testing, which costs time, money, and confidence in the data integration job. Prototyping is ideal for *confirming* user expectations and requirements as well as providing feedback on coding errors. Although this exercise may "feel" like unit testing, there are differences: Unit testing is stand-alone, and prototyping is done with the users, both technical and/or business.

Step 2: Develop User Test Cases

For brevity, we provide a unit test case for the Domestic Order Management System source system extract data integration job, as shown in Figure 12.6.

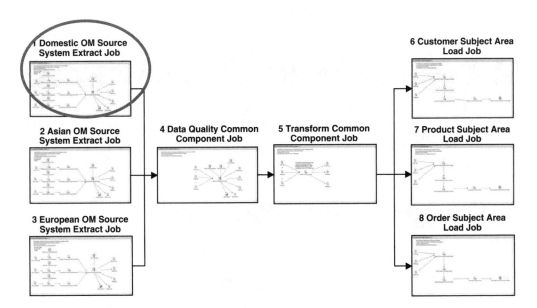

Figure 12.6   Selected Wheeler test cases

The primary verification technique for data integration jobs is verifying counts and amounts as follows:

- Counts include the number of expected rows, extracted, qualified, transformed, or loaded.
- Amounts are either
    - Control totals based on test-only aggregations
    - Predefined totals for business rule transformation types

For integration and system test purposes, it is important that the expected outputs for one set of data integration jobs are integrated and anticipated as expected inputs for down-stream data integration jobs.

Domestic OM Source System Extract Job Unit Test Case

This test case confirms the extraction of the three domestic order management files: SYS_1_CUST, SYS_1_PROD, and SYS_1_ORDR confirms the formatting into the three subject area files and then confirms the validation of the technical data quality for this source system extract job.

1. **Test method**—Verification of source-to-target column totals and record counts
2. **Expected input files**—The following files will be located in the \testing\initial staging directory:
    - SYS_1_CUST

System 1 Customer File

CUST_#	ORG	CUST_NAME	ADDRESS	CITY	STATE	ZIP
410	General Motors	Mr. Jones	1230 Main Street	Warren	Michigan	48010
520	Toyota	Ms. Smith	444 Elm Street	Pontiac	Michigan	48120
660	Ford Motor	Mr. Cartwright	510 Amber St	Detroit	Michigan	48434
200	Nissan	Ms. Wheelright	626 Anderson	Lansing	Michigan	48232
1790	**Control Total**					

- SYS_1_PROD

System 1 Rubber Product File

Item Number	Description	Cost	Price	Inventory
1301	Rubber Joints, Type 1	$7	$12	100,000
1302	Rubber Joints, Type 2	$8	$14	76,000
1303	Rubber Joints, Type 3	$10	$15	46,000
1301	**Rubber Joints, Type 1**	$5	$7	58,000
			Control Total	**280,000**

NOTE

Row 1301 is a known data issue used to confirm the technical data quality component.

- SYS_1_ORDR

| System 1 Order File | | | | | | | |
ORDER_NO	STATUS	DATE	CUST_#	TERMS_CD	ITEM_NO	PROD_ PRICE	AMNT_ ORDR
10001	Shipped	03032010	410	Fixd	1302	$14	2,000
10002	Ordered	03112010	520	Open	1303	$15	5,000
10003	Ordered	03122010	660	Open	1303	$15	3,000
10004	Shipped	03122010	200	Fixd	1301	$12	20,000
						Control Total	30,000

3. **Unit Test Case Steps**—The following steps will verify each component in the Wheeler Domestic Order Management System source system extract job.

3.1 **Source system extract verification steps**

Upon execution of the first step, the landed files should have four records per file and match the control total of 1,790 for the Customer File, 280,000 for the Product file, and 30,000 for the Order File.

3.2 **Format into subject area file verification steps**

For the subject area formatting component of the Wheeler Domestic source system extract, the following files will be located in the \testing\initial staging directory.

The expected output of the subject area files should include the following:

- CUST.dat

Customer Subject Area File: CUST.dat													
Customer_N umber	Source_System_ Identifier	Source_System_ Code	Customer_Org_ Name	Purchaser_F irst_Name	Purchaser_ Last_Name	Address_ Number	Address_ Line_1	Address_ Line_2	Address_ Line_3	City_Code	State	Zip_Code	Zip_Plus_4
Integer (10)	Varchar(10)	Varchar(4)	Varchar(20)	Varchar(20)	Varchar(20)	Integer(10)	Varchar(20)	Varchar(20)	Varchar(20)	Varchar(20)	Varchar(2)	Integer(5)	Integer(4)
1	SYS1		410 General Motors	<null>	Mr. Jones	1230 Main Street				Warren	MI	48010	<null>
2	SYS1		520 Toyota	<null>	Ms. Smith	444 Elm Street				Pontiac	MI	48120	<null>
3	SYS1		660 Ford Motor	<null>	Mr. Cartwright	510 Amber St				Detroit	MI	48434	<null>
4	SYS1		200 Nissan	<null>	Ms. Wheelright	626 Anderson				Lansing	MI	48232	<null>
10	Control Total												

Confirm the following in the CUST.dat output file:

- The new customer numbers are added and incremented by one.
- The source system identifier has been assigned as "SYS1."
- The Domestic OM customer primary key has been assigned to the Source_System_Code field.
- The Control Total should add to 10.

- PROD.dat

Product Subject Area File: PROD.dat								
Product_Id	Source_System_ Identifier	Source_System_ Code	Product_Name	Product_ Type	Product_ Code	Product_Cost	Product_ Price	Inventory
Integer(10)	Varchar(4)	Varchar(10)	Char(40)	Char(40)	Varchar(20)	Decimal(9)	Decimal(9)	Decimal(9)
1	SYS1		1301 Rubber Joints, Type 1		1	$7	$12	100,000
2	SYS1		1302 Rubber Joints, Type 2		2	$8	$14	76,000
3	SYS1		1303 Rubber Joints, Type 3		3	$10	$15	46,000
4	SYS1		1301 Rubber Joints, Type 1		4	$5	$7	58,000
10 Control Total								

Confirm the following in the PROD.dat output file:

- The new product numbers are added and incremented by one.
- The source system identifier has been assigned as "SYS1."
- The Domestic OM product primary key has been assigned to the Source_System_Code field.
- The Control Total should add to 10.
- ORDR.dat

Order_ Number	Source_System_ Identifier	Source_System_ Code	Status_Code	Order_Date	Effective_ Date	Cust_Id	Terms	Order_ Number	Order_Line_ Number	Product_Id	Product_P rice	Quantity_ Ordered	Line_ Amount
Integer(7)	Varchar(4)	Varchar(10)	Varchar(10)	Date(8)	Date(8)	Integer(10)	Varchar(30)	Integer(7)	Integer(4)	Integer(10)	Decimal(9)	Integer(7)	Decimal(11)
1	10001	SYS1	Shipped	03032010	03032010	410	Fixd	1302	1	1302	$14	2,000	$28,000
2	10002	SYS1	Ordered	03112010	03112010	520	Open	1303	1	1303	$15	5,000	$75,000
3	10003	SYS1	Ordered	03122010	03122010	660	Open	1303	1	1303	$15	3,000	$45,000
4	10004	SYS1	Shipped	03122010	03122010	200	Fixd	1301	1	1301	$12	20,000	$240,000
											Control Total		$388,000

Confirm the following in the ORDR.dat output file:

- The new order numbers are added and incremented by one.
- The source system identifier has been assigned as "SYS1."
- The Domestic OM order primary key has been assigned to the Source_System_Code field.
- The customer numbers have a corresponding customer number in the Customer Table Source_System_Code column.
- The order line numbers increment correctly.
- The product numbers have a corresponding product number in the Product Table Source_System_Code column.
- The Line Amount is calculated properly.
- The Control Total should add to $388,000.

3.3   Technical data quality verification steps

For the technical data quality component of the Wheeler source system extract job, verify the following:

- The following Reject Report file T_CUST_TDQ_REPORT will be located in the \testing\clean staging directory.

- The technical data quality process should produce one reject record, a primary key violation.

Technical Data Quality Error Report: T_CUST_TDQ_REPORT					
Record	Column	Value	Error Number	Severity	Error Message
4-SYS1-1301	Source_System_Code	1301	0014	002	Primary Key Violation - Duplicate Id

Summary

This chapter completed the Wheeler order management data integration project case study. This development phase case study walked through an example of how to prototype a slice of functionality by building out a common customer key transformation and building out the unit test case to support that data integration job.

This chapter also completed the part of the book on the Systems Development Life Cycle for data integration where each chapter covered the tasks' steps, techniques, and case study for each of the four phases of a data integration project, which in review are as follows:

- Data integration analysis
- Data integration logical design
- Data integration physical design
- Prototyping/development cycle

The final part of the book covers how data integration is used with other Information Management disciplines.

PART 3

Data Integration with Other Information Management Disciplines

289

Data Integration and Data Governance

The final part of this book covers how other Information Management disciplines influence the design and development of data integration processes. These disciplines are so important and have such an influence on data integration development and operations that they merit focus on what they are, their importance, and their impact on data integration.

As stated in Chapter 2, "An Architecture for Data Integration," data integration is simply a "layer" in the data warehouse reference architecture; it operates within the context of several other disciplines, as shown in Figure 13.1.

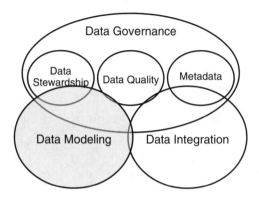

Figure 13.1   Data integration with other Information Management disciplines

Data governance is a particularly influential discipline in the business definition, metadata management, and data quality control aspects of data integration.

This chapter focuses on data governance, what it is, why it is important, its scope, what it influences, the processes that make up data governance, and its impact on the design and development of data integration processes. Chapters 14 and 15, "Metadata" and "Data Quality," respectively, focus on the data governance processes of metadata and data quality.

What Is Data Governance?

Data governance is an Information Management concept that includes very broad topics such as a business process definition, to very narrow topics such as technical metadata, depending on the author or audience. For this book, we use the following definition:

Data governance is the orchestration of people, processes, and technology to enable an organization to leverage data as an enterprise asset.

Despite the lofty goal of using and managing information as an enterprise asset, data governance has been a much talked about but poorly practiced, still-maturing discipline. It has been a topic of discussion in the Information Management community since the 1980s, and many organizations have attempted to implement data governance as a process with varying degrees of success. Much of the lack of success is due to a lack of ownership by the proper stakeholders and an understanding that it is an ongoing business process, not a one-time technology project.

Simply put, data governance is a business process that needs to be owned by the business community and managed by Information Technology (IT), but frequently it is owned and managed by IT, where the full value is not realized. The responsibilities for data governance include the following:

- Business owners defining and stating how they want their data created, managed, and used
- IT being responsible for supporting the businesses stewardship of the data and managing the content (the actual data) and definitions of data in its day-to-day usage

Business ownership also involves resolving ownership issues (e.g., is customer owned by the Accounting or Marketing Department), providing resolution to definitional and usage issues, as well defining and auditing security and privacy issues.

The relationship between business and Information Technology is illustrated in Figure 13.2.

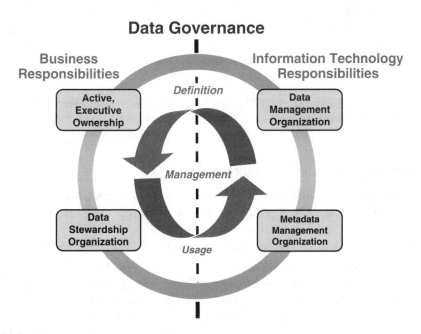

Figure 13.2   Data governance ownership

One of the challenges (illustrated in Figure 13.3) with making data governance a sustainable process is communicating to stakeholders the importance of the process, especially business stakeholders, such as the Finance or Marketing Departments. Chief financial officers might not understand their responsibilities in data stewardship, but they will be extremely focused when key financial metrics are not consistently interpreted such as *return on net assets*.

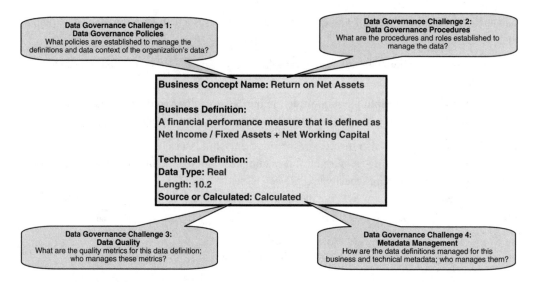

Figure 13.3   Data governance challenges

If there are not commonly agreed-upon definitions, such as *return on net assets* or *gross profit,* it is impossible to create those measures as transformation calculations in data integration processes.

Why Is Data Governance Important?

Although a difficult process to implement, it is critical that every organization, for both transactional and analytics purposes, have some level of data governance, even at a most rudimentary level.

Why? Because organizations that do not have data governance spend inordinate amounts of money and time reconciling data quality issues that have nothing to do with data integration or database design. They will spend weeks and months attempting to reconcile data definitional issues, which equates to hundreds of thousands of dollars. Organizations that have little or no data governance processes experience the following:

- Multiple versions of the truth
- Higher than necessary data management costs
- No ownership or accountability of data
- Internal audit concerns
- Lack of understanding and use of the information
- Loss of information credibility
- Intensive manual effort to respond to requests of information

- Difficulty complying with regulatory requirements such as Sarbanes-Oxley
- Management concerns about the quality of the information being used for decision making

Despite the slow growth of the discipline and the challenges in sustained performance of data governance processes, all IT environments have some level of data governance. Whether it is managing data definitions in data modeling tools or even managing technical metadata in COBOL copybooks, all IT organizations manage some level of data governance, regardless of whether it is recognized and embraced.

Whether it is passive or active, data governance is an organizational process that is found in all organizations using data. The goal is to have the business engaged in active data governance and reap the benefits of better information while saving on the organizational costs of not having an active data governance process.

Components of Data Governance

Implementing an active data governance process in an organization requires the implementation and execution of the following processes:

- Data governance policies and procedures
- Data governance organizational roles and responsibilities
- Data quality management
- Metadata management

The remainder of this chapter defines these foundational processes and their impact on data integration.

Foundational Data Governance Processes

Foundational data governance policies and standards must be defined and, equally important, executed in order to make data governance an ongoing, effective organizational process. Many organizations have committed to start a data governance organization with an executive commitment, but without the organizational processes put in place that will embed and sustain a data governance process, they inevitably fail. These foundational policies for data governance must be based on the recognition that corporate data is a critical corporate resource and will be managed as such. The foundational data governance processes include the following:

- **Policies**—The organizational mandates that will ensure that the stewardship of the data is ongoing
- **Standards**—The rules that frame and provide the audit criteria for the data governance policies that frame how an organization's data is important, ensure that the policy statements are from executive leadership of the organization, as well as provide guidance on how to follow the policies

- **Organization**—The staff and role models for Information Technology and the business that will be responsible for managing the data through the standards

The key to success in implementing data governance standards, organization, and policies is by ensuring that the entire organization is on the same page in terms of the purpose and mission of a data governance organization within an enterprise. A sample data governance mission statement is as follows:

> The data governance organization will support the mandated organizational process of data governance. This entails the definition, execution, and auditing of the creation and use of organizational data. This includes the clear and consistent application of the policies and standards in support of the business objective of having commonly understood information for our internal stakeholders, external clients, and regulatory agencies.

Best Practices, Operational Requirements, and Policies

To support this mission statement, there must be executive-level policies on the management of data that are supported and enforced from the very top of the organization. Although having executive-level mandates ensures a higher probability of success and buy-in, many organizations may have some levels of formalized data governance process but are not at a level of maturity yet to have formal policies in place. They usually have a set of best practices or guidelines, which are sometimes but not always adhered to.

Policies are executive management mandates, with the same rigor and enforcement as accounting policies or employment policies.

These policies are used as the guidelines for both business and IT data definition and analytic projects. In addition to the creation of the policies, there should be education and communication to management and staff about the reason for the data governance policies, the laws and regulations that are behind them, and the standards and processes that will be used to operationalize those policies.

The final section of this chapter discusses the need for formal change management in having organizations adopt the data governance policies.

There should also be monitoring and measuring activities that are put in place that will ensure compliance to the data governance policies. These organizational policies need to be enforced with policies, standards, guidelines, and requirements, which are defined as follows:

- **Policies**—A policy is typically a document or section of a document that states specific requirements or rules that must be met within an organization. Data governance policy statements are point-specific, covering a single area.

  For example: "Participants in the enterprise data governance program will follow a formal change control process for all policies, processes, databases, applications, and structures with the capacity to impact enterprise data from the perspective of Sarbanes-Oxley compliance or organizational accounting policies."

- **Standards**—A standard typically consists of collections of system-specific or procedural-specific requirements that must be met by everyone. All data governance policies should be accompanied by standards. Sometimes those standards are brief statements. In other cases, a single standard might require pages of text.
- **Guidelines**—A guideline is a collection of system-specific or procedural-specific "suggestions" for best practice. They are not requirements to be met but are strongly recommended.
- **Requirements and standards**—A requirement is just that—something that is not optional. Requirements are generally inputs to projects, both business and operational. They describe something that must be put in place by the project team.

Typical standards in data governance include the following:

- Governance of data modeling
- Governance of data definitions
- Governance of data integration mapping business rules
- Governance of metadata
- Governance of data quality controls

It is anticipated that requirements and standards will evolve as a data governance program matures and when appropriate, become policies.

Examples of Foundational Data Governance Policies

The following are examples of the policy statements for a data governance process. It is interesting to note the "thread" of data integration requirements and standards that support the policies. The commonly agreed-to definitions of the sources, target, and the business rules that rationalize the different definitions are pivotal to the design and development of data integration processes.

- **Management of data governance**—Data governance processes will be managed by a data governance organization and supported by a dedicated data governance services team.
- **Data as a corporate asset**—All data is owned by the business enterprise and will be managed as a corporate asset. Data is not owned by any individual functional area.
- **Adherence to data governance**—Adhering to the data governance policies and standards is the corporate responsibility of everyone within the organization. Although the formal data governance organization will include data owners and data stewards, all employees who use and manage data must understand how to interact with the data governance organization and the potential ramifications if policies are not followed.

- **Authority of the data governance program**—The data governance organization will have the authority to review projects for compliance with the organization's data governance policies and standards. The value of data governance can only be achieved if the organization is compliant. This requires ongoing monitoring and the ability to take corrective action with executive buy-in.

- **Documentation of data sources, transformations, and targets**—To be compliant with regulatory requirements such as Sarbanes-Oxley, data integration metadata must identify sources of data, transformation rules, and targets.

- **Enterprise data elements rationalization**—Source system data must be rationalized and linked to enterprise-defined data elements. Data requirements can be achieved by melding together existing accounting, servicing, processing, workout, and risk management system definitions, provided the linkages among these systems are well documented and include sufficient edit and integrity checks to ensure that the data can be used reliably. In the end, data and its analytic state information are strategic business resources owned by the enterprise. For the sake of efficiency, information should be created consistently and shared across the enterprise.

- **Documentation and management of enterprise data definitions**—Comprehensive business definitions for data elements must be defined, documented, and managed. Organizations must have comprehensive definitions for the data elements used within the organization.

- **Periodic data quality audits**—A data governance program should conduct regular audits to ensure that the policies, procedures, and metrics in place are maintaining/improving data quality. Audit team members will follow data quality audit guidelines.

These are only sample data governance policy statements that have been found in common in many organizations. They are by no means comprehensive or the correct policies for all organizations.

In fact, for an immature organization, it is recommended to start with a few policies that will be organizationally *and* publicly supported. Then, over time, increasing the scope and influence of the data governance policies can begin.

The next step is to define the organization for a data governance process.

Data Governance Organizational Structure

To implement and sustain the data governance policies and standards, an organization must be created and, most important, empowered to enforce and audit the data governance policy statements described previously. A data governance organization exists at three levels:

- **Executive level**—These are the C-level executives who have set a goal for a data governance organization, have set the mission statement, and have reviewed and approved the policy statements. They set and manage direction for the data governance office (DGO) that will manage the data governance process.

- **Management level**—The next level is the DGO, which is an ongoing program office that oversees the various data governance groups and committees within an organization such as the data stewardship community, the metadata management, and the various data-related projects such as data quality remediation projects.

- **Project/data stewardship level**—The project level consists of the data-related programs and projects that need to be reviewed and directed by the DGO. The data stewardship level is the data stewardship community, which addresses specific issues and concerns on a day-to-day basis and provides data quality information to the DGO.

Figure 13.4 depicts the three-tiered data governance organization discussed previously.

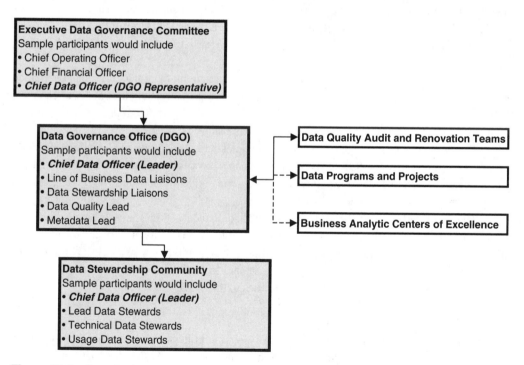

Figure 13.4   Sample data governance organization

This three-tiered model for a data governance process addresses the organizational and communications efforts required to ensure that decisions about data include all appropriate stakeholders and that impact analysis and issue resolution processes are conducted and documented and, when necessary, escalated to the appropriate levels, which are discussed in greater detail in the following sections.

Executive Data Governance Committee

The Executive Data Governance Committee is composed of the C-level executives who provide the mission and sponsorship for the data governance organizational process. They are expected to champion the organization across the enterprise and are responsible for setting the "tone from the top"; these executives must convey to their functional organizations the importance of a data governance process and the need for compliance and participation. It is typically chaired by the chief data officer who also leads the enterprise data governance office (DGO). This committee provides a forum for line-of-business-specific data concerns to be addressed by the DGO and data stewards.

Data Governance Office

The DGO runs the data governance program and is responsible for the day-to-day execution of the organizational data governance processes, which includes ensuring that creators and users of the data are in compliance with the data governance policies. The DGO is usually a thin organization from a full-time perspective; its primary purpose is translating policy to practice and ensuring compliance.

The DGO provides the entire enterprise with a single point of contact for data governance and serves as the central point of communication for governance-related decisions and changes. DGO staff facilitates sessions to identify and prioritize project and data-related issues and also facilitates impact analysis and issue resolution work sessions.

The DGO manages the data governance policies and works with technical and business groups to ensure understanding of the data governance process and its benefits. Although the Executive Data Governance Committee sets policy and standards, it is the DGO that executes many of the communication and audit activities.

The DGO staff serves as liaisons to technical and metadata staff. They work with data quality and compliance resources across the company to collect data quality metrics and to design and implement the controls used to ensure organizational data quality. They work closely with members of the data stewardship community: business and technical staff outside of the DGO who work with data and have dotted-line responsibilities to the DGO.

Chief Data Officer

One of the key roles in creating the interface between the policy-setting Executive Data Governance Committee and the day-to-day execution of those policies is the chief data officer. The chief data officer is responsible for the corporate data governance program and business data strategy. He or she provides oversight and provide final approval for the definition and execution of data governance policies and standards. Qualifications for a chief data officer include the following:

- Information Management and/or business experience
- C-level interaction experience

- Data quality and data risk management expertise
- Strong communication skills

Responsibilities would include the following:

- Owning and driving the organization's data strategy and enterprise-level data vision
- Driving data ownership and accountability in the business
- Aligning business and IT to support data quality
- Driving the organization to better business decisions through improved data quality and data practice
- Chairing Executive Data Governance Committee where data programs and projects are approved and sponsored to ensure data quality practices are embedded into those programs
- Integrating with business executives to understand their data quality requirements, objectives, and issues
- Working closely with the DGO's line-of-business data liaisons to evangelize data governance within a business unit

Data Quality Audit and Renovation Teams

One of the functions of a data governance program is the identification and renovation of bad data quality. The data quality audit and renovation teams can be semipermanent or virtual consisting of data stewards, data quality analysts, process experts, and data profilers. These teams collect, analyze, and report on data quality metrics based on subject area and/or line of business. These teams also provide business executives and system owners with recommendations for embedding data quality controls into systems and processes. An example of such a data quality report is shown in Figure 13.5.

Wheeler Source System Core Data Element List

Source File/ Table Name	Data Element Name	Subject Area	Domain	Data Quality Criteria			Additional fields from the data quality exercise task. Need to be verified with the business.
				Not Null	Key	Ranges/Rules	
System 1 Rubber Product File							
	Item Number	Product	Varchar(04)	Y	Y	Should be primary key	
	Description	Product	Char(30)	Y	N	Nonrepeating	
	Cost	Product	Decimal(12,2)	N	N	Cannot be negative	
	Price	Product	Decimal(12,2)	N	N	Cannot be negative	
	Inventory	Product	Decimal(12,2)	N	N		

Figure 13.5   Leveraging data integration profiling results

Often the results of the source systems analysis such as data profiling is used by data quality teams as input on source system data quality controls and business process improvements.

Ongoing Data-Related Programs and Projects

The data governance office has a dotted-line relationship with all data-related programs and projects. As data projects define new data elements for transactional and analytic data stores, define the source data mapping business rules, and define the measures and aggregations for analytic environments, the business definitions need to be vetted and approved with the DGO through data stewards assigned to the project, as displayed in Figure 13.6.

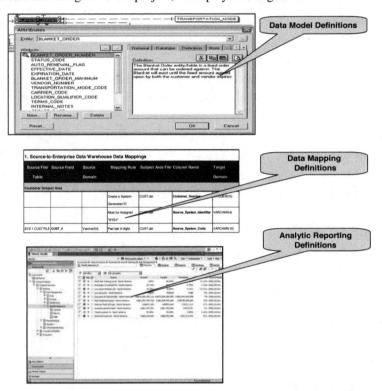

Figure 13.6   Data governance interfaces in data projects

Members of these teams also have responsibilities to embed enterprise data governance concepts into project design and activities. By working with the data programs and projects in their planning phases, data governance checkpoints and data governance roles can be embedded into the projects to provide the data stewardship, metadata, and data quality expertise and perspective needed to ensure that new and extended data definitions are managed and agreed to appropriately.

Business Analytics Centers of Excellence

Reporting is in many ways the objective of data governance. It ensures that the information that is reported through either traditional standard reports or queried in ad hoc environments is consistent and defined with commonly agreed-upon key reporting performance measures (e.g., raw data, calculations, and aggregations). It is important that as lines of businesses such as Accounting, Sales, or Marketing define and develop their reporting environments, they are using and getting approved any new key reporting performance measures and are in compliance with the DGO through the data stewardship process. Although the analytic key performance measure definitions are managed through data stewards, they are stored and controlled in metadata management environments that are further defined in Chapter 14.

Data Stewardship Community

The data stewardship community is a data governance organizational unit that ensures a common understanding and acceptance of the data. The data stewardship community includes individuals from each of the key business units with equal representation, which includes the business and IT. The ideal candidates are ones who understand both, but this is often difficult to find within the same individual.

Members should have the ability to understand and gain consensus from within their own business units with respect to the information needs and business definitions and rules within the data. It is important that the data stewardship team can rely on members to provide subject matter expertise for their subject areas. There has to be balance with what is technologically feasible, so an understanding of IT or having an IT member on the team is important.

A common challenge is to determine how many data stewards are needed in a data stewardship community. It is important to strike a balance between having too many data stewards, which could lead to elongated times for decision making and confusion around business priorities, and having too few. Having too few could result in data stewards who are too broad and can't speak to the needs of individual business units or subject areas.

The number of stewards will vary by organization. Some organizations will need to have one steward per subject area because it is difficult to find a single individual who understands multiple subjects.

For example, an insurance organization might have a data steward for Claims, Policy (perhaps broken down further by line of business), Actuary, Finance, HR, Marketing, and Agency. Also consider assigning someone to be the data steward for customer data. This tends to be the entity with the most cross-organizational issues.

The data stewardship community is often composed of two basic organization models with the various permutations of each, which include:

- **Lines of business**—Members of the data stewardship community are business and technical personnel who reside in their constituent organizations and lines of business and are responsible for their subject area data and have dotted-line responsibilities to the DGO.

- **Directly to DGO**—Data stewards directly report to the DGO in centralized data stewardship functions and are assigned to data governance project work by lines of business, performing activities such as gathering data quality metrics. They may also be responsible for monitoring controls for processes such as Sarbanes-Oxley compliance or data security.

Whether members of the data stewardship community exist within the lines of business or report directly to the DGO, each line of business should have a lead data steward who serves as the communications link between the DGO and those performing other stewardship functions. Lead data stewardship roles are critical for three reasons:

- They ensure that a consistent message is disseminated throughout the stewardship community and that important information reaches stewards.

- They ensure that data-related issues are communicated up from stewards directly to the enterprise data governance office.

- They provide continuity for data-related efforts and concerns.

Each line of business also has staff with responsibility for the following:

- Defining and managing data definitions

- Ensuring adherence to policy for data production and data usage

- Defining, gathering, and auditing data quality metrics

These stewardship responsibilities may be addressed by multiple individuals. Likewise, a single individual may perform multiple stewardship responsibilities.

Data Stewardship Processes

The main responsibility of data stewardship is the ownership and management of data within an organization. This includes what it means, how it is to be created, who creates it, and how it is used. It is also to facilitate a common understanding and acceptance of this data with the objective of maximizing the business return on the investment made in the data resources.

Another definition is the *formalization* of *accountability* for the management of definition, production, and usage of enterprise data assets. The expected results are improved reusability and quality of the data.

Responsibilities of Data Stewardship

Data stewardship responsibilities include the following:

- Documenting, implementing, and applying business-naming standards to existing and new data subject areas and elements

- Documenting standard calculations and calculations needed for key reporting performance measures

- Documenting the business rules related to the data, for example, data integration, required data quality, and transformation business rules

- Monitoring development efforts for adherence to standards

- Ensuring ownership and responsibility for the maintenance of data quality standards

Whether organizations have a formal data governance organizational process or program office, they are recognizing the critical role that the data stewardship function serves in providing higher quality data. Ensuring a common understanding of the data provides the foundation for sharing data across the organization with minimum disruption due to inconsistent definitions.

Data stewardship is an ongoing process with a data stewardship council as part of the data governance organization. This data stewardship council consists of both technical and business specialists as permanent members and data stewardship liaisons. The data stewardship council is responsible for overseeing conformity to organizational data standards as changes occur to data creation, maintenance, and usage activities, which affect business processes and the information systems that use that data.

Goals of Data Stewardship

The primary goal of data stewardship is to manage data as a strategic resource with a common set of definitions, usage patterns, and user access requirements.

For example, an insurance company that wants to understand customer or product profitability must be able to measure and monitor that profitability. If it is difficult to match claims to policies and identify the multiple types of transactions related to a policy, it becomes even more difficult to measure the costs related to the policy; therefore, it also becomes quite challenging to measure profitability.

When the quality of data is good, there often exist multiple definitions of the data across the organization. It is not uncommon for managers of multiple products to report a metric such as earned premium only to spend hours and days determining whether they all used the same calculation to arrive at their numbers. One of the costs associated with lack of stewardship is the time spent discussing and investigating how the numbers were created rather than acting upon the information.

Data Governance Functions in Data Warehousing

As stated in the introduction to this section, data governance processes interact with multiple facets of not only a data integration project, but also the entirety of the data warehousing project. The following sections detail known interfaces between a data governance organization and the development groups in a data warehousing development effort.

Oversight in Data Quality Development

The DGO through data stewards plays an important role in the definition of data quality standards and their implementation in the following:

- The DGO develops, publishes, and communicates data quality policies. The DGO manages a communication channel to provide consistent dissemination of information from the data council to the DGO and from the DGO to the lead stewards and, ultimately, those within business units who serve in stewardship functions. This data governance communication channel is available to disseminate data quality information.

- The DGO develops the data quality metrics and scorecard for the reporting of data quality metrics.

- The DGO provides issues resolution on data quality issues, such as data definition and other business data quality contentions.

Oversight in Master Data Management Development

The data governance organization manages all master data management policies and processes. Master data management or MDM is a particular focus for data governance because the definitions, lookup values, and common hierarchy data, such as customer, organization, and product, are critical to the creation update and delete of both transactional and analytic data.

Oversight in Metadata Management

Metadata is the pervasive construct that is found wherever data is created and used.

The data governance organization through data stewards is responsible for the definition of the business meaning of data structure and the business rules that create that data either directly or indirectly through reviewing and accepting data project work. The management of the metadata definitions, both business and technical, is kept in a metadata management repository often managed by IT.

The responsibilities for metadata management include the following:

- **Defining and managing initial base/calculation data definitions**—Responsibility for the initial population of data definitions and calculations associated with a project are generally performed by data project teams. The DGO has the final review and input to modify the process as necessary.

- **Performing and managing metadata capture**—As new data or data processes are defined or existing data and processes modified, the new metadata must be captured and the changes captured and versioned. This is also the responsibility of the project teams with specific oversight from the data stewards. Again, it is best to plan for these tasks and activities in the planning phase of the project so that they are not missed or rushed at the end of the project. At the end of this section is a sample Systems Development Life Cycle with data governance-specific tasks.

Fortunately, many commercial data integration and analytic packages have metadata management capabilities within them and also have the ability to export metadata to commercial enterprise metadata repositories.

Oversight in Data Integration Process Management

The data governance organization is responsible for the standards of the definitions for the source and target data, as well as the business rules that determine the quality and transformations for that data in data integration development, as shown in Figure 13.7.

Source Field	Source Domain	Mapping Rule	Subject File	Column Name	Column Definition	Target Domain
		Create a system-generated ID	CUST.dat	Customer_Number	The unique identifier assigned to a customer	INTEGER(10)
		Must be assigned "SYS1"	CUST.dat	Source_System_Identifier	The identifier of the source system that the data was sourced	VARCHAR(4)
CUST_#	Varchar(04)	Pad last 6 digits	CUST.dat	Source_System_Code	The unique identifier of the application or system from which the information last used to update the entity instance was populated	VARCHAR(10)
ORG	Varchar(40)	Populate the first 20 digits only	CUST.dat	Customer_Org_Name	The name of the customer organization	Varchar(20)
CUST_NAME	Varchar(40)	Populate the first 20 digits only	CUST.dat	Purchaser_First_Name	The first name of the purchaser	Varchar(20)
CUST_NAME	Varchar(40)	Populate the last 20 digits only	CUST.dat	Purchaser_Last_Name	The last name of the purchaser	Varchar(20)

Figure 13.7 Data governance management of data integration requirements

During a data integration project, it is often necessary to update metadata. Much of this work is managed by the project. For governance and stewardship data that is managed by the DGO, the project can pass information to the DGO, who will ensure that it is properly entered into the metadata repository.

Once in production, break/fix situations may uncover impacts to business metadata on a smaller scale. In these instances, it may be the production support team that may pass business metadata to data stewards who will ensure that it is entered into the metadata repository and is made available to resources performing future data integration tasks. Just as it is important to have formal interaction processes between the data stewards and the development teams, the same interaction processes must be documented and institutionalized with the production support teams.

Table 13.1 portrays the data governance tasks from analysis through physical design (which encompasses a majority of the interface points).

Table 13.1   Data Warehouse Development Life Cycle

Phase and DW Layer	Development Task	Data Governance Task
Analysis phase		
Analytics and reporting	Define key performance measures	Confirm key performance measures to data standards
Data repository	Build a conceptual data model	Confirm the data model subject areas to the enterprise data model and data standards
Data integration	Build a conceptual data integration model	Confirm that existing data integration processes do not exist to accommodate the requirements
	Perform source system profiling	Review source system profiling results for data quality issues
	Perform data mapping to source systems	1. Review and confirm source definitions 2. Review and confirm data quality and transform definitions and calculations 3. Review and confirm target definitions against the target data model and data standards
Logical design phase		
Analytics and reporting	Define analytic tool meta-data layer with key reporting performance measures	Audit and confirm the key reporting performance measures
Data repository	Build a logical data model	Confirm the entity, attribute, and relationship business definitions adhere to data standards
Data integration	Identify data quality criteria	Review and confirm the business and technical data quality checkpoints
	Create logical data integration models	1. Audit and confirm source definitions 2. Audit and confirm data quality and transform definitions and calculations 3. Audit and confirm target definitions

Table 13.1   Data Warehouse Development Life Cycle

Phase and DW Layer	Development Task	Data Governance Task
Physical design phase		
Data repository	Build a physical data model	Confirm the table, column, and constraints technical definitions adhere to data standards
Data integration	Create physical data integration models	1. Audit and confirm technical source definitions
		2. Audit and confirm technical data quality and transform definitions and calculations
		3. Audit and confirm technical target definitions

Compliance in Data Governance

In addition to the cost- and time-saving benefits of data governance, there is also the aspect of compliance. Based on industry, there are many regulatory reporting requirements that require common data definitions, hence data governance.

Regardless of industry, most private-sector organizations have to comply with regulatory agencies, such as the FASB for Accounting regulations, and Sarbanes-Oxley, which mandates a set of internal procedures designed to ensure accurate financial disclosure. The following is an example of data governance compliance.

Alignment with Sarbanes-Oxley

The data governance program will be supporting the organization's Sarbanes-Oxley compliance. To meet this compliance, the following five requirements must be met:

- **Formal data management risk assessments**
- **Documentation of the data management risk management approaches**
- **Formal controls**
- **Documentation proving that controls were implemented and successful**
- **Documentation of the data lineage of the documented changes in source data to the financial statements**

The data governance organization will be responsible for auditing and ensuring that the organization's Information Management reporting processes adhere to these requirements.

For regulatory agencies, the data governance organization will often work with internal organizations such as Accounting or Internal Audit to perform compliance testing and work with the external auditors during an audit.

Data Governance Change Management

Data governance efforts rarely fail due to technical challenges; they traditionally fail for one of two reasons:

- Lack of executive commitment
- Lack of or insufficient organizational change management

Simply dictating an executive mandate will not change the behavior of the organization. A major foundational process is a formal change management process, which is needed to communicate and educate the affected stakeholders of the new data governance organizational process.

Every data governance program needs to plan for a function in the DGO that is responsible for change management within the organization.

Based on experience in starting data governance organizations, change management issues can be anticipated at the executive, managerial, and project layers. At each layer of a data governance organization, change management activities will need to be determined with a set of critical success factors to monitor the success or lack of in the change of behavior toward managing data. These measures include the following:

- Executive challenges:
  - Executive buy-in and commitment
  - Realignment of data efforts
  - Project prioritization
  - Clear mission statement and communications
  - Adequate training support
  - Strong leadership and program management
- Managerial challenges:
  - Behavior change
  - Implementation and *ongoing* execution of data ownership
  - Adherence to new or changed policies and procedures
  - Implementation of new or changed procedures
  - Resourcing and role augmentation
- Project-level challenges:
  - Potential impact on timeline of existing project that had not considered data governance tasks
  - A lack of history in adhering to corporate standards
  - Skilled resources that are available to participate and audit on existing projects

- Turnover of data governance-trained resources
- Effective business and IT processes and practices realigned to support data governance projects and tasks

For the challenges at each of these levels, it is important to have both a senior executive mandate and a formal change management plan to overcome these risks as the data governance organization is being deployed.

It is also important to note the specification "on-going" in the managerial challenges. Many organizations have started a data governance organization only to see it diminish and die without both executive support and formal change management.

Summary

This chapter introduced the business (not technical) concept of data governance and its relevance to information disciplines such as data integration and the other data warehousing practices.

It covered why data governance is important and the hidden cost of not having some level of data governance processes in an organization.

The chapter reviewed the foundational processes and organizational model for an operational data governance office. It reviewed the interaction model for the DGO and the various groups it will need to interface with in DGO and data project work.

It focused on data stewardship in terms of the function and the organization model for data stewards reporting either to the DGO or existing within the organization's lines of business because the data stewards don't report to the lines of business.

The chapter then covered the interface points of a data warehousing development effort with special focus on data integration.

Finally, the chapter reviewed the need for change management and the organizational challenges of changing the organization behavior in regard to data governance.

Chapter 14 reviews in detail one of the key processes in data governance, metadata, the types of metadata, and its application in data integration.

End-of-Chapter Questions

Question 1.
Define data governance.

Question 2.
What data quality issues do organizations that have little or no data governance processes experience?

Question 3.
What is the impact/influence of data governance on data integration?

Question 4.
Explain the relationship between the business and Information Technology in the ongoing management of data governance. For example, who defines and who manages?

Question 5.

To implement a data governance organization, foundational processes must be defined and, equally important, executed in order to make data governance an ongoing, effective organizational process. Define these organizational processes and their roles in data governance.

Metadata

What Is Metadata?

Metadata is defined as "data about data," but it can also be explained as another layer of information created to help people use raw data as information.

Metadata provides context to raw data; it is the business and technical rules that provide that particular data element meaning, as illustrated in Figure 14.1.

Metadata has been referenced throughout this text, in fact in almost every chapter. It has discussed both the business and technical types of metadata. This chapter goes into detail into what constitutes business and technical metadata, how metadata is broken down into categories, who uses metadata, and the types of metadata created in data integration development and processing.

Metadata is created whenever data is created. When a data element is created, it contains information about what process was used to create it, along with rules, formulas, and settings, regardless of whether it is documented.

The goal is to capture this metadata information at creation to avoid having to re-discover it later or attempt to interpret it later.

The discipline of metadata management is to capture, control, and version metadata to provide users such as data stewards the ability to manage the organization's data definitions and data processing rules in a central location.

The tool to store and manage metadata is a metadata repository, which is a metadata "database" for use by stakeholders such as data stewards.

```
┌─────────────────────────────────────────────┐
│  What Is Metadata?                            │
│                                               │
│  Data Element Name: Customer Profitability    │
│                                               │
│  Business Definition:                         │
│  It is a key reporting performance measure that│
│  calculates the profitability of the organization's│
│  customers.                                    │
│                                               │
│  Technical Definition:                        │
│  Data Type: Real                              │
│  Length: 10.2                                 │
│  Source or Calculated: Calculated             │
│  Calculation: Total Customer Revenue - Expenses│
└─────────────────────────────────────────────┘
```

Figure 14.1   Example of business and structural metadata

The Role of Metadata in Data Integration

The discipline of data integration is simply metadata management. Quite frankly, if most Information Management organizations better managed their metadata in terms of common source system definitions, for example, then developing and extending data integration processes would be a much simpler exercise. The following shows where metadata is used in data integration development based on the data integration reference architecture:

- **Source system extracts**—Is the business and technical metadata documented? Is the documentation correct? Is it complete?

- **Data quality**—Are the technical checkpoints vetted and agreed to by IT? Is the business data quality vetted and agreed to by *all* the business stakeholders?

- **Transformations**—Are the transforms such as aggregations and calculations documented and commonly agreed to by the business stakeholders?

- **Load targets**—Are the business and technical definitions of the target data elements documented and agreed to?

Essentially, source system profiling is discovering the source metadata, and data mapping is matching that metadata with the analytic target metadata. Hence, the better documented the metadata, the easier the data integration development and maintenance efforts.

This chapter focuses not just on data integration metadata but also provides a broader view on the types or categories of metadata and how they all link.

Categories of Metadata

Metadata can be composed of any information that describes the actual data itself. For data warehousing purposes, metadata has been classified based on the purpose created and the functions it is used for and can be classified into the types or categories. In each of these categories, there are

relationships. For example, navigational, structural, and analytic all require the business definitions in the business metadata to provide context to the data, as demonstrated in Figure 14.2.

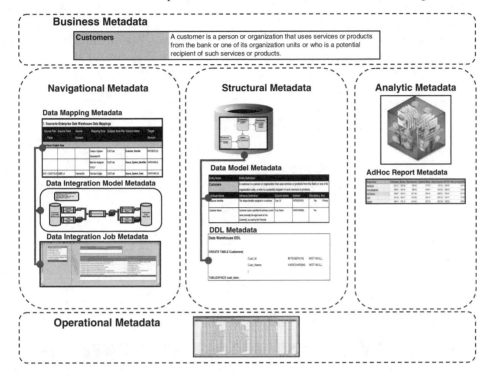

Figure 14.2 The relationships in the categories of metadata

Business Metadata

The business category of metadata defines the information that the data provides in a business
context. Examples of business metadata include subject area definitions (e.g., Product), entity
concept definitions, business attribute names, business attribute definitions, business attribute
valid values, data quality rules, and business rules.

One of the primary sources of business metadata includes conceptual data models, logical
data models, and data quality criteria workbooks.

Structural Metadata

Figure 14.3 portrays structural metadata, which contains the logical and technical descriptions of
the permanent data structures within the Information Management infrastructure. This metadata
includes structures such as flat files, hierarchical, and relational databases. Structural metadata
contains both logical and technical metadata.

Logical metadata consists of data models, entity, attribute, and relationship metadata.
There is a level of overlap between business and logical metadata, for example, business

attributes and physical attributes. Business attributes are defined by the business to describe an aspect of an entity. A physical attribute is defined by a data modeler or application database administrator to describe an aspect of the physical store of data. Some organizations only retain and manage the one type.

The technical metadata is the physical structures themselves, for example, databases/file groups, tables/views/files, keys, indices, columns/fields, source columns/fields, and target columns/fields. Often this type of information is found in Database Definition Language (DDL).

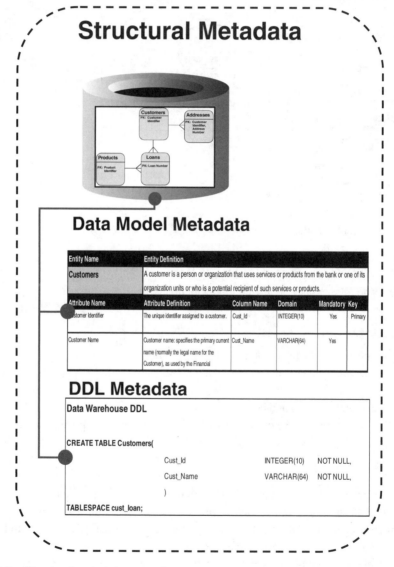

Figure 14.3   Structural metadata example

Navigational Metadata

Navigational metadata describes the process rules and data formats of the data extraction, transformation, and movements, as illustrated in Figure 14.4. Examples of navigational technical metadata are derived fields, business hierarchies, source columns and fields, transformations, data quality checkpoints, target columns and fields, and source and target locations. Primary sources of navigational metadata include data profiling results, data mappings, logical/physical data integration models, and Data Quality Criteria Workbooks.

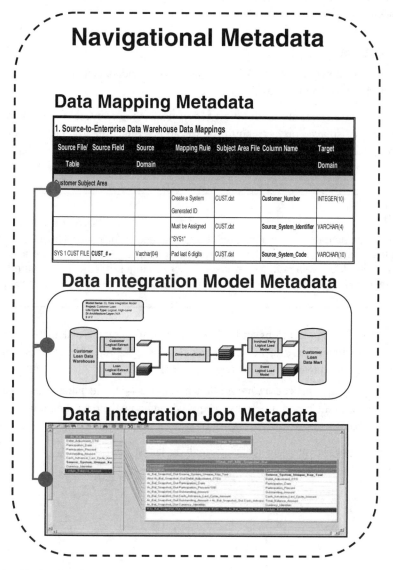

Figure 14.4   Navigational metadata example

Commercial data integration software vendors have addressed navigational metadata from two perspectives:

- **Integrated software suites**—IBM, Ab Initio, and Informatica have integrated profiling and data analysis tools into their design and development suites. This includes data mapping.
- **Metadata repositories**—The same vendors have metadata repositories for navigational metadata as well as the capabilities to integrate other types, which is discussed later in the chapter.

Analytic Metadata

Analytic metadata, shown in Figure 14.5, consists of the metadata that is used in a reporting and ad hoc environment, which includes:

- **Report data elements**—Within the report itself, the definition of the report-level data elements displayed on the report or in the ad hoc query environment is metadata to be created and managed. These elements are often the same technical and business definitions as the data warehouse or dimensional data mart.

NOTE

However, these data elements can and have changed technical and business metadata that is different from the data warehouse, leveraging the ability of the commercial analytic tool metadata capabilities. These changes should be captured and documented from both a data stewardship and metadata management perspective.

- **Report-level aggregations and calculations**—Most commercial analytic tools provide the ability to build aggregations and calculations at the report level. This topic was first discussed in Chapter 5, "Data Integration Analysis."
- **Report layout and report navigation metadata**—This technical metadata describes the layout of the report, the fonts to be used, and how the data should be portrayed and navigated.

Primary sources of analytic metadata include OLAP and reporting packages metadata environments.

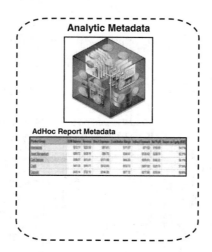

Figure 14.5 Analytic metadata example

Operational Metadata

The operational category of metadata, shown in Figure 14.6, describes the data integration applications and jobs through statistics, giving a full technical view of the environment. Examples of operational metadata include jobs statistics and data quality check results.

Figure 14.6 Operational metadata example

Whereas the prior categories are primarily used by business users, data stewards, and data management professionals, operational metadata is used by production support and systems administration for troubleshooting and performance tuning.

Sources of operational metadata include data integration job logs and data quality checks being generated either by the data integration jobs or the production scheduler.

Metadata as Part of a Reference Architecture

In Figure 14.7, which shows the business intelligence (BI) reference architecture, metadata is shown in two components:

- As a data store in the data repository layer; whether pursuing a build or buy scenario for a metadata repository, it will require its own data store
- As a stream in the data integration layer

Metadata management spans across the entire data warehouse reference architecture, due to the fact that metadata is a "by-product" of most of the disciplines. For example, defining a data model creates business and structural metadata. Defining source-to-target mappings creates navigational metadata. Additionally, metadata is part of the architecture in that the metadata provides communication and understanding between the disciplines.

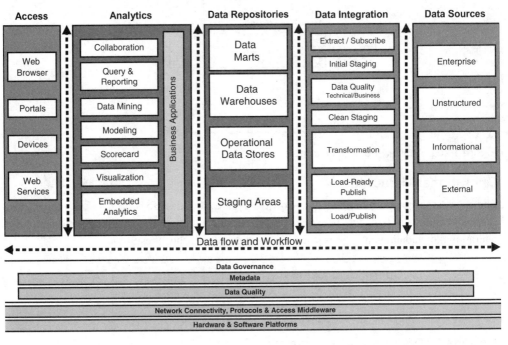

Figure 14.7   The business intelligence reference architecture

Metadata Users

Metadata provides value at a variety of levels to a range of users but can typically be divided into three categories:

- **Business users**—Business users of metadata need to understand the business meaning of the data in the systems they use. Additionally, they need to know the business rules and data access rules that apply to the data. Data stewards are typically classified as business users.

- **Technology users**—IT professionals who are responsible for planning and building the transactional and analytic systems need to understand the end-to-end picture of the data to manage change. These users need the technical metadata for the technical information about the data environment, such as physical data structures, extract-transform-load rules, reporting information, and impact analysis. Examples of technology users include data modelers, data integration architects, BI architects, designers, and developers.

- **Operational users**—IT operational professionals are those who are responsible for day-to-day operation of the data environment and are users of operational metadata. Operational metadata can assist them in identifying and resolving problems as well as managing change in the production environment by providing data information about the data integration processing and job processing impact analysis.

Managing Metadata

Because metadata is created in many places during the development of a system, it is important to understand and govern all the categories of metadata in the metadata life cycle. Information Management professionals have had the goal of a centrally managed metadata repository that governs all metadata, but that vision is difficult to achieve for a variety of factors. The reality is that metadata is created in many different tools used to develop data structures and process that data, as shown in Figure 14.8.

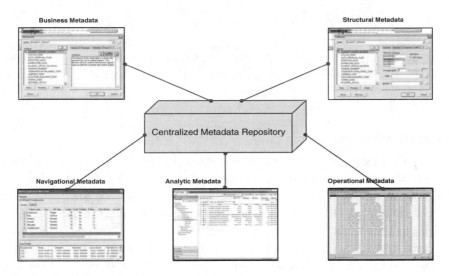

Figure 14.8   Centrally managing sources of metadata

At best, a centralized metadata repository should enhance metadata found in local repositories by building additional relationships between metadata. Additionally, this centralized metadata repository provides a place to store and manage additional metadata.

The Importance of Metadata Management in Data Governance

A centralized metadata repository is the "database" for all users of metadata, especially data stewards. Having an integrated metadata management environment is a far superior approach to performing data stewardship than with Microsoft Excel–based data dictionaries that might or might not be linked to the actual data elements with the same business and technical definitions.

Metadata Environment Current State

Metadata exists in many places, and the roles it plays throughout the system should be first understood in the IT environment. Begin by documenting ways metadata is created and governed (or not) today. An example of a current state inventory is shown in Table 14.1.

Table 14.1   Sample Current State Inventory

Artifact	Format Example	Governance Roles
Enterprise data model	Erwin	Enterprise data modelers
Logical data model	Erwin	Data stewards, data modelers
DDL	Database Catalog	Database administrators
Data quality workbook	Microsoft Excel	Data stewards, data quality analysts
Data mappings	Microsoft Excel	Data stewards, DI architects
Reports and ad hoc query environment	eCognos Framework Manager	Data stewards, BI architects

Metadata Management Plan

Consistency in the metadata is necessary to keep information organized. Consistent terminology helps communicate metadata, and it helps applications process the metadata. Bringing metadata together in either a consolidated or federated fashion provides that consistency. For example, commercial analytic tools have metadata repositories that provide function and meaning to the users of that tool. Understanding the report as it relates to commercial data integration packages and relational databases is often beyond the scope of that local repository. By bringing together key pieces of metadata, the complete heritage/lineage of the fields on a report can be understood.

Determining Metadata User Repository Requirements

Gathering and understanding requirements cannot be emphasized enough. Historically, metadata management efforts involved scanning in all known metadata and trying to derive meaning from the results. Not only does this waste resources, it often results in a metadata repository that isn't used because it lacks quality, organization, and simplicity.

Metadata management needs to be approached in a systematic manner with incremental benefit produced. Planning the end-to-end metadata architecture is necessary to identify and understand all integration points. Additionally, knowing what metadata is easy to obtain, load, and deploy identifies quick wins. Understanding the value each type of metadata provides helps to prioritize iterations of building the entire solution.

While reviewing requirements, identify the questions that can be answered once this metadata is loaded. Identify if a consolidated metadata repository is the best place to get that answer.

For example, users of the metadata repository might need to know the ultimate sources of a given column in a data warehouse and not necessarily all the technical details about transformations. A plain English textual explanation of what happens to the data is sufficient. For example, "Customer Number is from the Customer Data Hub," is preferred over "Field XX3234 is from Data Store CDH001." If more detail is required, the commercial data integration package's metadata repository can be accessed. This provides the appropriate level of information without transferring unneeded detail that is rarely used at a consolidated metadata repository level.

Additionally, while reviewing requirements, document both local- and consolidated-level metadata repository stores and the overall management of all metadata. The metadata repository should add value and not replace local metadata stores.

For each type of metadata, consider the following:

- **Where it will be stored**—Identify the data store requirements (e.g., commercial metadata repository, homegrown relational database).
- **What will be stored**—Identify metadata sources.
- **How it will be captured**—Identify load mechanism, CRUD (Create Read Update Delete) requirements, administration requirements, and audit and retention requirements.
- **Who will capture the data**—Identify the roles and responsibilities for managing the repository and levels of users.
- **When it will be captured**—Identify capture frequency, history, and versioning considerations.
- **Why it will be captured**—Identify the benefits of the requirements and the specific questions this metadata will answer and provide reporting/browsing requirements.

Metadata Management Repositories: Build Versus Buy

Enterprise metadata repositories can be implemented using customer-built applications on top of commercial relational databases or by purchasing commercial metadata repository solutions.

Many factors dictate which direction to take but, most commonly, budget and client requirements will drive most decisions.

Vendor solutions provide substantial out-of-the box functionality but need to be carefully mapped to requirements. Strengths of most vendor solutions include the following:

- Existing metamodels
- Ability to extend metamodels

- Scanners to read and populate from common metadata sources (e.g., Erwin, database catalogs, generic spreadsheet load facilities)
- Front ends (both a plus and a minus because they almost always require customization)

The main weaknesses of most vendor solutions are they are very costly in dollars and implementation time to configure and train on.

One advantage of building one's own solution is that when requirements are not too complex, they can be more quickly implemented and show immediate benefits compared with vendor solutions.

Metadata Management Life Cycle

The design of metadata is no different from the design of any other data. Therefore, metadata management applies the same Information Management design and development principles. Steps include the following:

1. **Prepare**—The preparation of metadata for centralized management involves identifying, gathering, and formatting for loading. It is highly important to obtain certification on the sources by sign-off or approval from appropriate data stewards. Metadata needs to be gathered in the format identified during planning (e.g., Erwin model, spreadsheet, database catalog). Preparation also involves obtaining access to these artifacts.

2. **Populate**—Population involves running the various population mechanisms (e.g., scanner, data integration job, interface, SQL loader) and verifying the results. Any problems or anomalies detected require correction before proceeding. Additionally, any enhancement or additional relationships need to be made via automated processes if possible.

3. **Publish**—The best way to deliver metadata reporting involves a standard "push" reporting technology and a standard Web interface with simple navigation. Reports and queries and Web access should be designed, vetted with the user community, and created during development of the metadata solution.

Administration

Metadata repositories require the same administration functionality that other databases and data stores need. Design and development of the metadata solution should have taken these into consideration, and ongoing administration should be established to provide current security and recovery capabilities. Administration involves the following:

- Security
- Backup/recovery
- Database monitoring and performance tuning
- Server maintenance

Metadata Management Administrator

The management of a centralized metadata repository requires a very specific role that is half IT (e.g., application database administrator) and half business (e.g., data steward). The person who fills this role will need to be able to perform the following tasks:

- Populate, maintain, and use the metadata repository content during the lifetime of a project.
- Provide metadata usage support for development projects.
- Ensure users are able to navigate and understand metadata based on their business requirements and perspective.
- Support the collection of business and technical metadata from queries and other uses of the data warehouse from end users.
- Approve that project deliverables meet metadata standards, guidelines, and tools during a project's QA control phase checkpoints.

Metadata Capture Tasks the Data Warehousing SDLC

Once the metadata is captured and maintained, it is critical to keep it up to date to keep it relevant. Data warehousing projects generate all the different categories of metadata. It is best to build metadata capture tasks into data warehouse development projects to capture the metadata at the time of approval for either new or changed metadata.

Table 14.2 portrays the metadata capture from analysis through physical design.

Table 14.2 Sample Metadata Capture

Phase and DW Layer	Development Task	Metadata Capture Task
Analysis phase		
Data repository	Build a conceptual data model	Capture the data model subject areas into the enterprise data model and metadata repository
Data integration	Perform source system profiling	Capture the profiling results in structural metadata under source systems
	Perform data mapping to source systems	1. Capture source definitions 2. Capture data quality and transform definitions and calculations 3. Capture target definitions

(continued)

Table 14.2   Sample Metadata Capture

Phase and DW Layer	Development Task	Metadata Capture Task
Logical design phase		
Analytics and reporting	Define analytic tool metadata layer with key reporting performance measures	Capture the key reporting performance measures
Data repository	Build a logical data model	Capture the data model, entity, attribute, and relationship business definitions
Data integration	Identify data quality criteria	Capture the business and technical data quality checkpoints
	Create logical data integration models	1. Capture the data integration model 2. Capture source definitions 3. Capture data quality and transform definitions and calculations 4. Capture target definitions
Physical design phase		
Data repository	Build a physical data model	Capture the DDL into the metadata repository
Data integration	Create physical data integration models	1. Capture technical source definitions 2. Capture technical data quality and transform definitions and calculations 3. Capture technical target definitions

Summary

This chapter provided a broad view of metadata in terms of the types of metadata created in a data warehouse environment. It also discussed the necessity for metadata management for effective data governance.

It covered the different categories or types of metadata in terms of how it is created and who uses it. It documented the importance of metadata in data integration design and maintenance and how, for example, source-to-target mapping is mostly a metadata management function.

The chapter covered the types of users of metadata, both business and technical, usually based on the category of metadata.

Finally, it covered what is needed to manage metadata in a repository in terms of planning population, usage, and maintenance.

The final chapter in the book covers another key data governance aspect, data quality and its application in data integration.

End-of-Chapter Questions

Question 1.
What are the two definitions of metadata?

Question 2.
There are several aspects of the impact or role of metadata in data integration definition and development. What are some of the examples based on the data integration reference architecture?

Question 3.
There is business metadata and several types of technical metadata. What are the different types of technical metadata and their relationship to business metadata?

Question 4.
What are the types of users of metadata?

Question 5.
What are the two prevalent factors in a build versus buy decision in a metadata repository?

CHAPTER 15

Data Quality

This chapter covers those aspects of data quality that have not been covered to provide a complete view of data quality management and its influence on data integration.

Several chapters throughout this book have addressed data quality. In Chapter 2, "An Architecture for Data Integration," data quality was defined as the commonly understood business and technical definition of data within defined ranges. In a prior chapter, flagging bad data quality was discussed through the definition and design of business and technical data quality checkpoints in the logical data quality data integration model using the Data Quality Criteria Workbook. Although identifying and flagging bad data quality is important, it is equally important to define what data is important to measure data quality on and how to define that data as key for data quality.

Once the key data is identified, it is important to periodically audit that data and when necessary clean or renovate bad data.

Data quality management is also one of the core disciplines within data governance. Like metadata, it is also one of the integral data governance threads within data integration. In fact, the line between data integration and data governance is often blurred because data quality is an integral process for data integration job processing and data stewardship processes, as portrayed in Figure 15.1.

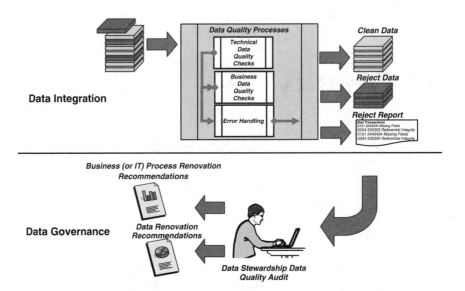

Figure 15.1   The data quality thread between data integration and data governance

The Data Quality Framework

Most Information Management disciplines have an architecture or framework by which to under-stand that model; data quality is no exception. The data quality framework illustrated in Figure 15.2 is a multidimensional reference model with the first dimension defining the key data quality elements, or what data is important to measure quality. The business and technical dimensions provide the rules that measure how well a data element meets a company's data quality goals and ultimately provides trusted and critical information.

We have made inference to the data quality framework throughout the book in terms of the types of data quality checkpoints that are required in the data quality data integration model. This framework consists of the following:

- Key data quality elements
- Technology defined data quality
- Business-process defined data quality
- Data quality processes

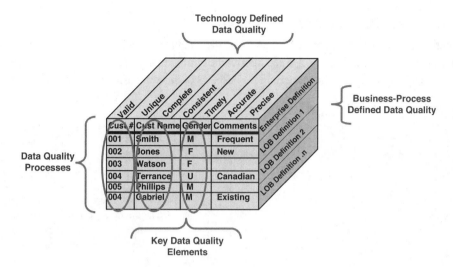

Figure 15.2   Aspects of the data quality framework

Leveraging all four aspects of this model in both the design of data repository databases and in the data quality components in the data quality layer of the data integration environments ensures the highest possible preventive data quality controls.

Key Data Quality Elements

With an organization, there are certain data elements that are critical to the business, for which the data quality should be identified, defined, and measured. These key data elements can be both base element data (for example, Customer Name) as well as derived data (for example, Net Profit).

These key data quality elements are often defined as such during data definition activities such as data modeling. Once identified as a key data quality element, the technical and business data quality criteria for that element are identified and defined in terms of ranges of compliance to requirements of a business.

For instance, the key data quality element Birth Date has a business data quality criteria defined as a date range, as follows:

Birth Date = Range: from 0 – 140

This business user-defined range reflects the probability that most people simply do not live beyond 140 years.

Although there is a relationship between relational key constraints, mandatory data, and key data quality elements, that relationship is not one-to-one. Not all mandatory and constraint data is necessarily key data quality data.

For instance, a Customer ID column may be both mandatory and a primary key constraint, but not a key data quality element based on that element's importance to the organization.

The Technical Data Quality Dimension

The technical data quality dimension refers to the data quality criteria found in the technical definition of the data, for example, as defined in both the entity integrity and referential integrity relational rules found in logical data modeling. Key aspects of this dimension are shown in Table 15.1.

Table 15.1   Technical Data Quality Dimensions

Name	Description	Examples of Poor Technical Data Quality
Valid	The data element passes all edits for acceptability.	A customer record has a name that contains numbers. The Social Security Number field should be a numeric integer but is populated with alphanumeric characters instead.
Unique	The data element is unique—there are no duplicate values.	Two customer records have the same Social Security number.
Complete	The data element is (1) always required or (2) required based on the condition of another data element.	A product record is missing a value such as weight. Married (y/n) field should have a nonnull value of "y" or "n" but is populated with a "null" value instead.
Consistent	The data element is free from variation and contradiction based on the condition of another data element.	A customer order record has a ship date preceding its order date.
Timely	The data element represents the most current information resulting from the output of a business event.	A customer record references an address that is no longer valid.
Accurate	The data element values are properly assigned, e.g., domain ranges.	A customer record has an inaccurate or invalid hierarchy.
Precise	The data element is used only for its intended purpose, i.e., the degree to which the data characteristics are well understood and correctly utilized.	Product codes are used for different product types between different records.

Each of these technical data quality rules or dimensions are instantiated against the key data quality elements with different methods. Many of the dimensions are enforced with simply relational database rules such as entity and referential integrity.

For instance, the precise dimension is enforced in the relational database by applying the primary key constraint.

Within each of these dimensions, technical data quality rules are applied against key data quality elements, as shown in Figure 15.3.

Data Quality Criteria Workbook

Table: Customer	Technical Dimension							Business Dimension
Column Name	Valid	Unique	Complete	Consistent	Timely	Accurate	Precise	Enterprise Business Definition
	Data element passes all edits for acceptability	Data element is unique—there are no duplicate values	Data element is (1) always required or (2) required based on the condition of another data element	Data element is free from variation and contradiction based on the condition of another data element	Data element represents the most current information resulting from the output of a business event	Data element values are properly assigned, e.g. domain ranges.	Data element is used only for its intended purpose	
Cust_Id	Must Be Numeric	Primary	Not Null	Relational rules on primary keys	Last update within the past month	Is a part of an involved party	Must be marketing or sales to create	The unique identifier assigned to a customer.
Cust_First_Name	N/A	Mandatory	Not Null	Cust_Id must exist	Last update within the past month	Is a part of an involved party	Must be marketing or sales to create	Specifies the first name of the party
Cust_Last_Name	N/A	Mandatory	Not Null	Cust_Id must exist	Last update within the past month	Is a part of an involved party	Must be marketing or sales to create	Specifies the last name of the party
Gender	Yes	Mandatory	Not Null	It must be "**Male**," "**Female**," or "**Unknown**"	Last update within the past month	Is a part of an involved party	Must be marketing or sales to create	Gender of the customer. Data Quality Criteria: Male, Female,

Figure 15.3   The applied technical data quality rules in a Data Quality Workbook

Data quality is not just about the structure and content of individual data attributes. Often, serious data quality issues exist due to the lack of integrity between data elements within or across separate tables that might be the result of a business rule or structural integrity violations.

Ultimately, the degree to which the data conforms to the dimensions that are relevant to it dictates the level of quality achieved by that particular data element.

The Business-Process Data Quality Dimension

The business-process data quality dimension in Table 15.2 defines the understanding of the key data quality elements in terms of what the business definition for a data quality element is and what the business rules are associated with that element.

As reviewed earlier, many organizations have inconsistent definitions and different business rules for similar data within each line of business, with each line of business having its own understanding of what that data element is. For example:

- Marketing Definition of Net Assets = Assets – Expenses
- Finance Definition of Net Assets = Assets – Expenses + Owners Equity

Table 15.2   The Business Dimensions of Data Quality

Name	Description	Examples of Poor Data Quality
Definitional	The data element has a commonly agreed-upon *enterprise* business definition and calculations.	Return on Net Assets (RONA), Net Present Value (NPV), and Earnings Before Interest, Taxes and Amortization of goodwill (EBITA) are calculated using different algorithms/equations and using different source data for each algorithm/equation for multiple departments within an enterprise.

Hence, with disparate views on what the definition and business rules of a data quality element are, when information is compared from different lines of business, the perception of bad quality is created.

Applying a consistently agreed-upon *common* business definition and rules against the data elements provides the insurance against inconsistent data quality issues.

It is the management of the common understanding of business definitions throughout the data stewardship community that is so critically important to not have misunderstood reporting issues.

Types of Data Quality Processes

The final aspect of the data quality framework are those processes that ensure good data quality or prevent bad quality from being created and those that find bad data quality for renovation.

Ensuring data quality is typically a *result* of solid adherence to the definition of data quality criteria from both a business process and data design perspective. As a result, there are *preventive* data quality best practices that focus on the development of new data sources and integration processes, and there are *detective* data quality best practices that focus on identification and remediation of poor data quality. Both of these types are found in the tasks and steps of the data quality life cycle, which is discussed in the next section.

The Data Quality Life Cycle

Data quality is an information discipline that has it own life cycle, which involves defining the data quality elements and the criteria for those elements, auditing and measuring the data quality for those elements, and renovating both the process and data (if appropriate).

As shown next, the data quality life cycle leverages the data quality framework throughout the phases, tasks, and activities:

Define Phase
1.   Define the data quality scope.
2.   Identify/define the data quality elements.
3.   Develop preventive data quality processes.

Audit Phase
1.   Develop a data quality measurement plan.
2.   Audit data quality by line of business or subject area.

Improve Phase
1.   Recommend strategic process renovations.
2.   Correct or flag existing data quality issues.
3.   Review business process and data renovations.

Similar to metadata, aspects of the data quality life cycle spans between data warehousing and data governance project life cycle tasks. An example is the data quality definition tasks in the data integration life cycle.

These are the data quality data integration tasks that were defined in the analysis phase that define business and technical data quality checkpoints and are examples of data integration tasks that are taken from the data quality life cycle as well as reflect the data quality framework.

The data quality life cycle is a highly iterative process that is executed by both data development project teams and that defines the data quality elements as well as data stewardship communities that monitor those elements, as illustrated in Figure 15.4.

Figure 15.4   The iterative nature of the data quality life cycle

Whereas the define phase focuses on the preventive data quality processes, the audit and improve phases focus on the detective data quality processes.

The remainder of this chapter reviews each of the phases of the data quality life cycle in terms of the tasks and best practices.

The Define Phase

The define phase describes the data quality elements needed with the organization, the scope of how these elements will be managed, and what processes will be used in the definition of data to ensure good data quality and prevent bad data quality. For example, is a full data quality program required, or is leveraging an existing data stewardship process sufficient?

Defining the Data Quality Scope

The first define phase task identifies the intended new or extended scope for a data quality process within an organization or line of business. Often, these efforts can be as expansive as enterprise data quality programs that are implemented and sustained by the data stewardship community or as narrow as data quality tasks embedded in other data governance activities.

This scope needs to be determined and vetted with an objective of pragmatism in terms of organizational capability and organization will in terms of the cost benefit of such an endeavor. One of the key determinants of that scope is the subject of budget. Initiatives that are project-funded usually have short life spans. Those that are funded as an organizational process (same as data governance budgets) are more likely to sustain.

Identifying/Defining the Data Quality Elements

This task determines what data elements should be considered as an element for which data quality criteria is required and measured. Typically, data quality elements are created from the same discipline that is used to design most structured data, data modeling. The entities, attributes, and relationships that are used to create a data model are also the primary sources to create data quality elements, as shown in Figure 15.5.

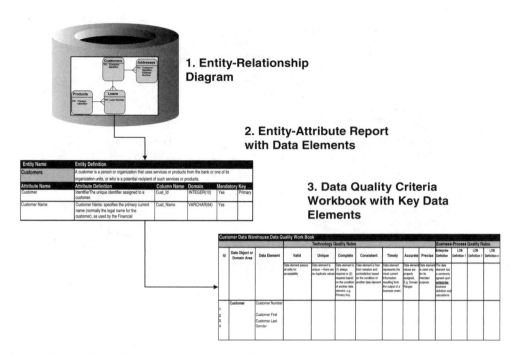

1. Entity-Relationship Diagram

2. Entity-Attribute Report with Data Elements

3. Data Quality Criteria Workbook with Key Data Elements

Figure 15.5   The data quality element sources

As discussed earlier in this chapter, not all defined columns, fields, and elements are relevant to data quality, only those that affect the structure and understanding of information. For example, within the Customer Entity, the "**Notes**" attribute will not affect data quality; therefore, this attribute will not be identified with any data quality rules or be considered a data quality element. Again, only those attributes that affect the structure and understanding of the data will be identified and quality criteria determined.

Developing Preventive Data Quality Processes

Based on the scope and the identification of the key data quality elements, the next step is to develop the preventive data quality process tasks in the data development process that will prevent data quality anomalies.

Data development projects such as data warehousing effort have two key areas of focus to ensure high levels of data integrity and data quality control, which are in the database and data integration processes, as shown in Figure 15.6.

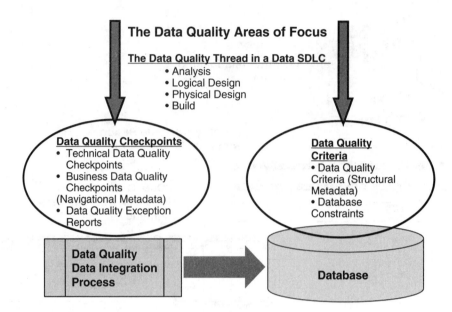

Figure 15.6   The preventive data quality areas of focus

By focusing on designing and building data quality checkpoint and reporting functions in the processes that move the data, and the constraints in the databases that contain the data, the overall integrity and confidence of the information is verified and improved substantially.

Please note, however, the real goal is to push data quality into the source systems and renovate those processes that are producing incorrect data.

Threading Data Quality Tasks into the Data Development Process

Preventive data quality processes are found throughout all phases of a data warehouse project. The data warehouse Systems Development Life Cycle includes the following major phases:

- Analysis
- Logical design
- Physical design
- Build

As discussed throughout the book, there are specific business intelligence disciplines or layers, each with specific tasks that manage and direct the definition, design, and development of data quality processes within the data integration processes and data structures (databases/data files). In the Systems Development Life Cycle for data integration and database development, data quality activities are a consistent thread in terms of additional tasks and deliverables, as shown in Table 15.3.

Table 15.3 Data Quality Development "Thread" Tasks

Phases/Disciplines	Data Repository Layer	Data Integration Layer
Analysis	Define key data quality elements DQ analysis QA checkpoint	Define key data quality elements DQ analysis QA checkpoint
Logical design	Identify DQ criteria Review/augment DQ criteria DQ logical design QA checkpoint	Define data quality criteria Review/assess source data quality Develop logical DQ data integration model with technical and business checkpoints DQ logical design QA checkpoint
Physical design	Validate DQ constraints in database DQ physical design QA checkpoint	Develop physical common DQ data integration model DQ physical design QA checkpoint
Build	Validate DQ constraints in database DQ build QA checkpoint	Build data quality data integration jobs DQ build QA checkpoint

These data quality-specific tasks leverage the key data quality elements to define data quality checks in both the data integration processes and database.

The following section provides further explanation of these data quality tasks. Although prior sections of the book have provided some level of detail on the data integration tasks on data quality, this section goes into detail for both the data integration and database development data quality–specific tasks. This information is useful for understanding the full scope of defining, designing, and developing preventive data quality processes in a data warehouse project.

High-Level Data Quality Data Integration Development Tasks

These tasks are a review of those data quality-focused data integration tasks found in the analysis, logical design, physical design, and build phases of the data integration life cycle:

1. **Review existing data quality information**—In this task, the data quality checkpoints in the existing data integration models related to the intended project are reviewed. The following best practices can be applied to this task:

   - Identify related sources and targets to assist in locating existing data integration models.

   - Review each data integration model to determine existing data quality checkpoints.

2. **Define project-level data quality requirements**—In this task, the existing data quality checkpoints in the existing data integration models related to the intended project are confirmed, a gap analysis is performed, and the high-level data quality requirements for a potential assessment are determined. The following best practices can be applied to this task:

   - Use previously identified sources and targets to assist in locating existing data integration models.

   - Review logical and physical data integration models to determine existing data quality checkpoints.

   - Work with business and IT subject matter experts to identify other sources of relevant data quality checkpoint information not included in the metadata repository.

   - Use previously identified potential new critical data elements to assist in determining the gap between current data quality checkpoints and potential new data quality checkpoints.

   - Use a percentage of new data quality checkpoints identified (new checkpoints / total checkpoints) and complexity (cleansing versus reporting) to assist in determining project risk.

3. **Review/assess source data quality**—In this task, the integrity and conformance of the data sources used to create the new data store is reviewed. The following best practices can be applied to this task:

   - Focus investigation on new sources and new critical data elements in existing sources.

   - Use the number of new sources and critical data elements to determine the level of effort.

   - Work with business and IT subject matter experts to determine the information value chain, overall quality of the source data store, and identify known data quality issues.

   - If this is an existing source, determine whether statistical sampling has been done.

   - Use source data store technical metadata to confirm structural integrity.

   - Use business definition and data quality criteria to verify sample data.

   - Work with business subject matter experts to determine absolute and optional data quality requirements for critical data elements.

   - Work with IT subject matter experts to determine file integrity check requirements and error threshold exceptions.

4. **Define logical data quality component model**—For this task, the data quality criteria should be gleaned from the Data Quality Criteria Workbook and used to

- Identify critical tables and data elements columns
- Identify technical and business data quality criteria
- Determine which identified data quality criteria is absolute
- Determine which identified data quality criteria is optional
- Determine cleanse requirements
- Capture DQ criteria into metadata repository

5. **Design physical data quality data integration model**—Apply source-specific technical data quality rules from the logical data quality data integration model, which includes

- Design file integrity checks
- Design record-level checks
- Design error threshold checks
- Design other checkpoint types
- Design cleansed file for clean staging area
- Design rejects file for clean staging area
- Design Rejects Report

6. **Build the data quality components**—Complete the build of the following components for the data quality jobs:

- File integrity cleansing components
- Record-level cleansing components
- Error threshold cleansing components
- Data quality error and exception handing reporting components

High-Level Data Quality Database Development Tasks

Just as critical as ensuring that there are controls on the data that is processed for a database, there need to be controls on the database itself to ensure that the key data quality elements are kept within the data quality criteria tolerances.

By not having proper data quality controls built in to the design of a database, the creation of technical data quality issues or data anomalies exists, such as incorrect, invalid, and missing data are allowed, as shown in Figure 15.7.

- **Incorrect data**—The database is allowing textual data to be created in the sales field (column) rather than numeric data.

- **Invalid data**—The database is allowing a negative or real number to be created in the sales field (column) rather than integer data.

- **Missing data**—The database is allowing a transaction to be created without a value or allowing a "null" value in a mandatory field.

Store Sales					
Store ID	Month in Qrt	Product ID	Scenario	Sales	Costs
1	1	1	Actuals	285	240
1	1	1	Plan	ABC	220
1	1	2	Actuals	270	260
1	1	2	Plan	265	255
1	1	3	Actuals	350	300
1	1	3	Plan	300	280
1	1	4	Actuals	220	230
1	1	4	Plan	230	235
1	1	5	Actuals	480	400
1	1	5	Plan	-100	366
1	2	6	Actuals	380	370
1	2	6	Plan	375	375
1	2	7	Actuals	313	264
1	2	7	Plan	308	253
1	3	8	Actuals	400	340
1	3	8	Plan	<null>	300
1	12		Actuals	2,698	2,404
1	12		Plan	#VALUE!	2,284

(Incorrect Data → ABC row; Invalid Data → -100 row; Missing Data → <null> row)

Figure 15.7   Database data quality anomalies

Developing data quality checks into data warehouse databases ensures that data that is created or changed meets the data quality criteria required of key data quality elements.

Preventive data quality checks for the database are traditionally implemented through database constraints. Having to correct incorrect, invalid, and missing data can be avoided by designing and implementing integrity constraints in the database. Integrity constraints physically enforce the business rules in the database. There are three types of constraints:

- **Primary key constraints**—Enforces the primary key rules, which states that each record in a table must be uniquely identified and cannot be null

- **Foreign key constraints**—Enforces the foreign key and referential integrity rules in the manner that it has to reference the primary key and match in value to another table or be null

- **Unique key constraints**—Enforces unique business rules such as domain values (e.g., a lookup table where the number is from 1 to 5)

The database development Systems Development Life Cycle has the following data quality–specific tasks and steps to ensure that data quality constraints are identified, designed, implemented, and verified:

1. **Review existing data quality information**—In this task, the existing data quality information for the intended project's data stores is reviewed. Be sure to review the data

quality criteria of each data store for completeness and accuracy. Is record count accurate? Is uniqueness correct?

2. **Review existing data against the data quality framework**—Review each element against the data quality framework to determine existing data quality coverage. For descriptions of each dimension, see the data quality framework.

   Work with business and technical subject matter experts to determine whether any relevant business or technical data quality metadata exists outside the metadata repository and review if available.

3. **Identify data quality criteria**—In this task, the data modeler identifies the data quality criteria in the logical data model. They identify the critical entities and data elements, the domain values, and the business rule ranges. Use facilitated sessions with business subject matter experts to identify critical entities and data elements. Use the following sample questions to assist in this effort:

   - What critical entities/elements are used for reporting?
   - What critical entities/elements are used for forecasting?
   - What critical entities/elements are used for decision making?
   - What is the impact of not having these critical entities/elements?
   - Are you willing to add staff to review/process exceptions associated with this entity/element?
   - What is the overall importance of this entity/element?
   - What is the importance of this entity/element in downstream processes?
   - What is the importance of this entity/element in processes?
   - What is the legal risk associated with this entity/element?
   - What is the regulatory risk associated with this entity/element?
   - What is the financial risk associated with this entity/element?
   - What is the customer service risk associated with this entity/element?
   - What is the decision risk associated with this entity/element?

   Then use follow-up facilitated sessions with business and IT subject matter experts to determine the data quality criteria and refine the list of critical entities/data elements. If available, profiles of source data for critical entities/elements would be helpful. The following directional questions will help to identify the current data quality condition with the following:

   - What is the impact of bad data on this element? Can it still be used? If it contains bad data, can it be cleaned up?
   - Have the criteria for each entity/element been validated against the dimensions of data quality?

- Confirm the specific information on the tables, which includes:
    - What are the record counts?
    - What rules are in place to ensure uniqueness?
- Confirm the specific information on the columns, which includes finding the following actual values:
    - Domain values
    - Range values
    - Valid values
    - Unique values
    - Completeness values
- Define the data quality metrics for each entity/element. Use the following questions to assist in this effort:
    - What is the target level of data quality required for this entity/element? Examples for entities include expected record count and tolerance for duplicate records. Examples for elements include tolerance for sparsity (nulls) and valid dates.
    - Should this element be combined with any other elements to determine its metric?
    - What are the business impacts of this entity/element falling below the target metric?
    - If the quality of the entity/element is below the target, is the element still usable?

It is important to note that this data quality information is very valuable metadata that should be captured and stored with other business metadata.

4. **Review/augment data quality criteria**—In this task, the database administrator reviews the physical data model to ensure completeness and accuracy of data quality criteria that was extracted from the logical data model and perpetuated during the transformation of the logical data model into the physical data model. It includes the review from a data quality perspective of any additional entities, attributes, and relationships added for the physical model and the database-specific augmentations. The same best practices used for identifying data quality criteria can be applied to the data elements added or updated in this task.

5. **Validate the data quality constraints in the database**—In this task, the application DBA reviews the database to ensure that the entity, referential constraints, and defined data quality criteria perpetuated from the physical data model to the database are in fact in place and functional. The following best practices can be applied to this task:

- When validating primary key constraints, the element(s) that make up the key cannot be null, and the key must be unique. Each table can have one primary key. A primary key allows each row in a table to be uniquely identified and ensures that no duplicate rows exist.

- When validating foreign key constraints, the element(s) that make up the key must be null or contain the value of a primary key in another table.

- When validating unique key constraints, the element(s) that make up the key cannot be duplicated in the table. Do not confuse the concept of a unique key with that of a primary key. Primary keys are used to identify each row of the table uniquely. Therefore, unique keys should not have the purpose of identifying rows in the table. Some examples of good unique keys include the following:

- Employee's Social Security number (the primary key is the employee number)

- Customer's phone number, consisting of the two columns AREA and PHONE (the primary key is the customer number)

- Department's name and location (the primary key is the department number)

- When validating data range constraints, the column that the constraint is on should only contain values in the range specified by the constraint.

These data quality tasks are not unique. In fact, they are simply best practices in data modeling. These are the traditional data model development tasks that define and design the constraints that prevent create, read, update, and delete database anomalies.

The Audit Phase

The next phase of a data quality life cycle is the audit phase. A key data governance process is for organizations to periodically detect, measure, and assess the quality of the data that it uses for analytics and reporting. Despite all the controls that are put into place both at the data integration and database layers, periodic data quality audits ensure not only real data quality, but perceived data quality, which are both important measures of success. Periodic measurement of data quality also ensures ongoing group and staff performance in this area, thereby enabling an effective data stewardship community that can execute a data quality policy. This phase defines the approaches to review ongoing quality of the key data quality elements with the data quality criteria that had been established with data quality reporting and auditing processes.

Developing a Data Quality Measurement Process

The measurement of data quality occurs at many levels. At the lowest level, the quality of individual data elements can be measured to ensure that all of the data quality categories are being met. At a higher level, aggregation of key data quality measures can be used to determine the quality of a specific data object, data table, or data source.

The first step is to define the data quality measurements and metrics that the measurements support.

Data quality measurement is the collection of data quality element performance information that supports the data quality reporting metrics that provides the ongoing success of an organization's data quality accuracy. There are two types of performance information that can be collected:

- **Direct measures**—Direct measures are those that are gathered from diagnostics and other tools that directly relate to data quality. An example is the count of active accounts across two or more systems.

- **Indirect measures**—Indirect measures are those based on inferences made from events occurring within the organization. For example, the number of applications being accepted with low credit scores or the number of calls being received by the customer service center. They are not directly generated in the data management environment.

Metrics are the different types of measures that can be obtained for the critical data elements and data entities:

- Generic/entity metrics, which include:
  - Record count
  - Uniqueness
- Specific/column metrics, which include:
  - Accuracy
  - Sparsity (nulls, blank)
  - Uniqueness
  - Validity
  - Completeness
  - Date validation (day, month, year, date)
  - Categorical distribution
  - Numeric (maximum, minimum)
  - Relational consistency

Measures are the actual values obtained specific to each metric and are described as follows:

- **Quality measures**—Contain calculated metrics, which refer to a single entity (e.g., CUSTOMER) or to a single column (e.g., SSN) of a table or file
- **Distribution measures**—Contain calculated metrics, which refer to both relational and associative consistency
- **Consistency measures**—Contain calculated metrics, which refer to the distribution of categorical, date, and numeric attributes

Different types of measures and metrics apply to the various critical data elements and entities across the lines of business, as depicted in Figure 15.8.

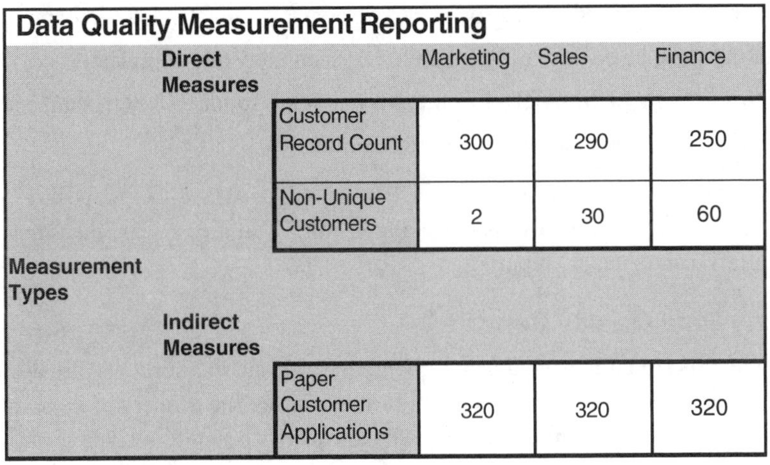

Data Quality Measurement Reporting

Measurement Types			Marketing	Sales	Finance
Direct Measures					
	Customer Record Count		300	290	250
	Non-Unique Customers		2	30	60
Indirect Measures					
	Paper Customer Applications		320	320	320

Figure 15.8   Direct and indirect data quality measures

These metrics and the associated measures are used to develop data quality measurement reports. These metrics are intended to be used for many different roles in an organization, especially a data governance organization, as portrayed in Table 15.4.

Table 15.4   Data Quality Metric Users

DQ Metric Users	Area	Action
Chief data quality officer	Executive	Interpret business impact on organization. Communicate impact and recommend action to a data governance group.
Line-of-business data owner	Operate	Interpret business impact and develop report for chief data quality officer.
Line-of-business data steward	Operate	Interpret business impact and develop report for line-of-business owner.

Table 15.4   Data Quality Metric Users

DQ Metric Users	Area	Action
Data quality SWAT projects Long-term projects	Projects	Understand technical problem related to data quality issue.

In developing data quality metrics, the following guiding principles should be considered:

- Organizations that want to succeed and remain profitable need to continually assess and improve their business and information processes; metrics are the critical component of this assessment and lay the groundwork for organizational enhancement.
- Metrics must be capable of being collected accurately and completely.
- Metrics should be SMART: **S**pecific, **M**easurable, **A**ctionable, **R**elevant, and **T**imely.
- Metrics should be intuitive and not overly complex.

Metrics and their associated measures will be stored in a data quality repository database or in the data quality domain areas of a metadata repository. The metrics and measures will subsequently manifest in data quality reports.

Developing Data Quality Reports

Data quality reports are built using the data quality metrics and measures and are designed based on the types of users as defined previously. Data stewards are the primary users of these reports, who interpret the results to identify and escalate data quality issues to all data quality stakeholders. These reports should focus on both the quality current and trend data quality results. When communicating these results, the reports should be tailored to the stakeholder audiences so that they can act upon them.

Data quality scorecards are often used as a high-level Red-Yellow-Green risk identification approach to data quality reporting and facilitate the communication of current performance and the identification of quality trends.

Figures 15.9 and 15.10 illustrate sample data quality reports in a standard report and scorecard format.

Data Quality Measurement Report: Subject Area View by Key Data Quality Element									
Subject Area: Customer Application									
Source: Data Warehouse Customer_Application table									
Rows Processed: 45,345									
Key Data Quality Element	Weight (1- 10)	Valid	Unique	Complete	Consistent	Timely	Accurate	Precise	Data Quality Total
Application ID	10	100.00%	99.30%	N/A	N/A	N/A	N/A	N/A	
Customer ID	10	99.22%	100.00%	100.00%	99.58%	N/A	N/A	N/A	99.62%
Customer First Name	8	99.00%	100.00%	94.76%	100.00%	N/A	N/A	N/A	91.90%
Customer Last Name	9	100.00%	100.00%	96.78%	100.00%	N/A	N/A	N/A	99.22%
SSN	9	99.00%	N/A	94.52%	N/A	N/A	N/A	N/A	98.11%
Annual Gross Income	7	100.00%	N/A	94.76%	100.00%	N/A	N/A	N/A	100.00%

Figure 15.9 Data quality sample report: key DQ metrics by subject area

The following data quality scorecard in Figure 15.10 is prepared for the line-of-business data owner who requires highly summarized data quality information across the information value chain.

This report provides the data owner with a quick assessment of the data quality levels by subject area for each of the four systems within the scope of the data quality pilot project.

This data quality dashboard uses a traffic signal color scheme to immediately provide the data owner with data quality levels in each system. In Figure 15.10, the systems within the data environment of the data quality management framework pilot project are displayed. These types of dashboards can be produced using most reporting packages provided by vendors such as Business Objects, MicroStrategy, and Cognos.

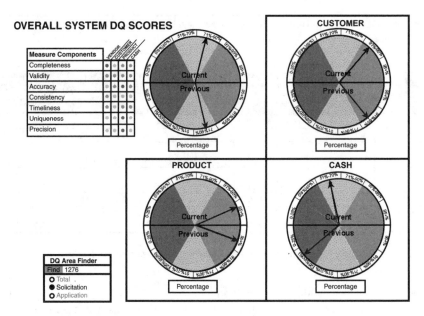

Figure 15.10   Data quality scorecard—subject area by system view

Figure 15.11 shows a sample Data Quality Trend Report, which can be used by a very wide audience to gauge and promote the data quality levels across the enterprise or within a specific application or line of business.

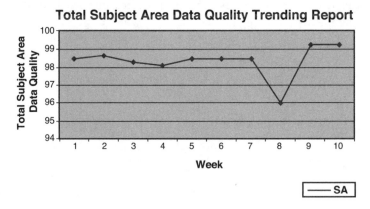

Figure 15.11   Data Quality Trend Report

Auditing Data Quality by LOB or Subject Area

There are two primary methods to audit data quality within the lines of business or subject area, as shown in Figure 15.12.

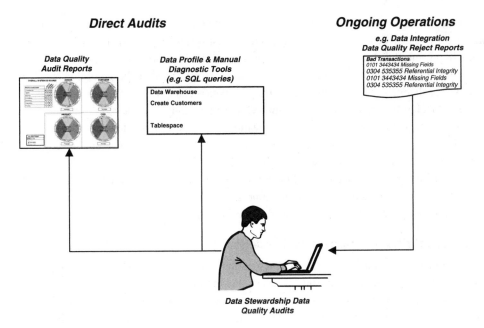

Figure 15.12   Data quality auditing

- **Direct audits**—Data stewards perform periodic audits of data quality in lines of business or subject areas using both data quality reports and diagnostic tests to individual data elements. The diagnostics are designed to test specific quality categories (validity, completeness, etc.), and the results can be aggregated into overall quantitative measures. These diagnostics are applied to all data unless performance issues result in the need to apply additional sampling algorithms.

- **Ongoing processing**—Figure 15.12 portrays the data quality reject reports that are generated when data integration application jobs are run. The volume of rejected records, contact information changes, and call center traffic could all be used as barometers related to data quality. The results can give overall measures of quality and can identify when the enterprise is experiencing difficultly, but they seldom identify specific data issues that need to be addressed.

The Renovate Phase

The final phase of a data quality life cycle is the renovate phase. When sets of data fail in the audit phase, there are two primary options: One is to simply flag the data with the error (which is the recommended option in data Integration processing), and the second option is to correct or renovate the data.

Data quality renovation efforts typically involve the remediation of bad data and the processes that produced the bad data so that historical data is cleansed. Proactive data governance organizations have special data quality teams to "hot spot" areas within an enterprise to analyze data quality issues, determine root causes, and suggest system and/or business processes changes that will prevent the data quality issues from occurring in the future.

It is important to note that these renovation efforts need to be carefully reviewed and approved at all levels of the organization. Changing data is changing history; it is important that key internal stakeholders such as the Accounting Department and the Audit Committee are in agreement with what data is being changed and how those changes are logged for regulatory purposes.

Data quality renovation is a very expensive and time-consuming operation, where the adage "an ounce of prevention is worth a pound of cure" is very appropriate.

Based on the type of data quality renovation required and the types of data governance organizations in place, there are different approaches and organizational structures that are best suited to work on these efforts as discussed in the following sections.

Data Quality Assessment and Remediation Projects

The type of team required to assess and remediate data typically consists of both Information Technology and business participants. These teams require leadership and management from the data stewardship community as well as participation from business users who can review and confirm changes to the data. These projects usually require participation from database administrators, data profilers, and data quality analysts who work on the actual changing of data. It cannot be stressed enough that any change to the actual data needs to be extensively documented for both internal and external auditing.

In terms of scope of these efforts, for organizations with issues that are specific to an application system or process, a temporary team such as a data quality SWAT team can identify the nature of the data quality issue and its probable resolution, usually a system or process fix. Once complete, these teams revert back to their constituent organizations.

For data environments where the accuracy of the data is critical for both financial and regulatory purposes, many organizations fund the creation of a permanent data quality program. These programs are often created as a function within a data governance organization and are used for performing data quality assessments and renovations based on assigned subject areas within an organization.

The following sections discuss the types of data quality renovation projects that are typically performed.

Data Quality SWAT Renovation Projects

SWAT renovation projects are temporary project teams pulled together for quick hit cleanup projects, usually in response to a crisis.

- **Duration**—Short, usually 6–12 weeks
- **Area of focus**—Narrow, usually a single application system or business process
- **Roles**—Business data analyst, application DBA, data quality analyst

Data Quality Programs

Data quality programs are permanent organizations that are often instantiated within a data governance organization to assess, document, and, when necessary, renovate data.

- **Duration**—Semipermanent to permanent
- **Area of focus**—Broad, usually a significant portion of a business process flow (information value chain) or an entire business process flow
- **Roles**—Business system analyst, business data analyst, application DBA

Final Thoughts on Data Quality

Data quality is directly related to the accuracy with which the data reflects reality. An organization's actions, if based on a "flawed reality" may create costly mistakes for themselves, their customers, and their stakeholders.

Organizations need to recognize that not all data is relevant and assess what data is critical to their operations. Focusing on this "critical" data allows an organization to assess the quality of its data without overwhelming the organization.

Data should be treated with the same respect as any other corporate asset. It should be protected, and impacts to it should be analyzed for risks to the organization.

Many organizations simply do not have a significant focus on ensuring data quality in either their source system processes or their analytic data stores with the excuse that "it costs too much." In the cost-benefit section of a project charter or scoping document for any data quality initiative, there should be a section of the cost of not performing the data quality tasks. Again, in data quality projects, the "ounce of prevention is usually worth a pound of cure."

Summary

This chapter provided a broad view on the functions of data quality that had not been covered in earlier chapters.

It explained the data quality framework and the dimensions of that framework that have been used in the data quality data integration model for business and technical data quality checkpoints.

The chapter reviewed the data quality life cycle and its iterative nature of how to define, assess, and, when necessary, renovate data quality. It covered the connection between data integration processing and data stewardship in data quality reject reporting.

Finally, it described the organizational structures to perform data quality renovation efforts.

End-of-Chapter Questions

Question 1.
Most Information Management disciplines have an architecture or framework by which to understand that model; data quality is no exception. What is the data quality framework?

Question 2.
With an organization, there are certain data elements that are critical to the business, for which the data quality should be identified, defined, and measured. What types of data can they be?

Question 3.
The technical data quality dimension refers to the data quality criteria found in the technical definition of the data; what are they and their definitions?

Question 4.
What is the definition of the business-process data quality dimension?

Question 5.
The last phase of the data quality life cycle is the renovate phase. When data fails in the audit phase, there are two primary options; what are they?

Chapter Exercise Answers

Chapter 1 Answers

Question 1

What is the formal definition of data integration?

Data integration is a set of maturing processes, techniques, and technologies used to extract, restructure, move, and load data in either operational or analytic data stores either in real time or in batch mode.

Question 2

What are the three issues in the Introduction that are caused by the complexity of simply integrating the Loan Type attribute for commercial loans and retail loans into a common Loan Type field in the data warehouse?

- **Issue 1. Matching and confirming the fields to the EDW loan type**
- **Issue 2. Conforming the types and sizes of the field length**
- **Issue 3. Conforming different loan types into one field (e.g., commercial, retail)**

Question 3

What are the four data integration architectural patterns?

- **EAI provides transactional data integration for disparate source systems, both custom and package.**
- **SOA is a standard framework for components to interact over a network.**
- **ETL is the collection and aggregation of bulk, disparate data to be conformed into databases used for reporting and analytics.**
- **Federation combines disparate data into a common logical data structure, typically a relational database.**

Question 4

Regardless of data integration purpose (transactional or business intelligence), what are the clear and common functions in each of the patterns?

- **Capture/extract**
- **Quality checking**
- **Move**
- **Load/publish**

Question 5

For two of the four data integration architectural patterns, provide a rationale of when it is appropriate to use that particular pattern.

- **EAI as a data integration architectural pattern is best leveraged in environments with multiple, disparate transactional systems.**
- **SOA is for organizations that have some level of maturity in their development and architecture processes.**
- **Federation should be used for expediency when developing a solution that requires data from disparate environments.**
- **ETL should be considered when the requirement is nonreal-time transactional data that accumulates.**

Chapter 2 Answers

Question 1

Identify and name the staging processes of the data integration reference architecture.

- **Extract/subscribe**
- **Data quality**
- **Transform**
- **Load/publish**

Question 2

Identify and name the staging layers of the data integration reference architecture.

- **Initial staging**
- **Clean staging**
- **Load-ready publish**

Question 3

What are the two primary uses of the data integration architecture?

- **Framework for establishing a data integration environment**
- **Providing a blueprint for development and operations**

Question 4

What are the four types of bad data quality?

- **Invalid data—By not applying constraints, alphanumeric data is allowed in a numeric data field (or column).**
- **Missing data—By not applying key constraints in the database, a not-null field has been left null.**
- **Inaccurate data—By inaccurately creating a record for "Ms. Anthony Jones," rather than "Mr. Anthony Jones," poor data quality is created. Inaccurate data is also demonstrated by the "duplicate data" phenomenon. For example, an organization has a customer record for both "Anthony Jones" and "Tony Jones," both the same person.**
- **Inconsistent definitions—By having disparate views on what the definition of poor data quality is, perceived bad quality is created.**

Question 5

Define and explain the transformation types discussed.

- **Change Data Capture—Identifies changed records from a source data set by comparing the values with the prior set from the source**
- **Calculations—Processes data in a data set to produce derived data based on data transforms and computations**
- **Aggregations—Creates new data sets that are derived from the combination of multiple sources and/or records**
- **Joins—Combines data fields from multiple sources and stores the combined data set**
- **Lookups—Combines data fields from records with values from reference tables and stores the combined data set**
- **Conforming—Maps or translates data from multiple data types into a common data type**
- **Splits—Divides a data set into subsets of fields that are then stored individually**

Question 6

What are the two key areas to consider for the load-ready publish layer?

- **Sizing—Just as with the clean staging land zone, it is important to determine sizing. In this stage, there may be justification for keeping more than one generation of the load-ready files.**
- **Disaster recovery—Load-ready files are essentially flat-file images of the tables that are going to be loaded. Saving these files on a data integration server that is separated from the database provides another "layer" of database recovery.**

Chapter 3 Answers

Question 1

Data integration modeling is based on what other modeling paradigm?

Data integration modeling is a type of process modeling technique that is focused on engineering data integration processes into a common data integration architecture.

Question 2

List and describe the types of logical data integration models.

- **High-level logical data integration model**—A high-level logical data integration model defines the scope and the boundaries for the project and the system, usually derived and augmented from the conceptual data integration model.

- **Logical extract data integration model**—A logical extraction data integration model determines what subject areas need to be extracted from sources, such as *what* applications, databases, flat files, and unstructured sources.

- **Logical data quality data integration model**—A logical data quality data integration model contains the business and technical data quality checkpoints for the intended data integration process.

- **Logical transform data integration model**—A logical transform data integration model identifies at a logical level what transformations (in terms of calculations, splits, processing, and enrichment) are needed to be performed on the extracted data to meet the business intelligence requirements in terms of aggregation, calculation, and structure.

- **Logical load data integration model**—A logical load data integration model determines at a logical level what is needed to load the transformed and cleansed data into the target data repositories by subject area.

Question 3

List and describe the types of physical data integration models.

- **Physical source system extract data integration model**—A source system extract data integration model extracts the data from a source system, performs source system data quality checks, and then conforms that data into the specific subject area file formats.

- **Physical common component data integration model**—A physical common component data integration model contains the enterprise-level business data quality rules and common transformations that will be leveraged by multiple data integration applications.

- **Physical subject area load data integration model**—A subject area load data integration model logically groups target tables together based on subject area (grouping of targets) dependencies and serves as a simplification for source system processing (layer of indirection).

Question 4

Using the target-based design technique, document where the logical data quality logic is moved to and why in the physical data integration model layers.

Source system-specific data quality checks logic is moved to the physical source system extract data integration models; the remainder is considered enterprise or common.

Question 5

Using the target-based design technique, document where the logical transformation logic is moved to and why in the physical data integration model layers.

Local transformations are moved to the physical subject area load data integration models; the remainder is considered enterprise or common.

Chapter 5 Answers

Question 1

How does a conceptual data integration model help define scope?

A conceptual data integration model provides that pictorial, high-level representation of how the data integration requirements will be met for the proposed system that will serve as a basis for determining how they are to be satisfied.

Question 2

What are the reasons why source system data discovery is so difficult?

- **Undocumented and complex source formats**
- **Data formatting differences**
- **Lack of client subject matter knowledge**

Question 3

Define data profiling.

Data profiling uncovers source systems' structural information, such as the data elements (fields or database columns), their format, dependencies between those data elements, relationships between the tables (if they exist via primary and foreign keys), data redundancies both known and unknown, and technical data quality issues.

Question 4

Define data mapping.

Data mapping is the process of conforming data elements between one or (usually) more sources to a target data model.

Question 5

Using the following diagram, what type of data mapping scenario is this?

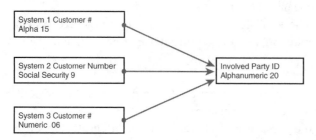

The diagram represents a one-to-many data mapping scenario, where the elements will need to be analyzed both horizontally and vertically to have a complete picture of the data relationships.

Chapter 7 Answers

Question 1

What are the two primary reasons to determine volumetrics?
- **Extract sizing—How the extracts are going to affect the network**
- **Disk space sizing—How the extracts are going to affect the disk space**

Question 2

What are the reasons for having an active data integration environment as early as possible in the Systems Development Life Cycle?
To take advantage of technical design tuning and prototyping opportunities

Question 3

Why should the data quality criteria be defined for the target rather than the source?
Unlike the source systems that will have varying levels of data quality, the data warehouse must have both consistent levels of data quality from all source systems for accurate reporting detail and reporting rollups; therefore, the target data warehouse model must be used.

Question 4

The source-to-target data mapping document portrayed in the following image is used as input to build what logical data integration models?

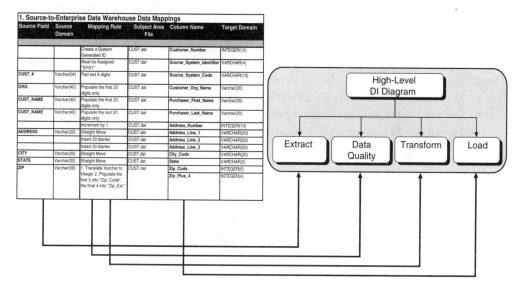

Question 5

Identify and explain the reasons for converting or not converting history.

- **Reasons for history conversion**
- **Historical data required for historical projections and forecasting**
- **Regulatory requirements**
- **Reasons for not converting history**
- **Relevance—Increasingly bad data year over year.**
- **Cost—The cost/benefit in terms of effort and business involvement on how to interpret older data in context of the current definition is often cost-prohibitive.**

Chapter 9 Answers

Question 1

Define coupling and cohesion.

- **Cohesion is determined by how tightly related or focused a single component is.**
- **Coupling is the degree to which components of a design depend on each other.**

Question 2

Define the two types of parallel processing discussed in the chapter.
- **Between data integration processes—running these processes in parallel**
- **Within a data integration process—parallel processing large data sets with a data integration process**

Question 3

What are the factors on which parallelization design is based?
- **The number of available CPUs in the server**
- **The number of potential logical partitions in the CPU**
- **The total data volumes and frequencies**

Question 4

For Change Data Capture, what are three of the methods discussed on capturing the changed transactions?
- **Log scrapers take the changed data from the transaction logs.**
- **File-to-file matching files and sorts the changes into a CDC file.**
- **Commercial Change Data Capture applications.**

Question 5

What would be appropriate candidates for leveraging data integration jobs in an SOA environment?
- **Source system extract data integration jobs**
- **Common component data integration jobs**
- **Data access processes**

Chapter 11 Answers

Question 1

What are two of the benefits of prototyping?
1. **Adjusting for fluid requirements**
2. **Developing buy-in**

Question 2

Why is the testing required to verify the correctness and completeness of a transactional system much more comprehensive and different than that of a data warehouse?
- **A transactional system must test**
  - **Whether a transaction has been created properly**
  - **Whether the transaction was created in the right sequence, at the right time, and at the right speed (e.g., service-level agreements)**

- **A data warehouse must test**
  - **Whether the transactions were collected at the right time, in the right format, and in the right quantity**
  - **Whether the calculations were necessary to aggregate the data performed correctly**

Question 3

What are the four types of data integration unit testing?
- **Source system extraction completeness and correctness**
- **Data quality completeness and correctness**
- **Transformation completeness and correctness**
- **Subject area load completeness and correctness**

Question 4

What are the common types of data integration defects found in testing?
- **Formatting defects**
- **Source-to-subject area mapping defects**
- **Subject area-to-load mapping defects**
- **Incorrect common or subject area calculation defects**

Question 5

Configuration management in the context of data integration primarily addresses what two key areas?
- **Data integration job migration**
- **Data integration job recovery**

Chapter 13 Answers

Question 1

Define data governance.
Data governance is the orchestration of people, processes, and technology to enable an organization to leverage data as an enterprise asset.

Question 2

What data quality issues do organizations that have little or no data governance processes experience?
- **Multiple versions of the truth**
- **Higher than necessary data management costs**
- **No ownership or accountability of data**
- **Internal audit's concerns**

- Lack of understanding and use of the information
- Loss of information credibility
- Intensive manual effort to respond to requests for information
- Difficulty complying with regulatory requirements such as Sarbanes-Oxley
- Management concerns about quality of the information being used for decision making

Question 3

What is the impact/influence of data governance on data integration?

Data governance influences the business definitions, metadata management, and data quality control aspects of data integration.

Question 4

Explain the relationship between the business and Information Technology in the ongoing management of data governance. For example, who defines and who manages?

The business through data stewards defines data; Information Technology manages both the content and the definitions of data.

Question 5

To implement a data governance organization, foundational processes must be defined and, equally important, executed in order to make data governance an ongoing, effective organizational process. Define these organizational processes and their roles in data governance.

- **Policies—The organizational mandates that will ensure that the stewardship of the data is ongoing**
- **Standards—The rules that frame and provide the audit criteria for the data governance policies that frame how an organization's data is important, ensure that the policy statements are from executive leadership of the organization, as well as provide guidance on how to follow the policies**
- **Organization—The staff and role models for Information Technology and the business that will be responsible for managing the data through the standards**

Chapter 14 Answers

Question 1

What are the two definitions of metadata?

- **Metadata is the "data about data."**
- **It is also explained as another layer of information created to help people use raw data as information.**

Question 2

There are several aspects of the impact or role of metadata in data integration definition and development. What are some of the examples based on the data integration reference architecture?

- **Source system extracts—Is the business and technical metadata documented?**
- **Data quality—Are the technical checkpoints vetted and agreed to by IT? Is the business data quality vetted and agreed to by all the business stakeholders?**
- **Transformations—Are the transforms such as aggregations and calculations documented and commonly agreed to by the business stakeholders?**
- **Load targets—Are the business and technical definitions of the target data elements documented and agreed to?**

Question 3

There is business metadata and several types of technical metadata. What are the different types of technical metadata and their relationship to business metadata?

- **Structural metadata—Contains the logical and technical descriptions of the permanent data structures within the Information Management infrastructure**
- **Navigational metadata—Describes the process rules and data formats of the data extraction, transformation, and movements**
- **Analytic metadata—Consists of the metadata that is used in a reporting and ad hoc environment**
- **Operational metadata—Describes the data integration applications and jobs through statistics, giving a full technical view of the environment**
- **Their relationship to business metadata? Navigational, structural, and analytic, all require business definitions to provide context to the data.**

Question 4

What are the types of users of metadata?

- **Business users—Business users of metadata need to understand the business meaning of the data in the systems they use.**
- **Technology users—IT professionals are responsible for planning and building the transactional and analytic systems and need to understand the end-to-end picture of the data to manage change.**
- **Operational users—IT operational professionals are those who are responsible for day-to-day operation of the data environment and are users of operational metadata.**

Question 5

What are the two prevalent factors in a build versus buy decision in a metadata repository?
Budget and client requirements will drive most metadata repository package decisions.

Chapter 15 Answers

Question 1

Most Information Management disciplines have an architecture or framework by which to understand that model; data quality is no exception. What is the data quality framework?
A multidimensional framework that consists of
- **Key data quality elements**
- **Technology defined data quality**
- **Business-process defined data quality**
- **Data quality processes**

Question 2

With an organization, there are certain data elements that are critical to the business, for which the data quality should be identified, defined, and measured. What types of data can they be?
These key data elements can be both base element data as well as derived data:
- **Customer name**
- **Customer profitability**

Question 3

The technical data quality dimension refers to the data quality criteria found in the technical definition of the data; what are they and their definitions?
- **Valid—The data element passes all edits for acceptability.**
- **Unique—A data element is unique, and there are no duplicate values.**
- **Complete—A data element is always required or required based on the condition of another data element.**
- **Consistent—The data element is free from variation and contradiction based on the condition of another data element.**
- **Timely—The data element represents the most current information resulting from the output of a business event.**
- **Accurate—The data element values are properly assigned, for example, domain ranges.**
- **Precise—The data element is used only for its intended purpose, that is, the degree to which the data characteristics are well understood and correctly utilized.**

Question 4

What is the definition of the business-process data quality dimension?
The business-process data quality dimension defines the understanding of the key data quality elements in terms of what the business definition for a data quality element is and what the business rules are associated with that element.

Question 5

The last phase of the data quality life cycle is the renovate phase. When data fails in the audit phase, there are two primary options; what are they?

- **One is to simply flag the data with the error (which is the recommended option in data integration processing).**
- **The second is to correct or renovate the data.**

Data Integration Guiding Principles

This appendix contains the guiding principles of data integration that were referenced throughout the book.

Write Once, Read Many

There is a reason why source system owners are so cranky. It is often the result of requests for multiple extracts from their source systems for the same data. One of the major issues in terms of cost and maintenance data integration is the number of uncontrolled, undocumented, and duplicative data integration extraction routines for the same data. The goal is to have one data integration component per source type (flat file, relational, etc.).

Grab Everything

When developing extract requirements, it is easy to focus on only extracting the fields needed for the intended application or database. A best practice is to evaluate the data source in its entirety and consider extracting all potentially relevant data for the current and potential future sourcing needs. When extracting only data needed for a single application or database, it is highly probable that there will be the need to extend the application or rewrite the application or in the worst case, write another extract from the same source system. It also helps in resource planning to have sufficient space planned for in the initial staging landing zone.

Data Quality before Transforms

Data quality should be checked before any transformation processing because there is usually no reason to process bad data.

Transformation Componentization

Most common transforms are those that conform data to a common data model. Those transformations needed for specific aggregations and calculations are moved to the subject area loads or "where they are needed." In terms of enterprise-level aggregations and calculations, there are usually very few. Most aggregations and calculations occur in the data warehouse to dimensional data mart data integration processes.

Where to Perform Aggregations and Calculations

The default rule of thumb is to aggregate (or perform the transform) as far back as possible and store in the dimensional data mart, thereby pushing the workload on the data integration server and managing the metadata in the data integration processes. Despite the default rule of thumb, there are exceptions to each rule. A review is needed for each of the business rules in the user requirements, logical data integration models, as well as other documentation to determine the types of transforms and where they would best occur.

Data Integration Environment Volumetric Sizing

It is recommended to add an additional 30% to the estimate to account for system overhead in the estimate, so for an extract estimate of 1,000 bytes, add an additional 300 bytes for a total of 1,300 bytes.

Subject Area Volumetric Sizing

A guiding principle is that subject area loads should be directionally the same size as the sum total of the sources. For example:

File	Number of Records	Probable Size of the Target Customer Table
Customer File 1	1,000	
Customer File 2	200	
Customer File 3	300	
	1,500	

Even if there is de-duping, the number of target customer records should be directional, equal to the source records.

Glossary

The terms in this glossary are ordered according to the data integration reference architecture.

business intelligence

Focuses on the collection of those transactions and forming them into a database structure that facilitates analysis.

data quality criteria

The defined business and technical standards for those data elements associated with every entity in the logical data model. For each of these data elements, data quality criteria include concepts such as business definitions, domain values, and formatting rules.

transactional data integration

Focuses on how transactions are created, updated, and deleted.

data integration architecture

Focuses on the methods and constructs that deal with the processing and movement of data to prepare it for storage in the operational data stores, data warehouses, data marts, and other databases to share it with the analytical/access applications and systems. This architecture may process data in scheduled batch intervals or in near-real-time/"just-in-time" intervals, depending on the nature of the data and the business purpose for its use.

Process and landing areas of the data integration architecture include:

extract/subscribe process

The set of processes that capture data, transactional or bulk, structured or unstructured, from various sources and lands it on an initial staging area. It follows the architectural principle of "read once, write many" to ensure that impact on source systems is minimized, and data lineage is managed.

initial staging area

The area where the copy of the data from sources persists as a result of the extract/data movement process. (Data from real-time sources that is intended for real-time targets only is not passed through extract/data movement and does not land in the initial staging area.) The major purpose for the initial staging area is to persist source data in nonvolatile storage to achieve the "pull it once from source" goal.

data quality process

Provides for common and consistent data quality capabilities. To accomplish this, a standard set of data quality reusable components will be created to manage different types of quality checking. The outputs of the data quality functions or components will link with exception handling.

clean staging area

Contains records that have passed all DQ checks. This data may be passed to processes that build load-ready files. The data may also become input to join, split, or calculation processes, which, in turn, produce new data sets. The data integration architecture should include an archiving facility for the files in the clean staging area.

transform processes

A transformation is a data integration function that modifies existing data or creates new data through functions such as calculations and aggregations. Types of transforms include the following:

- **Calculations and splits**—The data integration architecture supports a data enrichment capability that allows for the creation of new data elements (that extend the data set), or new data sets, that are derived from the source data. The enrichment capability includes the following functions:

  - **Calculations**—The architecture supports the use of calculations developed in the tool. Calculations process data in a data set to produce derived data based on data transforms and computations.

  - **Splits**—The architecture supports splitting data sets. Splitting is an optional technique, developed in the tool, to divide a data set into subsets of fields that are then stored individually.

process and enrichment

A transformation operational type that creates new data at the end of the process; these operational types includes the following functions:

- **Joins**—Combines fields from multiple sources and storing the combined set.
- **Lookups**—Combines fields from records with values from reference tables and storing the combined set.
- **Aggregations**—Creates new data sets derived from the combination of multiple sources and/or records.
- **Delta processing**—Identifies changed records from a source data set by comparing the values with the prior set from the source.

target filtering

The first target-specific component to receive data. Target filters format and filter multiuse data sources from the clean staging area, making them load-ready for targets. Both vertical and horizontal filtering is performed:

- **Vertical filtering**—Passes only the data elements the target needs.
- **Horizontal filtering**—Passes only the records that conform to the target's rules.

load-ready staging area

Utilized to store target-specific load-ready files. If a target can take a direct output from the data integration tool first without storing the data first, storing it in a load-ready staging area may not be required.

load/publish processing

A set of standardized processes. Loads are structured by subject area by data store, for example, subject areas in the data warehouse such as involved party. There are five types of physical load architectures, including the following:

- **FTP to target**—In this type of load, data integration is only responsible for depositing the output to the target environment.
- **Piped data**—The data integration tool is utilized to execute a load routine on the target that takes the data directly piped from the target-specific filter.
- **RDBMS utilities**—For example, DB2's bulk loader on the target, but the source is the load-ready staging area.
- **SQL**—Writes directly to the target database.
- **Messaging**—Real-time data feeds from the message data quality component.

process modeling

A means of representing the interrelated processes of a system at any level of detail with a graphic network of symbols, showing data flows, data stores, data processes, and data sources/destinations. Process modeling techniques are used to represent processes graphically for clearer understanding, communication, and refinement.

data integration modeling

A type of process modeling technique that is focused on engineering data integration processes into a common data integration architecture.

conceptual data integration model

A high-level implementation-free representation of the data integration requirements for the proposed system that will serve as a basis for determining how they are to be satisfied.

logical data integration model

A detailed representation of the data integration requirements at the data set (entity/table) level that details the transformation rules and target logical data sets (entity/tables). These models are still considered to be technology-independent. The focus at the logical level is on the capture of actual source tables, proposed target stores, and the business rules required to conform the source information to meet the data requirements of the target data model.

physical data integration model

Produces a detailed representation of the data integration specifications at the component level. They should be represented in terms of the component-based approach and be able to represent how the data will optimally flow through the data integration environment in the selected development technology.

data integration job

A data integration process that has been fully designed, constructed, tested, and ready for production.

data integration application

One to many data integration jobs that perform an entire logical unit of work.

data volumetrics

The technique of determining the potential file sizes of the source and target files that will flow through the data integration environment.

Index

A

absolute data quality checkpoints, data integration modeling case study, 80

accurate dimension (data quality), 332

administration of metadata repositories, 324-325

aggregation transformations, 37
in data warehouses, 120-122
defined, 373
where to perform, 370

analysis. *See* data integration analysis

analytic metadata, 318

analytics layer (data warehouses)
aggregations in, 121-122
unit testing, 271-272

Append Change Data Capture approach in physical design phase, 217-219

application development cycle, data integration development cycle versus, 251-252

architectural patterns
common functionality in, 15-16

EAI (Enterprise Application Integration), 8-9

ETL (Extract, Transform, Load), 14-15

federation, 12-13

layers of, 26-27

within overall architecture, 41-42

physical load architectures, 41

reference architecture
data integration modeling to, 48-49
defined, 19-20
modularity of, 22-24
objectives of, 21-22
purposes of, 26
scalability of, 24-25
structuring models on, 50

SOA (Service-Oriented Architecture), 9-12

assessing
data quality, 352
source data quality, 109-111, 130-134

audit phase (data quality life cycle), 335, 345-351
data quality measurement process, developing, 346-348
data quality reports, developing, 348-350
direct audits, 351
ongoing processing, 351

B

best practices for data governance policies, 294

build phase. *See* development cycle phase

building metadata management repositories versus buying, 323-324

business, relationship with Information Technology, 293

business analytics centers of excellence, 302-303

business case for data integration modeling, 45-47

This could be the best advice you get all day

The IBM® International Technical Support Organization (ITSO) develops and delivers high-quality technical materials and education for IT and business professionals.

These value-add deliverables are IBM Redbooks® publications, Redpapers™ and workshops that can help you implement and use IBM products and solutions on today's leading platforms and operating environments.

See a sample of what we have to offer

Get free downloads

See how easy it is ...

ibm.com/redbooks

- ➤ Select from hundreds of technical deliverables
- ➤ Purchase bound hardcopy Redbooks publications
- ➤ Sign up for our workshops
- ➤ Keep informed by subscribing to our weekly newsletter
- ➤ See how *you* can become a published author

We can also develop deliverables for your business. To find out how we can work together, send a note today to: redbooks@us.ibm.com

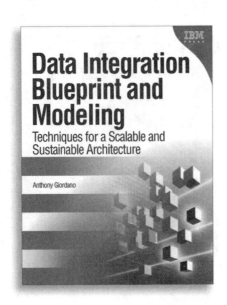

FREE Online Edition

Your purchase of *Data Integration Blueprint and Modeling* includes access to a free online edition for 120 days through the Safari Books Online subscription service. Nearly every IBM Press book is available online through Safari Books Online, along with more than 5,000 other technical books and videos from publishers such as Addison-Wesley Professional, Cisco Press, Exam Cram, O'Reilly, Prentice Hall, Que, and Sams.

SAFARI BOOKS ONLINE allows you to search for a specific answer, cut and paste code, download chapters, and stay current with emerging technologies.

Activate your FREE Online Edition at
www.informit.com/safarifree

> **STEP 1:** Enter the coupon code: KKPHQVH.

> **STEP 2:** New Safari users, complete the brief registration form.
> Safari subscribers, just log in.

If you have difficulty registering on Safari or accessing the online edition, please e-mail customer-service@safaribooksonline.com